SOCIOLOGY AND THEOLOGY

Alliance and Conflict

SOCIOLOGY
AND
THEOLOGY

Alliance and Conflict

EDITED BY

DAVID MARTIN

Professor of Sociology,
The London School of Economics and Political Science

JOHN ORME MILLS O.P.

W.S.F. PICKERING

Senior Lecturer in Social Studies,
University of Newcastle-upon-Tyne

With an Introduction by John Orme Mills

ST. MARTIN'S PRESS
NEW YORK

All rights reserved. For information write:
St. Martin's Press, Inc., 175 Fifth Avenue, New York, N.Y. 10010
Printed in Great Britian
First published in the United States of America 1980

ISBN 0-312-74007-7

Library of Congress Cataloguing in Publication Data
Main entry under title:

Sociology and theology, alliance and conflict.

  Bibliography: p.
  Includes index.
  1. Sociology, Christian-Addresses,
  Essays, lectures.
I. Martin, David, 1929-
II. Mills, John Orme.
III. Pickering, W.S.F.
BT738.S62 1980   261.8   79-27012
ISBN 0-312-74007-7

CONTENTS

ACKNOWLEDGEMENTS

The Editors thank The Christendom Trust, which gave grants towards financing the meetings of the Symposium at Oxford in 1978 and 1979 from which this book came. They also express their gratitude to the Dominican Order – to the Master of the Order and the General Council in Rome, for enabling John O. Mills, O.P., to carry a considerable amount of the burden of editing, to the Prior and Community of Blackfriars, Oxford, for their hospitality in permitting the Symposium to meet there, and to the theologian, the late Cornelius Ernst, O.P., who, shortly before his death, when the first meeting of the Symposium was being prepared, gave invaluable advice. Contributors as well as Editors regret that it is impossible to mention individually the numerous sociologists, anthropologists, philosophers and theologians in Europe and America for whose comments during the writing of this text they are most grateful. Peter Moscarella is thanked for helping to prepare part of the text. The Editors also extend their appreciation to Rodney Needham in quoting from his *Belief, Language and Experience*.

Oxford, January 1979   D.M.
                                                              J.O.M.
                                                             W.S.F.P.

CONTRIBUTORS

Eileen Barker
Lecturer in Sociology, The London School of Economics and Political Science. Has written on the Unification Church; science and religion; sociological theory and social philosophy.

Gregory Baum
Professor of Sociology, University of Toronto. Author of *Man Becoming: God in Secular Experience* and *Religion and Alienation*

Robin Gill
Lecturer in Christian Ethics and Practical Theology, University of Edinburgh. Author of *The Social Context of Theology* and *Theology and Social Structure.*

Christopher Harris
Senior Lecturer in Sociology, University College of Swansea. Has published primarily on the family and social change. Interested in sociological methodology.

Mary Hesse
Professor of Philosophy of Science, University of Cambridge. Stanton Lecturer (philosophy of religion) 1978–80. Has written on the history and philosophy of physics; the philosophy of social science and religion.

W. Donald Hudson
Reader in Moral Philosophy, University of Exeter. Author of Studies on Wittgenstein.

Fergus Kerr O.P.
Dominican theologian, Gunning Lecturer (philosophy of religion), University of Edinburgh, 1976–7. Has written on Heidegger and modern French philosophy.

Nicholas Lash
Norris-Hulse Professor of Divinity, Cambridge. Interested in problems of theological method. Has published most recently *Theology on Dover Beach*.

Antoine Lion O.P.
Chargé de mission pour la recherche, Direction de l'Action Sociale, Ministère de la Santé, Paris; formerly lecturer in sociology, Institut Catholique, Paris. Has researched on utopias. Dominican.

David Martin
Professor of Sociology, The London School of Economics and Political Science. Has published books on the secularization process, the student movement and Christian symbolism.

John Orme Mills O.P.
Councillor to the Master of the Dominican Order on the Means of Social Communication, Rome. Has published on modern religious movements and theologians.

W.S.F. Pickering
Senior Lecturer in Social Studies, University of Newcastle upon Tyne. Has published on Durkheim and aspects of religious belief and practice. He originally took a degree in theology.

Timothy Radcliffe O.P.
Vice-Regent of Studies for the Dominicans in England. Is teaching systematic theology in the Dominican study house at Oxford. Interested in theological hermeneutics.

Robert Towler
Lecturer in Sociology, University of Leeds. Author of *Homo Religiosus: sociological problems in the study of religion*.

Introduction

OF TWO MINDS

THIS book is a product of the 1970s. It is the product of a particular time: the time of the simultaneous waning of a great variety of certainties; of new certainties as well as old ones, and of frequently conflicting certainties.

The theme of the book is, of course, one that has been explored before, as our bibliography shows. It is, after all, a theme likely to catch the attention of a fairly wide range of people. For at the deepest level what it is concerned with is not simply how two particular academic disciplines meet (or fail to meet or do not need to meet) and the practical consequences; what it is concerned with ultimately is the difficulties we have today in organizing our understanding of the human world. Yet, in the English-speaking countries especially, the activities of scholars researching the confrontations and interactions of these two particular disciplines, sociology and theology, have in the past more often than not been distrusted by fellow-workers in one discipline and ignored in the other. Not surprisingly, the explorations have, then, been few and scattered. What we have done here may also be distrusted or ignored. If so, however, this will surely not be because its appearance is premature. The time has surely come now for a fresh examination of an inter-disciplinary area which (we believe) helps to put in focus urgent central questions about the future possibilities of sociology as well as of theology, and can help us look with new eyes at certain problems in the sociology of knowledge.

According to Heidegger, the level which a science has reached may be determined by how far it is capable of a crisis in its basic concepts. In that case (said an ironic observer) sociology and theology, assuming they truly are sciences, must have both reached very advanced levels indeed. As we are untiringly told, both disciplines have gone through a period of vigorous self-questioning, and there is no sign that this has ended. The ferocious debates in American sociological circles which followed the publication in 1970 of Alvin Gouldner's *The Coming Crisis of Western Sociology*, and the storms in the churches raised by the conclusions of some theologians on the meaning for men today of basic Christian ideas like incarnation and resurrection, are themselves only symptomatic.

Of course, the fact that two disciplines are simultaneously passing through a time of self-questioning and are shifting their perspectives in the process is not necessarily a reason for reconsidering what they have to say to each other. Sociology and theology are both concerned with the human condition, but they have different frames of reference. They belong to distinct universes of discourse. Questions raised in terms of one cannot be answered in terms of the other. The opening contribution to this book, on the limits of sociological explanation of religion, underlines this elementary truth; the second and fourth contributions stress how dangerous it is in any case to talk loosely about 'points of contact between sociology and theology', seeing that the reality is a great variety of 'sociologies' and a great variety of 'theologies'. If the two disciplines are not strictly comparable because of differences in methodology, and if in any case lack of homogeneity makes it very difficult to define the boundaries of the disciplines, no 'shifts in perspective' within the disciplines are going to move them closer together in the way that scientific research is constantly bringing about the merging (and diverging) of the boundaries of the various natural sciences.

Our concern in this book is not, in fact, to wed two bodies of knowledge nor to calculate the chances of one body of knowledge being able to envelop the other. All the same, it is (we reiterate) sometimes foolish and occasionally disastrous for practitioners in one of these disciplines to work as if the other discipline did not even exist. A study of some of the most imaginative architecture of the Renaissance raises questions for the art critic and the engineer which belong to wholly different universes of discourse and yet can only be properly put and satisfactorily answered if art critic and engineer are overhearing each other. And, similarly, although the responses of sociologist and theologian to social reality belong to different universes of discourse, sociologist and theologian can and do affect each other and sometimes (not always, but sometimes) they will talk better sense if they overhear one another or, equally important, are aware when they are overhearing one another. So initial objectives must be to explore from a variety of angles the ways in which they can in this indirect manner affect each other and to what extent. And this means investigating not only the ways in which workers in these two disciplines can benefit (or, on the other hand, be confused and threatened) by overhearing each other, but also the advantages of looking at the area of one's own activity from the point of the other discipline.

A further objective, based on this preliminary work and only outlined here, probably ought to be the very much more exacting task of exploring the direct interrelations between what can be seen as two distinct ways of thinking, or as two 'minds' you might say, the 'sociological mind' and the 'theological mind', the tensions between them, and the possibilities of mutual enrichment. For, arguably, fruitful long-term progress in genuine dialogue will demand advances on these lines especially, which are not bedevilled by the old interminable arguments over what are 'admissible' data and categories – the arguments that have made past attempts at dialogue so often arid from the start. The focus of attention might then, for a time at least, be directed not so much at 'the disciplines' themselves (in short, at what can end up in print) as at the way these people labelled 'sociologist' and 'theologian' think and live, and the extent to which they mirror a wider world and its needs and hopes. Men have different universes of discourse, but the sources of sympathy, conflict and misunderstanding are only partly rooted in the particular universes of discourse of our professional disciplines (see, in this context, what is said in Chapter 5, on rationality and belief).

Yet can 'dialogue' of any kind even begin unless the people in it are able to accept each other as equals? So far this Introduction has been written as if the time of self-questioning and shiftings of perspective had not altered the range of influence of one discipline in relation to the other. But the truth is, of course, that nearly everybody agrees that ever since the Enlightenment and especially recently the influence of theology as an autonomous academic discipline has been in decline, so much so that in this book, for example, Antoine Lion can seriously question the usefulness of preserving a distinction between theology and sociology.

At the beginning of this century, during sociology's so-called 'classical' period, men like Durkheim still saw theology as a rival to be contested as a basis for morality, 'between God and society lies the choice', he wrote.[1] Comte, the inventor of the word 'sociology' had pictured the sociologist in an overtly religious role: he was the priest to serve the new faith centred on Man. It was he who was called to uncover for man's salvation 'the rational co-ordination of the fundamental sequence of the various events of human history according to a single design'. Most modern sociologists firmly dissociate themselves from Comte's crypto-religious aims, but most would nevertheless concede that 'classical' sociology had its roots in theology as well as in political theory and in the methodology of post-Newtonian natural science. And even in the 1960s, for example, Hans Albert was saying (in his essay 'Hermeneutik und Realwissenschaft') that what he regarded as the false claim of the human sciences to be autonomous of the natural sciences had a 'theological ancestry'.

Here, of course, is an example of how the words 'theological' and 'metaphysical' are often assumed to be interchangeable. The churches in the industrialized West may be empty or emptying, but the fear persists, maybe justifiably, that the ancient Greek hiding in every Western man, however consciously atheist in conviction or in professional practice, will slip disguised metaphysics into even apparently thoroughly materialist, seemingly scientific explanations of social reality. Even when sociologists – for example, Durkheim and Lévi-Strauss – at some point even explicitly deny being metaphysical, they have time and again been accused of being precisely that.

All the same, at least in the West it is generally assumed that it can now be no more than theology's ghost that is still occasionally frightening the social scientists. Paul Tillich was possibly the last theologian who in his lifetime exercised a significant intellectual influence as theologian well outside the Christian community and in the academic world at large, and this may be at least partly attributed to his close associations with the Frankfurt School. The quantity and quality of theological activity in this century has in fact been remarkable, and most sociological theorists of the older generation have at least heard of Barth and Bultmann, *Honest to God* and the Second Vatican Council. But the repercussions of all this activity are hardly discernible outside the ranks of the educated middle-class committed Christians. One of the reasons for this is that theology's language and structure of concepts are no longer generally shared by the academic community, but this is only another way of saying that the much-discussed process of secularization, which has so dramatically undermined the influence of Christianity in the industrialized West, has simultaneously undermined the influence of Christian theology as an academic discipline. Furthermore, the gravest threat to the status of theology, most scholars seem to agree, has not come from the direct onslaughts of the geneticists, the exegetes, the historians and the linguistic philosophers. No, the gravest threat is of a kind that cannot be met solely by intelligent scholarship: namely, the spread of cultural pluralism and the associated 'privatization' and present extreme subjectivization of religious beliefs. And, although this is largely an outcome of transformations in society itself, it is the social sciences which have supplied the language and concepts in which it has been possible to describe and explain what has happened and to pose the painful questions.

So it would appear that the theologian, confronting the social sciences and what seems to be their rival picture of 'man', almost invariably takes the world's diagnosis of his own condition for granted and assumes that he is speaking from the weaker position. (A controlled survey has not to our knowledge been made, but studies of the effects on modern theologians of changes in moral attitudes in the wider society suggest this.) The theologian feels he is on the defensive in a way that he does not now feel when he confronts, say, a cosmologist's predictions on the future of the universe and is asked to square these with what the Bible says. Even if we leave aside psychology and anthropology, concentrating on sociology in the British academic's fairly narrow sense of the term, this is still what we widely observe. So, in some colleges training people for the Christian ministry, Durkheim is spoken of with a reverence which would have bewildered and shocked him; in others, all brands of sociology are still dismissively banned altogether. And, when theologians speak about sociology, they nearly always speak of it as a thing that may either help or else hinder them. Is this a package of food providentially sent to a hungry man? Or is it a probably dud parcel-bomb? Here we have an approach quite unlike that of (shall we say) Aquinas to Aristotle or even Rahner to existentialism. And the sociologist, when he bothers to speak to the theologian at all, nearly always sounds the stronger man, the man on firmer ground. Peter Berger (who in a non-professional capacity has quite a lot of sympathy for religion) wrote in *The Sacred Canopy*: 'The Christian theologian is ill-advised if he simply views sociology as an ancillary discipline . . . *Existentially,* in terms of the theologian as a living person with a social location and a social biography, sociology can be a very dangerous business indeed.'[2]

Berger is right: it is a foolish theologian who sees sociology merely as a useful tool. But, if Berger's strong word 'dangerous' is repeated out of its context (and this has happened), it is only likely to reinforce the illusions many non-sociologists – theologians especially – have already got about what sociology can and cannot do and is and is not doing . . . the illusions which are a major concern of this book. Perhaps the most important point for the theologian to realize is that, in terms of *practical day-to-day working*, he and the sociologist are now further apart than they have ever been, but not because of disputes over God.

Most theologians still think that the fundamental task of theology is to speak about the *whole* of things. All talk about, for instance, 'creation', 'sin', 'salvation', 'church' presumes this. And even up to approximately World War II most sociologists, both in Europe and America, saw at least the very final aim of their task as being an account of society as a *whole*. It was, of course, precisely because the sociologist's aims were so close to the theologian's, however different might be his presuppositions and methodology, that (in Europe especially) the two could so easily see themselves as in confrontation. But the post-war shift in sociology towards increasing specialization, (a consequence partly, perhaps, of the influence of empiricists like Paul Lazarsfeld, but primarily of the emergence in

the West of the welfare state and its needs) has profoundly altered
the situation.

The man whose life is, for example, devoted wholly to analyzing
patterns of deviance in medium-size low-cost housing complexes
can, if he wishes, contentedly go through his whole career without
seriously facing a Durkheim-type assertion. This is not to be criti-
cized on the grounds that all sociologists should be concentrating
solely on cosmic questions, but on the grounds that only too easily
many sociologists can consequently go through their careers with
their basic presuppositions remaining overlooked and unanalyzed.
All too often (we hear) what passes, then, for sociology is little more
than 'social engineering'.

Yet there are also negative reasons to deter the sociologist from
rigorous reflection on what fundamentally he is doing. They are
strong negative reasons. For, in spite of sociology's growth in power
and status, the soundness of the foundations of sociological theory
are still often attacked. The difference is that today most of the
attackers are themselves sociologists. There has been what some see
as a disappointing absence of 'pay-off'. To take the most outstand-
ing example: the theories of Marx, however important, have not got
the elegance of those of Newton and Einstein, as most Marxists
would now agree. And Marx himself probably supplies the reason.
There is widening doubt and unease about both Parsonian Grand
Theory and neo-Marxist Critical Theory, about attempts of every
kind to construct very ambitious large-scale theory. Some sociologists have suggested that one reason for a decline in theology's
academic influence is the difficulty theologians have in satisfactorily
interpreting the world theologically simply because of the span and
complexity of modern knowledge. But this is a difficulty that also
confronts the sociologist. There is an increasingly persistent awareness that a difficult question which sociology has put to theology –
how can you evaluate and explain what you are part of yourself, and
what you are conditioned by? – sociology has to put to itself. How
many social scientists can hear with comfort what the quantum
physicist Heisenberg has to say about natural science: 'What we
observe is not nature itself, but nature exposed to our method of
questioning'?[3] Some young sociologists are attacking sociology for a
frequently unanalyzed dependence on a philosophy of science
which scientists have largely abandoned themselves, and for a tendency to be ahistorical. And the problem of the irreducibility of
sociology's basic concept 'society' in specifically sociological terms
continues to be a question-mark over sociology's claim to be a
science in its own right.

These are, perhaps, the most familiar of the seemingly intractable problems which hamper the sociologist who is reflecting on basic questions about the nature of the human world. The limitations they threaten to impose on him have often been exaggerated, but they are sufficient to encourage him to restrict himself to the small and statistically easily definable and verifiable: in short, to stay well away from the spaces where the paths of sociologist and theologian are likely to cross.

But, if, in spite of whatever they might gain by 'overhearing' each other, the gap in understanding between these two disciplines shows no signs of narrowing, and rather the contrary, what is the point of this book? We can join the ecologists and say that the all-important common ground which the sociologist, theologian, and others too, could and should share, ought to be entered for the sake of man's survival. But if a dwindling number of us are equipped to enter that space, equipped to meet each other and assist each other, what is the point of saying this sort of thing?

As was remarked earlier on, it is possible that advances in studies on the ways sociologist and theologian may meet will for a time rewardingly focus less on the disciplines themselves than on the possibilities and consequences of the meetings of two different minds, of two different ways of thinking. But what, in outline, could this mean? What, to start with, are these 'two different ways of thinking'? Here is sketched what is undoubtedly only one interpretation – that of the author of this Introduction – and even this, for simplicity's sake, centres on only one type of sociologizing and only on Christian theologizing.

Sociological literature has a reputation for being unreadable, being all too often written in a hermetic over-jargonized language, and yet there are very few adults today shaped by middle-class Western culture who do not, in at least a clumsy unsophisticated way, 'think sociologically', if only because it is impossible to be a modern human being without being part of a post-Marxian, post-Freudian world. We cannot avoid thinking in its categories. But that is only the beginning. C. Wright Mills, in *The Sociological Imagination* (1959), says that the first fruit of this 'imagination' is 'the idea that the individual can understand his own experience and gauge his own fate only by locating himself within his period, that he can know his own chances in life only by becoming aware of those of all individuals in his circumstances', and 'what is specifically "sociological" in the study of any particular feature of a total society is the continual effort to relate that feature to others, in order to gain a conception of the whole'. Indeed, the sociologist should have a capacity 'to shift from one perspective to another, and in the process to build up an adequate view of a total society'.[4]

Wright Mills had plenty of enemies as well as admirers, and by no means all sociologists today are prepared to write as confidently as he did about the potential liberating humanizing power of sociological knowledge, but these basic ideas are commonplace enough. The anthropology student is frequently warned that his field-work cannot be too thorough, for, when trying to understand a society profoundly different from his own, he can only reliably make sense of an institution or pattern of behaviour he observes there in the context of the life and structure of that society *as a whole*. In the course of a very different line of thought, T.W. Adorno (in his essay 'Soziologie und empirische Forschung' – 'Sociology and Empirical Research') even argues that 'isolated social research becomes false as soon as it conceives the wish to eradicate totality as a crypto-metaphysical superstition, simply because that totality systematically eludes its methodology'.[5]

The man who is 'thinking sociologically' (and he is not necessarily a person who identifies himself as a professional sociologist) sees social structures and changes within them as patterns to be analyzed, defined, explained in terms of each other and of their past. Inevitably in his explanation he is saying something not merely about the phenomenon calling for explanation (which most of humanity is still tempted to treat as a distinct object which could be put upon a laboratory bench if only there was one of the right shape and size), but he is also saying something about the whole world it belongs to, and quite often this means the entire society. Understanding of the wider society and understanding of the specific phenomenon to be explained interact. Here is a way of thinking that undoubtedly can reveal strikingly the diversities in the structure of society. Yet – and this is the point to be emphasized – the focus is bound to be on similarities, on parallels, on the classifiable, *on the alike*.

And the man who is 'thinking theologically'? The theologian also aims to articulate a 'comprehensive sense' of reality, but in a different way from the social theorist. Consciously or unconsciously, he sets out to do it by acting as 'go-between' – as a creative interpreter – between, on the one hand, the wider society and its culture, and, on the other hand, the life-giving meaning-determining communication (for the Christian 'the gospel') simultaneously motivating and preserved by the believing worshipping group to which he is linked. Each is seen as deepening understanding of the other. The person who is thinking theologically is engaged in an on-going attempt, which is not solely cerebral, to comprehend each in terms of the other. But the kind of tension which the person who is seriously theologizing is consequently bound to know is not peculiar to him: it is also often known by, for example, the anthropologist (see what Lévi-Strauss has to say in Part Nine of *Tristes Tropiques*!). The tension that the theologian has to cope with is unique only because the essence of the 'life-giving, meaning-determining communication' that it is his task to articulate in the categories of the 'wider society' is seen by the 'believing worshipping group' not as a creation of the group itself but as 'wholly given', and it is this 'givenness' that characterizes the communication. One can try to articulate this communication in the categories of the wider society but (claims the believing group) it is not reducible to conditioning factors within the society . . . and this is precisely why it is 'life-giving, meaning-determining'.

Now, whether this 'givenness', this 'otherness', is 'God's grace' or 'group projection' is not relevant to our purpose here. The point here is that the basic task of the theologian can be seen as the paradoxical one of mediating 'otherness' – or, more exactly, a sense of it. If, through this activity, he facilitates the growth – the growth in himself, in the believing group, in the listener – of a 'comprehensive sense of reality', arguably this is at least partly because what he is conveying does not terminate in but actually begins from a sense of the impossibility of conveying everything, explaining everything, appropriating everything: a sense, moreover, that the truth is distorted if one tries to do these things because one is then claiming to eradicate what are discerned as the ineradicable differences which structure reality (those differences men have traditionally talked about primarily but not solely by using 'God-talk'). The specifically religious message may speak of forgiveness, reconciliation, love and unity, of being 'made in God's image' and 'sharing Christ's life', but (in Western theological thinking, at least) these ideas presuppose the fundamental irreducible distinctiveness of beings. And so the articulation of much of this thinking is in symbolic, logical and linguistic forms which bring into focus the boundaries of classification and of measuring, and what resists classification and measuring. To put things in a dangerously simple way: in their attempt to comprehend reality as a whole in all its complexity, while sociological thinking focuses initially and ultimately on territories, on the alike, theological thinking on the other hand focuses initially and ultimately on frontiers, on the different. Parts of this definition are expanded and carried further in Chapter 8. (pp.142-9)

There are, of course, plenty of other ways of depicting these two kinds of thinking. But this one emphasizes simultaneously the dissimilarity and the possibilities for comparison and mutual stimulus, and there is surely no need to present here the arguments for believing that a sensitive awareness of a way of thinking not our own, of its procedures and its current problems, can help us acquire a more critical understanding of our own way of thinking, of its potentialities and its limitations (and even, perhaps, how we can transcend these).

However, if this growth in critical self-awareness is not to stay confined to the area of theory, but is to be integrated into our working lives, it must be accompanied by an on-going rigorous examining of a range of specific questions.

But which ones? In 1975 one of the contributors to the present volume (a theologian) asked another (a sociologist) to review for a journal the book *The Social Context of Theology,* the first of the studies in this area to be written by yet another contributor here, Dr Robin Gill. The sociologist asked the theologian to comment on the review he wrote; a lively correspondence on the relationship between sociology and theology ensued, and its outcome was the meeting in January 1978 of twelve sociologists and theologians, of different denominations, and a philosopher, at Blackfriars, the Dominican house of studies at Oxford, in order to debate the matter further. This book is based on some of the papers given at that meeting and at the subsequent one, in January 1979, most of them revised or rewritten in the light of what was said at those meetings. What we believe to be the crucial, specific questions that we must return to again and again if our theorizings are ever to turn into practice became clear to us as we prepared to meet for the Symposium. The extent to which we, in our contributions to this book, met the questions inevitably varies, but the numbers of what are possibly the most relevant contributions (Chapter numbers printed in brackets) accompany each of the questions which are detailed below. Theses or observations of Symposium participants not writing in the book are also mentioned here.

First of all we found we had to ask what is the scope of the two disciplines? From his studies of conversion to Roman Catholicism in the north-east of England Antony Archer, O.P. of Newcastle-upon-Tyne, a member of the Symposium, argued that tension and potential conflict between the disciplines had been overstressed by some writers; in his research he had normally found sociological and theological descriptions to be, on analysis, virtually identical (but see also on this question 1, 2, 3, 9). Next, how fragile are the boundaries between the disciplines? (8,10) In what ways, owing to the plurality of approaches within them both, do they interrelate – at certain points only or is the interrelationship more profound than that? (2, 4) What are the social determinants of theology? (5, 6, 7) And in what ways are theological categories influencing the sociologist or social anthropologist attempting to analyze what he identifies as religious phenomena? (8, Epilogue)

Assuming sociologist and theologian do indeed share some important common ground, we found we had further questions to ask. What are the basic requirements for constructive dialogue between the two disciplines? Professor G. Dekker of Amsterdam, a member of the Symposium, argued the thesis that cooperation is not possible if fundamentally different values are held by the sociologist and the theologian. (See also Introduction, 4, 5, Epilogue.) To be more precise, what chances are there of finding a common conceptual language, and what benefits – and problems – would it bring? On this question Professor John Bowker of Lancaster, a member of the Symposium, drew attention to the common language of concepts being supplied by Information Process. (See also 4, 8.) Further, are there reasons for thinking that theological procedure is likely to be of growing interest to at least some social theorists? Regarding this, the late Professor Oliver R. Whitley of Denver, Colorado, a correspondent to the Symposium, said that hermeneutics is likely to be a tool of growing future importance to sociologists, and that here the experience of theologians may well be found invaluable. (See also Introduction, 9.) In what ways, on the other hand, is sociological methodology likely to influence theology and may perhaps already be contributing to an adjustment of theology's character, scope and aims? (2, 3, 6, 9, 10, Epilogue) Is sociology in fact an aid to the theologian or the opposite? (Introduction, 1, 2, 6, 9) And is the theologian, for his part, able to clarify issues for the sociologist and social anthropologist, or is he more likely to obscure them? This question was raised in the Symposium by Canon David E. Jenkins, now Professor of Theology at Leeds; and Professor Mary Douglas of London and New York, a correspondent to the Symposium, suggested that it should assess the case for provision by one of the professional institutes of facilities to help anthropologists to be aware when preparing their fieldwork of what might be theologically interesting.

We also concluded it was useful to confront basically the same issues from a negative point of view . . . in other words, to consider what inadequacies are most frequently evident in sociological and theological practice owing to ignorance of the other discipline. For instance, how adequate have been the assumptions of theologians about society and its functioning, and how aware have they been of the social context of theology? On this point, Dr Bill McSweeney of York, a member of the Symposium, argued that because of their failure to see the reality of sociological bounds marking the limits of change, Roman Catholic theologians had not anticipated the basic crises of faith precipitated by alterations in church organization and practice which they had advocated. (See also 3, 6, 7, 8, Epilogue.) And have the investigations of religious phenomena carried out by some sociologists been vitiated because they have assumed such enquiries can be conducted relying on theologically naïve descriptions of related ideologies, and because of ignorance of their own theological presuppositions? (Again see Epilogue.) Finally, a warning to ourselves. Doubtless it is desirable for sociologist and theologian to know more about each other's work and areas of knowledge, but is it always desirable to be seeking common ground in inter-disciplinary encounters? Cannot more sometimes be learned by abrasive exchanges?

Each of the contributions is complete in itself, but they are thematically linked. The earlier ones map out the area of the debate. In *The Sociological Mode and the Theological Vocabulary* (3) and *Theodicy and Social Theory* (4) two of the editors, Professor David Martin and Dr W.S.F. Pickering, write on the problem of disciplinary overlaps (on the need, especially, for clarifying different language levels) and on the limits of collaboration between the disciplines. The need not only for ways of advancing conceptual clarity but also for ways of ensuring sociologist and theologian genuinely are 'in dialogue' – that they are concerned with the same object – raises questions explored in *The Rational System of Beliefs* (5), Dr W. Donald Hudson's chapter on how concepts of the rational are socially conditioned, and also in the chapter that follows, *From Sociology to Theology* (6), where Dr Robin Gill examines the need for sociological tests of theological truth. After this comes a case-study: Professor Gregory Baum, in *The Sociology of Roman Catholic Theology* (7), depicts the changes in a century of theological activity, which has also been a time of major social change, as these appear from a sociological viewpoint. And the kind of danger – and creative challenge – that can face the present-day theologian trying to talk about 'modern society' is the subject of this editor's own contribution, *God, Man and Media* (8). It is followed by Timothy Radcliffe's essay in theological hermeneutics, *Relativizing the Relativizers* (9), which examines the role of sociological explanation, and what is seen as sociology's important liberating role today, specifically from a theologian's point of view. Finally, in *Theology and Sociology: what point is there in keeping the distinction?* (10), a French sociologist, Antoine Lion, shows how for certain Christian groups in France the distinction between sociology and theology has lost its meaning. The Epilogue, *Many Voices*, written by Dr Robert Towler, is, partially, a response to this closing chapter, and shows how our debate is restricted by our shared ignorance of that figure we foolishly call 'the ordinary believer'.

One of our objects is to show that this discussion we have entered is not in fact one that can be satisfactorily rounded off, one that can be brought to a seemingly final conclusion, and the Epilogue locates the debate in a wider context. However, the book also starts with a reminder that the debate must always be seen as part of a greater one. From different approaches the first two chapters consider how sociology might be said to be a threat to theology. In *The Limits of Displacement* (1), Eileen Barker writes on the scope of sociological procedure; Dr Christopher Harris, in *Displacements and Reinstatements* (2), first of all writes about the way the relationship between sociology and theology needs to be seen within the context of general movements of thought, and then (in the second part of the chapter) joins in a discussion of the more important questions he has raised with the philosopher of science, Professor Mary Hesse, and two theologians, the Dominican, Fergus Kerr, and Professor Nicholas Lash. For the question which is being put in basically negative terms at the opening of our book clearly cannot be considered apart from the even broader and much-pondered question: do the social sciences (and the world of thought from which they come) truly invade the world of faith and, if so, how? Our book is not about where the divisions ought to go in a university curriculum. At least, not primarily. If the relationship between these two particular disciplines, sociology and theology, has been an astonishingly confused mixture of hostility, aloofness and frequently misplaced expectation, surely one reason for this is that, however obliquely, both of us, sociologist and theologian, are trying to identify and explain what moves men most deeply. And we are trying to do this with the confident assumptions of the nineteenth century, as well as of the thirteenth century, radically shaken. If the debate is not to be barren we must constantly remind ourselves of where it begins: fairly deep in the fear, hopes and searchings for comprehension of the 'believing, self-reflecting animal'.

And that is where, in this book, we begin.

JOHN ORME MILLS *March 1979*

Notes

1   Durkheim, E. English translation: *Sociology and Philosophy* (London, 1953) p. 52.
2   Berger, P.L. *The Sacred Canopy* (New York, 1967); Eng. edn. *The Social Reality of Religion* (London, 1969) pp. 182–3.
3   Heisenberg, W. *Physics and Philosophy* (London, 1963) p. 57.
4   Mills, C.W. *The Sociological Imagination* (New York, 1959); Eng. edn. (Harmondsworth) p. 12.

5 Adorno, T.W. 1962 'Soziologie und empirisch Forschung' in M. Horkheimer &
   T.W. Adorno, Sociologica II, Europäische Verlagsantalt, Frankfurt; English
   translation in P. Connerton ed. *Critical Sociology* (Harmondsworth, 1976)
   p. 249.

Chapter 1

THE LIMITS OF DISPLACEMENT: TWO DISCIPLINES FACE EACH OTHER

Eileen Barker

There was a young man who said, 'God
Must think it exceedingly odd
  If he finds that this tree
  Continues to be
When there's no one about in the Quad.'

              (Ronald Knox)

Dear Sir:
  Your astonishment's odd:
I am always about in the Quad.
  An that's why the tree
  Will continue to be,
Since observed by
    Yours faithfully,
      God.

              (anon.)

Far more basic than trees in the Quad
Is a thought which may strike you as odd:
  Without Us to see
  You continue to be
You are Dead, dear omniscient God.
          (Eileen Barker)

THE theme is a dramatic one. There is a suggestion that the idealism of Bishop Berkeley has been transferred from reality lying in the mind of God to God merely lying in the *'conscience collective'* of society – and perhaps, even then, only in that *'conscience collective'* which is the cultural left-over of primitive society.

My own belief is that social science *does* present a challenge to religious faith, but it need not be the negative one of challenging any ontological reality which transcends such a world as science can explore. It is instead a positive challenge to the manner in which that faith is held and the way in which it is lived. Religion, not God, is challenged. But of course to make such a distinction is to assume a theological position which many theists (and atheists) would not accept.

What is not being offered in this chapter is any discussion about the possible outcome of those challenges which social science does present. That may be found elsewhere in this book. All that is being attempted here is to evaluate, from the point of view of the social scientist, the possibility of a claim that social science could explain religion as a sociological phenomenon. In other words, all you will find here is an attempt to explore the extent to which the claim, in so far as it exists, could, from *within* social science, be considered legitimate. It is hoped thus to clarify the position presented *to* theology rather than to evaluate it theologically. Any theological positions will therefore be presented here in a rough elliptical fashion to indicate starting points for discussion.

First of all it might be helpful to look at the concept of 'explanation' in social science in so far as it is relevant. For various reasons (several of which apply equally to the natural sciences), sociology is only rarely, if ever, in a position to provide explanations in the hard sense of offering the *explicans* of an invariable law together with a set of initial conditions from which one could logically deduce the *explicandum*, or thing to be explained. In what follows, three types of partial explanations which are used in the sociology of religion are briefly described. These are (a) correlative descriptions, (b) functional explanations and (c) *Verstehen* or empathic understanding.

(a) *Correlations*

Much of the empiricist tradition of the sociology of religion is concerned with little more than descriptive head counting. Such variables as age, sex, class, occupation, and geographical or cultural areas are correlated with particular beliefs and practices. By means of various statistical techniques, such as multi-variate analysis, it is possible to work out the relative 'strengths' of the different variables as indices of behaviour. Occasionally it is believed that this means the variables are determinants in some causal way and that by describing the relevant correlates one has explained away the belief. It should however be remembered that no such sociology ever predicts with certainty the behaviour of any particular individual; statistically the techniques involved are only viable when dealing with large numbers and at all times even descriptions of degrees of probability rely heavily on a '*ceteris paribus*' clause. There is always the possibility other variables can intervene and change the situation. Quite apart from the complexity of the subject matter, it can also be argued that the *nature* of the subject matter (man) is such that he can change the situation through knowledge *of* the situation becoming a new variable. This last point can be elaborated into arguments concerning man's 'reflexive' capacities which lead us into the free will/determinism debate.

An even less reliable (methodologically speaking) but possibly more challenging set of correlations are indicated by social scientists at a macro-level. An example of this can be found in the work of

Mary Douglas[1] where she suggests that such phenomena as the religious beliefs of a society reflect (and perhaps are reflected by) the kind of social organization which the society has. For example, the greater the degree of control the society has over its members the more ritualistic will be its religious practices; dietary rules may be related to kinship rules through classificatory rules. Such correlations as those elaborated by Professor Douglas can undoubtedly be seen as presenting a challenge of relativism (see below) to religious faith, but just as ethical relativism is only one possible answer to the problem of moral diversity, it can certainly be argued that the fact (and it should be remembered it is not a very 'hard' fact) that religious faiths can be correlated with social variables does not in itself prove religion is ontologically *nothing but* a social epiphenomenon. It can still be argued that God 'gets in' as an independent variable in various ways according to the faith. He may, for example, be a First Cause; he may be a subjectively received 'force' or experience, the source of an Invisible Religion; he may be an immanent social relationship himself, or the qualitative aspect of the whole. Furthermore, the descriptive 'how' does not necessarily imply an ultimately explanatory 'why'.

(b) Functionalist Explanations

This covers a group of explanations which are associated with Emile Durkheim's *The Elementary Forms of the Religious Life*[2] in which (to put it with unfair crudeness) he explains religious phenomena as mirror images whereby societies worship themselves, and by which they acquire an additional quality which gives them power over the individual. Religious rites impose the self-discipline necessary for social life; ceremonies, by bringing believers together, affirm group membership and reinforce group solidarity; religious observance maintains and revitalizes the social heritage of the group and helps in the transmission of values from one generation to another. As a social institution religion gives meaning to man's existential predicaments by tying the individual to that supra-individual sphere of transcendent values which is ultimately rooted in his own society.[3]

The concept of function is used in a variety of ways in the literature, and this has led to considerable confusion. It is perhaps helpful to separate out three of the meanings: consequence, contribution and (most teleologically) purpose.

To say y is a consequence of x (for example, social cohesion is a consequence of religion) may give some sort of a limited explanation for the *persistence* of religion but not for its origin. It can be seen as a 'negative-causal' explanation in the sense that natural selection is a negative-causal explanation – that is, if x did not 'work' or 'fit' in some way then x would not survive. This is an argument that can be circular but need not be vacuous if the temporal dimension is observed.

To say the purpose of religion is to produce cohesion does indeed provide a kind of explanation of religion but it is surprisingly often forgotten that (1) purpose implies a mind (human or superhuman) that *has* the purpose (and, of course, knowledge of the connection between x and y) and (2) it is the purpose-to-bring-about-cohesion which is the *cause* of the religion, not the cohesion itself, which is a consequence.

(c) Verstehen

Another kind of explanation in social science (which is associated with the work of Max Weber)[4] is to make people's behaviour seem more rational and understandable, in the empathic sense, than it might otherwise have been. From such knowledge as that of the assumptions with which people view the world and the situations in which they see themselves as being, the social scientist tries to make sense of their actions. For example, at the time of writing this chapter I am engaged in research on the Reverend Moon's Unification Church. If one reads about the 'Moonies' in the press it would appear inconceivable that any intelligent person who was not suffering from a psychotic illness would possibly want to join, far less stay inside, the movement. No rational reason can be offered, and so it is assumed Moonies must be brainwashed.[5] By going through the 'brainwashing process' myself, by staying in their communities and talking to members for hours on end I hope to 'explain' their actions in terms of rational behaviour. For the study, the religious faith is *datum* – it is something which is given and social science has no competence to judge its truth or falsity, only its correlates and its effects. However, even with avowed methodological agnosticism, the fact that one hopes empathically to understand why there will be a differential receptivity to acceptance (for example, why are the young more receptive than the middle-aged) has been seen as some kind of challenge. Still, it might be argued that the challenge is to the efficacy of God's means of revelation – the fault being either his or ours if his message does not get through with sufficient universality. It could also, of course, be argued that only certain types of peoples are *meant* to be among the elect.

For some kinds of theology (including that of some of the leaders of the Unification Church) the social explanation is not just insufficient but is actually wrong. They offer an alternative rather than additional reason or redescription of something. For example, if I ask why the Church has had such a success the answer will be 'because God is helping us', and this explanation is seen as *competing* with that offered by the social scientist. Similarly, explanations in terms of 'He was filled with the Holy Ghost' or 'He felt a vocation' can have different claims made on them for completeness by adherents of various religious faiths and thus can give rise to social science being seen as presenting a challenge.

However, *within* the social sciences none of the three types of explanation that have been mentioned needs to be incompatible with the other two. It can indeed be argued that it is only by combining them together that we can begin to build up a full picture, each type being complementary, contributing something the others do not to our understanding of a social phenomenon. But even with all the correlations, *Verstehen* and knowledge of functions we can muster we can never hope to have a complete picture. Our psychological and social satisfaction with an explanation must always depend on the particular questions that are being asked and the assumptions that have to be made in order to ask those questions. *In* any scientific explanation certain ontologically relevant variables are held constant. For *that* explanation they are considered non-problematic, but this does not mean they cannot be problematic for another inquiry into exactly the same phenomenon (always assuming one can define the phenomenon independently of the question being asked of it). The method must be reductionist, but methodological reductionism does not imply ontological reductionism. This is something social science has been long proclaiming in its attempts to establish itself as a discipline *sui generis*. While bearing in mind that it would be dishonest for social science to claim any absolute power of explanation, it might be helpful to stress the kind of phenomena social science *can* legitimately claim to study and which are frequently ignored by both lower-level (such as psychological) and higher-level (theological) inquiries into religious faith.

Reductionism and Emergence

Reductionism takes many forms, but for the present purpose it is only necessary to say that while some social phenomena can be partially explained in terms of psychological, biological, chemical or even physical phenomena, such explanations will never be sufficient, as there emerge at the social level both constraints and possibilities which are not present at the level of individual action. The emergent properties can be roughly divided into (1) those of *structure* – relationships between two people have different properties (potentialities or constraints) from those between three people; communication through a bureaucratic structure has different possibilities and constraints from communication through a despotic structure – and (2) those of *meaning* – the language of a community provides a shared perspective which both constrains its members and offers them potentialities unobtainable to the individual.[6] Similarly one can perhaps argue that higher level explanations (such as those in which God is seen as an independent variable) cannot in themselves be complete if they do not include awareness of the social context and lower levels. Just as knowledge of the structure of DNA helps a particular explanation of how inheritance works, so knowledge of the role of structures and socially mediated meanings helps an understanding of the process of religion. Whether or not one believes there *is* a higher level is a theological question. Some will deny its existence altogether, some will believe it exists but depends on a relationship with a lower level to some degree, others may see it as completely independent. The various permutations and combinations involved in the mind/body debate have their equivalents here. Social science, however, can go little beyond the pragmatic statement that *belief* in a higher level has an *effect* – it is a reality that exists and 'works' in *that* sense.

In talking about different levels one is of course oversimplifying, and it is sometimes assumed a simple additive process can produce a grand total explanation. This is to forget the feedback which occurs between the levels and the fact that the relationships between the levels can themselves have properties independent of the levels themselves. The complexity of the inter-relationships may be covered by some overall meta-theory which may itself be secular or religious and will be more or less informed – but not dictated – by science.

All this must be borne in mind as we turn to consider more fully what some think to be the most serious challenge to belief.

Relativism

One of the basic tenets of the sociology of knowledge is that what is known is related to the social context in which it is known. In its extreme form relativism denies any ontological reality independent of the knowing subject (which can be extended to a more or less well defined group). Such absolute relativism is of course endangering its own validity like a snake eating its own tail, but even relative relativism has its problems of infinite regress. To try to separate out epistemological and ontological statements is frequently considered analytical *mauvaise foi*, but not to do so is to take us back to a position where knowledge of the concept of relativism itself becomes impossible.

There can be no doubt that comparative studies have since at least the time of Durkheim and Mauss shown that the degree to which knowledge of an object depends on the socially conditioned subjective knower, rather than on the object itself, is far greater than most subjective knowers would accept. Mary Douglas for example has suggested that there is no natural way of viewing the human body,[7] and much recent work by ethnomethodologists has pointed to similar 'socio-centric' world views.

Frequently a sharp division is drawn between the kinds of thought to be found in primitive societies where relatively few options are available and advanced societies where there is what Berger and Luckmann have described as a veritable supermarket of beliefs from which to choose.[8] Sometimes it is assumed that because religion is related to mythopoeic modes of thought in primitive societies, this means there is a sharp division between subjective and non-rational thought and modern rational, scientific thought.[9] For several years I have been looking at the role of science in relation to modern religion, and the study suggests that while science *as* a theology or religious faith is possibly on the wane, modern religious faith has turned to science for justifications that are considered unnecessary in more primitive societies. Science is the new myth which has taken on the role of a priesthood of expertise and scientists can be found 'proving' practically any theological position one cares to imagine.[10]

Again, whether this is seen as presenting the negative challenge to a legitimation of a religious faith, or the positive challenge to an understanding of the ways in which, in different contexts, different 'resonances' spark off or mediate the faith, will depend on the theology. That social science can illuminate the ways in which knowledge is known, the process whereby practices 'work', need not be seen as constraining knowledge but as enlarging it.

But is it the cause of uniquely acute problems in the area of morality? This is a subject that cannot be left out of any survey of the challenges of social science to religious faith, however brief, although much of what is relevant to it I have touched on already.

Morality

In reviewing the question as to whether or not social science presents any challenge to religious morality, one finds oneself basically rehearsing most of the old familiar arguments. For example: 'Should we do what God says because what he says is good, or is it because God says it, it is therefore good?' If the first is the case then presumably there are criteria apart from God which make it good, and if these are to be found in a social science one is not challenging a religious faith particularly. If the second case holds, then social science is hardly in a position to challenge God with respect to an absolute morality.

It is certainly true that some sociologists and philosophers believe they can produce an ethic from social science. However, one can apply most of the 'Naturalistic Fallacy' arguments here – one cannot logically derive an 'ought' from a social 'is' any more than from any other kind of 'is'. One can go further and say that *in so far as* one believes that one knows what is right or wrong by looking at what 'is', one has denied a possibility of choice and therefore abrogated responsibility to a particular interpretation of society. For morality to have any meaning it implies that what is *pro*scribed must be as available as what is *pre*scribed and some criterion has to be found from beyond what 'is' in order to choose between them. In other words, even assuming social science can really tell us what *is* the case, an 'is' must include the potentiality of an 'ought' *and* an 'ought not' if 'ought' is to provide any meaningful constraint, or indeed be a meaningful concept. By putting it this way, it is perhaps possible to see morality as consisting of an emergent property beyond the level of a descriptive (or even explanatory) social science.[11]

That said, however, morality is concerned with how people live together, and the real challenge to religious people that a social science can offer is to open their eyes to the *context* within which they try to live their lives and achieve their valued goals (on this earth). There are severe limitations to the realization of Utopia, but these are not perhaps so limiting when we have knowledge of them as when we are in ignorance of their existence. Social science can for example warn us of likely unintended consequences and make us more aware of the structural constraints which impede – or could facilitate – the implementation of chosen ends. An all too obvious example springs to mind when one considers the role of legal, political, religious, scientific and bureaucratic institutions in the implementation of aid to Third World countries. There is, another, related, challenge which is neatly summed up in the opening paragraph of Reinhold Niebuhr's *Moral Man and Immoral Society* '. . . a sharp distinction must be drawn between the moral and social behaviour of individuals and of social groups, national, racial and economic; and . . . this distinction justifies and necessitates political policies which a purely individualistic ethic must always find embarrassing'.[12]

What has been suggested is that social science cannot challenge any ontological theological reality. It cannot offer the content of a theology but it can survey the context. It can throw down a gauntlet to those religions which hold a 'Many-are-the-Keys-to-the-Kingdom-of-Heaven' theology. As for a religious faith which is exclusive in providing its own description of the world, the gauntlet will not be picked up, but social science may raise a sceptical eyebrow in its direction.

Notes

1 Douglas, M. *Natural Symbols: Explorations in Cosmology* (London, 1970).
2 Durkheim, E. *The Elementary Forms of the Religious Life* (London, 1915).
3 Coser, L. *Masters of Sociological Thought: Ideas in Historical and Social Context* (New York, 1971) p. 139.
4 Weber, M. *The Methodology of the Social Sciences* ed. E. Shils and H. Finch, (New York, 1949).
5 Barker, E. 'Living the Divine Principle: Inside the Reverend Sun Myung Moon's Unification Church in Britain' *Archives de Sciences Sociales des Religions* Vol. 45, No. 1, 1978.
6 Barker, E. 'Apes and Angels: Reductionism, Selection and Emergence in the Study of Man' *Inquiry* Vol. 19, 1976, pp. 367–99.
7 Douglas, M. *op. cit.*
8 Berger, P. and Luckmann, T. *The Social Construction of Reality: Everything that Passes for Knowledge in Society* (London, 1967).
9 Needham, R. *Belief, Language and Experience* (Oxford, 1972).
10 Barker, E. 'Science and Theology: Diverse Resolutions of an Interdisciplinary Gap by the New Priesthood of Science' *Interdisciplinary Science Reviews* Vol. 4, No. 1, March 1979.
11 Barker, E. 'Value Systems Generated by Biologists' *Contact* Vol. 55, No. 4, 1976.
12 Niebuhr, R. *Moral Man and Immoral Society: A Study in Ethics and Politics* (London, 1963).

Chapter 2

DISPLACEMENTS AND REINSTATEMENTS: THE RELATIONS BETWEEN SOCIOLOGY AND THEOLOGY CONSIDERED IN THEIR CHANGING INTELLECTUAL CONTEXT

Christopher Harris

Responses by
Mary Hesse, Fergus Kerr, Nicholas Lash

Clarifying a question

BEFORE the meeting of the Symposium at Oxford from which this book emerged, a list of questions was circulated to participants to help focus discussion. One of them was not wisely worded. 'To what extent', it read, 'is sociology "theology's greatest enemy", presenting a highly relativized world-picture in which there is no place for God?' Basically the present chapter is concerned with some of the problems which arise if we try to reflect seriously on this impossible question. Many of the difficulties met in doing so can be traced to the fact that the meaning of the statement depends on the character of the discourse in which it is situated. Here an attempt will be made to locate and to describe a number of frames of reference within which the question can be put. In so doing we shall be considering the changing intellectual context of both theology and sociology.

First, what do we mean when we talk about 'theology' and 'sociology'? The complexities quickly appear. Let us briefly consider 'theology'. In Britain much of what is called 'theology' is not, I would urge, theology at all. Biblical criticism and church history are an essential basis for theological work but they are not 'theology', which term I shall use to refer exclusively to what is conventionally called in Britain systematic and philosophical theology. Within the area thus defined, however, there are obviously not one but many theologies. Of what is sociology supposed to be the enemy – Thomism, Calvinism, Lutheranism? Is it supposed to be repugnant to the world-view of Kierkegaard or Barth, Niebuhr or Tillich, Teilhard de Chardin or Küng? Equally briefly, let us consider 'sociology'. In my view, one of the chief defects of sociology is that (putting the problem crudely) there are still, in spite of the developments of the last decade, two sorts of sociology – theoretical and empirical – and these two kinds exist in the area of religion as the sociology of religion and religious sociology respectively. The second of these poses no problems itself for theology; it is largely sociographic. When I use the term 'sociology' I shall be referring to the theoretical kind only. Even so, what sort of sociology is supposed to be the enemy of theology: Marxian, Weberian, Durkheimian, Parsonian, symbolic interactionist, structuralist, phenomenological, structural functional, radical or critical? And if it is Marxian, what sort – existentialist, structuralist, positivist? Engels', Lenin's, Lukács', Sartre's, Althusser's, Marcuse's and now Kolakowski's Marx is each rather different.

The point I am trying to make is this. The fundamental concepts of each discipline, 'God' and 'society', are theoretical terms, and the precise meaning of each depends on its definition in terms of other concepts in a distinct theoretical system, in a distinct universe of discourse. Therefore it is impossible to ask whether sociology is inimical to theology without specifying the socio-centred and theo-centred theoretical system between which incompatibility is held to exist. 'Sociology' and 'theology', simply considered in the abstract, cannot possibly be 'enemies' of each other.

There are, then, major problems about the terms of the question. There are also problems about the substance of the question itself. The nineteenth-century question was 'To what extent is *science* "theology's greatest enemy"', presenting a highly *materialistic* world-picture in which there is no place for God?' There has, in other words, been a replacement of 'sociology' for 'science', and 'relativism' for 'materialism'. Why is this?

Here is one possible answer. As is the case throughout this chapter, it regrettably must (owing to lack of space) be presented in very generalized terms, without the nuancing and supporting documentation it needs, but this will at least mean that the issues will appear starkly. The nineteenth-century conflict between 'science' and 'religion' was resolved by a positivist philosophy which divided the world neatly into two. There were two types of statement: analytic and synthetic. There were two types of entity: ideal and material. There were two types of study: arts and sciences, or, in Germany, two types of *Wissenschaft* – *Geisteswissenschaften* and *Naturwissenschaften* – beyond which lay philosophy, which grounded both epistemologically. Science, understood as an empiricist enterprise in which knowledge was acquired by means of experiment and observation, was confined to the natural world in which these can be practised. The cultural, *'geistig'*, disciplines were also concerned with 'factual' knowledge; being empirical, they were *wissenschaftlich*, but they differed from the *Naturwissenschaften* in

being descriptive, not explanatory. This meant that cultural
phenomena were immune from *explanation* by either types of discipline. The *Geisteswissenschaften* could establish their existence,
analyze, relate and compare them, but made no claim to explain
them in any way which was analagous to the way in which science
claimed to explain natural phenomena. Cultural phenomena constituted an autonomous realm, and because statements about them
were incapable of translation without loss into the language of
description of physical objects, they did not constitute appropriate
explananda for the *Naturwissenschaften*.

Arts-type disciplines were in consequence apparently immune
from natural-scientific investigation. Investigations of this kind
stopped short at an autonomous world of *Geist,* and to this autonomous world theology belonged. Theology, thus protected from
being falsified by science, swiftly laid its claim to be an authentic
Wissenschaft by concentrating on academically acceptable activities
like church history and biblical criticism, to the neglect, especially in
the English-speaking world, of theology proper.

Here was a state of affairs that could not fail to be disrupted by the
emergence of the so-called 'human sciences', anthropology (cultural and social), sociology and psychology, in so far as they attempted to study the facts of *moral* life after the manner of the *natural*
sciences, and so undermined the basic division between the two
types of intellectual enterprise. Such sciences posed, then, not only
a threat to theology but a threat to all the *Geisteswissenschaften,* to
all the 'sciences of meaning'. Moreover, the threat served to bring
into the open the implicit ideology of the *Geisteswissenschaften*.
(Here, incidentally, I use the term 'ideology' to connote any unreflective world-view or form of consciousness which arises unself-
consciously out of engagement in a type of social practice.) Hindess
has called this ideology 'the rationalist conception of action', for as
he correctly writes, 'In its most general form [it] presents a realm of
ideas, a realm of nature, and a mechanism for the realisation of the
realm of ideas in the realm of nature, namely, human action.'[1]

I favour calling it *subjectivist humanism*, for the following
reasons. First, it is 'humanist' in the sense that it is man-centred. The
different elements of the world are not seen as 'man' and 'nature',
with the relation between them understood in terms of a third entity
that created both, but as ideas and things, and these are related
through man, who engenders ideas and embodies these meanings in
action, thereby transforming nature. Second, it is 'subjectivist' in
the sense that the division of the world it postulates reflects a
fundamental division, in man as subject, between thought and
experience. It is a 'subjectivist humanism' because it allows for no
meaning being in anything except that which is embodied in it by its

author, and it is historically-conditioned man, not God, who confers meaning on the world. (It follows, of course, that the meaning of the world will vary from epoch to epoch and culture to culture, and consequently that there is no absolute standard by which interpretation can be judged, and individual interpretations can be judged relative to standards peculiar to a particular culture, discipline or language game.)

However, subjectivist humanism was not only the ideology of the *Geisteswissenschaften*: it was also the world view which made possible the division of the intellectual world into the two types of *Wissenschaften*. So I am basically saying two things which are distinct but clearly very intimately related. If it is true that any sociology both 'leaves no place for God' and 'presents a highly relativized world-picture', that is not necessarily because of anything distinctively sociological about it, but rather because it participates in a culture (the post-Enlightenment culture) which, because it is subject-centred rather than object-centred and because it chooses man as its subject, both 'leaves no place for God' (or at least makes the idea of God dispensable) and necessarily relativizes thought. Nevertheless, in so far as, within the framework of this world-picture, sociology claims to be a 'science' – or, rather, in so far as sociology attempts to combine a positivistic conception of science with a naturalistic attitude to the study of social phenomena – sociology is indeed necessarily going to be inimical to theology of every description (for reasons to be developed below) and equally to all the *Geisteswissenschaften*.

Science and the challenge to theology

I am opposed to a positivistic conception of science. Very briefly, I believe it to be sufficiently demonstrated that all scientific enterprises are only possible on the basis of metaphysical assumptions about the nature of the phenomena which they study, and that these assumptions, being metaphysical, are not open to investigation by the same sort of methods as those which are conventional in the physical sciences, and consequently have no more 'scientific' warrant than the metaphysical assumptions which ground theological investigation. At the same time, while wholeheartedly advocating scholarly examination of the evidence in favour of statements having empirical import, I can find no cogent reasons for denying either meaning or truth to statements which do not have direct empirical import, whether they occur in natural-scientific or sociological or theological discourse. And I consider the naturalistic positivistic school in sociology has not produced what might count, on any criteria, as a scientific 'explanation' of religion (or, indeed, anything else).

I make these personal observations only to point out that whether or not one considers the invasion by 'science' of the province of the *Geisteswissenschaften* is really a threat depends at least partly on the nature of one's understanding of science and the metaphysical presuppositions of the *soi-disant* 'science' concerned. However, even if the shortcomings of a positivistic view of science are (to one's view) clear, the fact remains that even a 'realist' conception of science (which rejects positivistic assumptions and conceives science as having for its object the uncovering of the mechanisms which produce observed regularities in the world) is potentially inimical to the *Geisteswissenschaften* as long as they are rooted in what I have called a subjectivist humanistic ideology, which regards meaning as something mysteriously created by the human individual. For this precludes the investigation of the process of the production of meaning, so that subjectivist humanistic studies of cultural phenomena are merely descriptive and therefore unscientific. If a discipline espousing a realist conception of science emerged which was able to describe the process of meaning-production it would have uncovered the mechanism producing what the *Geisteswissenschaften* study. Then that which previously could only be understood would truly be explained after the manner of the natural sciences. And that *would* constitute a threat to theology (at least theology of the kind we have seen produced since the Enlightenment).

As long as the divide between culture and nature is maintained, and science distinguished by its empirical content, it remains possible for cultural disciplines to retain their status as sciences while denying the possibility of the scientific explanation of their facts. Once an empiricist characterization of science is abandoned and it is claimed possible to discover the mechanisms of meaning-production, the paradigm of meaning-production in which meaning is *given* by the subject is immediately threatened, and it matters not whether the subject is the human individual, the group, or God.

Theology has accommodated itself to the subjectivist humanist world-view by claiming historical truth for its authority and proposing an absolute subject, God, in addition to the human subject himself. The humanist paradigm in which man unites culture and nature has the same structure as the theological paradigm in which God unites man and nature. Similarly, a humanist philosophy of history, in which history is understood as the process of man's becoming, has easily replaced a salvation history, in which history is the story of God's redemptive activity towards man. The replacement is easy because both presuppose an author of history and presuppose that the answer to the riddle of history lies in the nature of the being of the author. The destruction of this paradigm leaves

'God' as a theoretical term without any function, and the paradigm is destroyed once science claims to explain the production of meaning. The true enemy of theology is not necessarily sociology, but any discipline which claims to displace the problematic of the subject, thus leaving room for neither God nor man.

The question then becomes: how far does sociology participate in the attempt to displace the problematic of the subject? Certainly this was not one of Weber's objectives, but in my view it was an objective of both Marx and Durkheim, in so far as they both attempted to derive the forms of consciousness from the structure of society. Marx's conception of ideology as a reflection of the character of a social formation in the minds of its inhabitants parallels the Durkheimian notion of collective thought as a representation of a shared social milieu, and his later attempts to understand the Kantian categories as originating in social structure. However, the works of both these authors pale into insignificance before Lévi-Strauss's and Althusser's explicit and determined attempts to destroy the subjectivist problematic.

The importance of recent developments in sociology

The overthrow of the problematic of the subject involves its replacement by another problematic, that of the object. Surely the sequence God as subject, man as subject, object as structure, chronicles the progressive demystification of the world, a process of *Entzauberung* in which structuralism in its various forms constitutes the terminal point?

Here, however, we are faced with a paradox. A world which is mere appearance, behind and beyond which lies a structure which gives it phenomenal form, is not a bit like most modern conceptions of the world, informed as they are by the empiricist conception of science. It is, rather, a world of signs which point to something beyond themselves and which exists independently of our conception of it. In this sense it resembles the pre-seventeenth-century world-view which Foucault describes thus:

The face of the world is covered with blazons, with characters, with ciphers and obscure words . . . and the space inhabited by immediate resemblances becomes like a vast open book; it bristles with written signs . . . Paracelsus says: 'It is not God's will that what he creates for man's benefit and what he has given us should remain hidden . . . And even though He has hidden certain things, he has allowed nothing to remain without exterior and visible signs in the form of special marks.'[2]

For the pre-seventeenth-century world-view (as depicted by Foucault) religious belief in a divine subject ensured the intelligibility of the object to the human subject by guaranteeing that the reality of objects was manifested by signs. We find here a combination of an objectivism supported by subjectivist guarantees. Hence there is a sense in which modern structuralist objectivism is the new form of an old solution. But the old solution could not do without a divine author to guarantee it. We may ask: is structuralism in any better situation? For while it is true in one sense that structure has replaced God as the reality which all forms of being share, the notion of structure itself requires metaphysical guarantees just as certainly as empiricism requires a metaphysical belief in the uniformity of nature.

Lévi-Straussian structuralism has been described as Kantianism without a subject, and this judgment makes sense if one recalls Lévi-Strauss's inheritance from Durkheim and Mauss, and Gellner's judgment on Durkheim. But to me the work of both Althusser and Lévi-Strauss seems to be in many ways more reminiscent of Hegel than of Kant, and what Marx, Hegel and Althusser, the sixteenth-century world-view and certain kinds of theology have in common is their underlying Aristotelianism. And this mention of Aristotle reminds us that theology and science have not always been opposed. There has been opposition of the kind I have written about in this chapter only since the time that the scientist's understanding of his task became positivist, and I do not think this is an historical accident. I am not suggesting that the natural sciences are now returning to an Aristotelian world-view even if some branches of the social sciences are. There does, however, seem to be a move in the philosophy of science towards a realist conception of science, and arguably realist conceptions are less antipathetic to theology than phenomenalist conceptions.

My reason for making this claim is that a scientific view of the world which seeks to abolish by fiat the questioning of appearances, and identifies knowledge with phenomenal regularity, describes and does not explain. Things are as they are. Science is simply finding out *how* they are. *Why* they are like that is a metaphysical (that is, metaphenomenal) question. A scientific world-view which seeks to explain phenomena in terms of hidden causal mechanisms forges a chain of explanation which must end in a description of a causal mechanism which is not explained, thus generating a tension between the satisfactorily explicated and the fundamentally inexplicable which engenders truly metaphysical questioning.

Now, various forms of structuralist objectivism in sociology attempt to account 'scientifically' for the process of meaning-production, and in so doing reduce the human individual to a mere carrier of a meaning-structure which mutates according to its own laws. But this movement from phenomena to surface structure and then to deep structure involves a movement of explication which would be frustrated once it reached its goal, and could only be taken further, in Lévi-Strauss's case, by recourse to natural scientific explanation which merely postpones the point of frustration. The structuralist interpretation of Marxism runs into similar difficulties. Here the object which exhibits the structure is not an a-historical one (*l'esprit humaine*) but an historical one (capitalist societies). Here the demand for explanation cannot result in the production of a natural scientific mechanism, but requires for its satisfaction an ontogenetic type of explanation. Such an explanation would require that capitalist social formations be shown to originate in earlier formations, or be one moment in the development of an entity. In the first case such a sequence would have to have a term. In the second the entity itself would demand an ontogenetic explanation. By one route or another the demand for explanation must be frustrated, thus generating a demand for metaphysical explanation.

I conclude, therefore, that *only* positivist science (and hence positivist sociology) 'leaves no place for God', and consequently no Place for theology of any description, and this it succeeds in doing simply because it leaves no room for explanation and 'God' is a theoretical term which serves an explanatory purpose. What purpose it serves depends, of course, on the nature of the problematic. The collapse of a given problematic obviously abolishes that particular conception of God which the problematic had called forth. But the death of a particular God-concept should be no more mistaken for the death of all God-concepts than it should be mistaken for the death of that of which it is a concept.

It may be objected that I have totally ignored other developments in sociology which retain the subjectivist-humanist problematic and the positivist conception of science. I have not discussed them above because in these there is found a real but special problem. If one retains a subjectivist problematic but makes meaning not the private and mysterious creation of the individual but the product of the associative activity of individuals, and claims to have explicated this process, then a world-view results in which man is both cultural subject and object, creating and created by culture. On this view the creation of meaning is a natural (that is, unintended) process, in which the resultant product requires human intentionality and makes human intentionality possible but is not identified with it. The realm of mind ceases to be mysterious and becomes rooted in sociality, which is in turn rooted in nature. Now, this solution promises more than it can deliver, since it can never succeed in explaining specific instances of meaning-creation; it can only show how it is possible for meaning-creation to take place. Hence it tends either to develop into a form of structuralist semiotics, or else lapses into a romantic individualism. This suggests that there is no third way between the problematics of subject and object. So-called phenomenological and ethnomethodological new directions in sociology do not, then, threaten the *Geisteswissenschaften* with scientific take-over. They undoubtedly do constitute an attempt to use sociology as a means of ridding the subjectivist-humanist world-view of the last remnants of 'enchantment', of removing the remaining element of mystery from the humanist world-view, but these developments seem to me to threaten only a 'God of the gaps' type of theology, rather than theology itself.

The relation of meaning between sociology and theology

The serious complaint is likely to be, however, that all I have said somehow misses the central point of conflict between the two disciplines.

Popularly, sociology is seen as a world-view which, by explaining human action in terms of determining social conditions, leaves no room for individual responsibility and moral choice. Now, it is not possible here to discuss the relation between individual responsibility, moral choice and the belief in God. Let us suppose, however, that belief in the reality of the first two of these are psychologically necessary conditions for religious belief. Is sociology antipathetic to belief in the first two? The answer to this must be 'Yes' if sociology claims to be a science, and claims that science simultaneously discovers causal regularities and subscribes to a social-realist ontology. However, this particular amalgam of claims is so confused that it would be difficult to discover any reputable scholar that holds them in conjunction. On the contrary, sociology finds itself in every generation confronted anew with the problem of attempting to clear up the relationship between statements about structure and statements about action, and it was precisely the claim to have resolved this problem that made early Parsonian sociology such an influential theoretical standpoint.

Nonetheless, the confused notion that social conditions ('structure') somehow cause individual human actions is at the bottom of the second point of conflict with theology: the Enlightenment belief that the heavenly city belongs not to another world but to the future. This belief is certainly antipathetic to any Christian understanding of history. However, although many sociologists are utopianists there is nothing particularly sociological about utopianism. Sociology is implicated only in so far as it is used as a possible means of arriving at this utopia, whether by Popperian social engineering or Marxist revolution. Sociology, that is, comes to have a certain meaning when located as part of an historical movement of human thought, which begins with the Enlightenment. And this draws our attention to a potential source of conflict and misunderstanding between the disciplines whose origins do not lie in theoretical confusion.

I began this chapter by drawing attention to the diversity of the two areas of human thought – sociology and theology – whose relations we were about to discuss. There is, however, an additional sense in which they are diverse: they each carry diverse meanings which vary systematically with their context, and conflicts within sociology over what sociology is derive in part from the different wider frames of reference within which sociology is located. If one accepts a Comtian view of history, thought and knowledge, the antipathy of sociology to theology naturally follows, not because of their intrinsic nature but because of the way they are defined by the Comtian framework and become meaningful in it. Sociology may symbolize rationality, scientific disinterest, objectivity and the attempt of man to control his social as well as natural environments; it may symbolize a stage in the development of man's self-consciousness; it may symbolize the bureaucratization of knowledge and society and be seen as an instrument of oppression. But which it symbolizes will depend as much upon the historical perspective within which it is located as upon its intrinsic characteristics.

Similarly, theology has a variety of meanings: in a Comtian schema it is associated with the childlike faculty of imagination rather than reason, whereas for Durkheim it is a primitive form of rationality, and for Weber it is the locus of the development of rationality. It may symbolize superstition, authority and oppression, or, alternatively, the human capacity for transcendence and man's search for ultimate meaning.

These variations in the externally determined meaning of each discipline are paralleled by variations over time within each discipline itself. Obviously I simplify a great deal, but I believe it is nonetheless true to say that within theology there is an oscillation between emphasis on different types of authority (church or bible, prophecy or conscience), between faith and reason, between faith and works, between the first and second of the 'Great Commandments' (that is, between pietism and humanitarianism), between 'church' as community and 'church' as an aggregate of individual believers; and that these oscillations parallel those in sociology between methodological individualism and methodological collectivism, between social realism and social atomism, between emphases on diachrony and synchrony, on structure and process, on structure and action, on purposes and consequences, on situations and outcomes, on thought and conditions, on values and categories.

There is, of course, not only a parallelism between these oscillations but also a relation. There is an obvious structural similarity between, for example, social realism and a 'high' doctrine of the Church, and social atomism and a 'low' doctrine of the Church. The fascination of tracing connections of this kind between sociological and theological doctrines should not however distract our attention from the fact that the oscillations in both disciplines are part of a wider movement of thought which embraces them both and through which they are related. The spreading humanitarianism of the churches since the eighteenth century does not mirror the spreading of humanistic secular thought-systems like sociology, socialism and Marxism. Both, rather, are reflections of a fundamental change in man's conception of himself and of his place in the universe, which provides the basic framework within which both sociology and theology operate.

Locating the disciplines

If we regard sociology and theology as forms of knowlege-production within society, we may ask what sort of knowledge does each produce and what function does each product perform? To answer the first question I shall adopt Habermas's classification of disciplines.[3] The empirical analytical sciences are informed by a technical interest and rooted in work, the historical-hermeneutic sciences are informed by a practical interest and are grounded in interaction, and the critical sciences are informed by an emancipatory interest which is rooted in power.

Using this classification, we can see that it has been claimed that sociology belongs to each of these three different types of discipline, and certainly it has been informed by the methods and results of all three types of enquiry. Hence it is amenable to interpretation as a member of each of these three categories. At the same time, sociology has and does serve technical, practical and emancipatory functions. And what of theology? Clearly it is not an empirical analytic discipline serving a technical function. Obviously it is an historical hermeneutic discipline. But what interest informs it? Is it a practical interest rooted in interaction or an emancipatory one grounded in power?

There is not room here for further discussion of the place of sociology and theology in Habermas's scheme. I have raised the problems, however, because I think they illuminate the cultural situation of both sociology and theology. The demand for critical, committed, radical sociologies is a demand that sociology should play a part in human emancipation. This it can do on one of only two conditions. Either it must adopt an Aristotelian position and presuppose, first, that a careful study of what something at present is can reveal what it has the potentiality to become, and, second, that the realization of potentialities is good, or else it must put forward its own view of the good society and seek to provide the means whereby it can be realized. I, personally, have difficulties with both of these positions. Alternatively, it must be blind to questions of value and concentrate on providing the technical means for the manipulation of social conditions to achieve whatever men choose as their good. I am equally unhappy with the abdication of moral responsibility this involves, the manipulative attitude towards others that it implies, and the social-deterministic position it assumes. Like most liberal sociologists, I am happier with a sociology that is informed by a practical interest rooted in interaction. I understand the function of this sociology to be the creation of self-awareness and self-understanding among its subjects. Yet as soon as one admits, as Habermas does, that such self-understanding is only possible under the appropriate social conditions, which in inegalitarian societies are not realized, the achievement of this practical aim generates an emancipatory interest which in turn requires a specification of a 'better' society and an interest in the technical means of creating the conditions under which the realization of the practical aim is possible.

This situation parallels that of theology very closely. For theology too has a clear practical interest, is concerned to foster a kind of self-understanding, and finds barriers to its achievement of this aim in social conditions, this state of affairs leading in turn to a demand that it play a role in changing those conditions so that the aim may be realized. (Recognition of this necessity is, I would add, distinct from, though frequently confused with, what I have argued to be the mistaken belief that Christianity should seek to create a this-worldly heavenly city.)

Consequently, far from seeing sociology as a humanist and relativizing discipline which threatens an absolutist theology, I see both as disciplines concerned with enlarging human self-consciousness and sensibility, but struggling with the problems which the pursuit of this aim involves under social conditions which militate against its realization.

There is, however, a further question that has to be faced: the question whether or not theology is *necessarily* absolutist (the major question raised by a colleague who is not a Christian on reading this chapter). Is theology not concerned with final truths, final solutions, does it not have a totalizing character, and does not *this* character therefore radically demarcate it from that of science or sociology, whose interpretations of the world are necessarily partial, provisional and infinitely revisable in the light of experience? Central to the definition of theology I have been using is the thesis that any claim that God can be encompassed by a human system of thought (even one based on the incarnation and divine revelation) is a form of idolatry which confuses the object of knowledge (as defined in and through the terms of a theoretical system) with the real object. Compared with the reality which the theologian as a religious person seeks to know, his or her theological formulations are inevitably 'all straw'. What theologians call 'divine revelation' is conditioned by the life experiences provided by a particular social formation, and its formulation conditioned by the available cultural resources for its interpretation. It is, I consider, the task of theology to synthesize these partial revelations; that is, to relate them and universalize them so that, freed from the specific socio-historical references they embody, they may serve to enrich the understanding of the inhabitants of social formations other than those in which they originated. 'God', within a definition of theology of this kind, is identified as a living reality operating effectively in the world. Without the descriptive frame of reference which theology elaborates, this activity cannot be recognized as such, but that is true of any theoretical observation. Descriptive frames of reference are never falsifiable by experience; they are abandoned when they fail to make sense of experience.

By this same definition, an absolutist theology is, on the contrary, essentially the theology of an unbeliever, since it reduces 'God' to a formal explanatory principle. Therefore the growth of a scientific world-view which renders absolutist and closed theology impossible is (I would suggest to Christians) surely something only to be welcomed?

Responses by

Mary Hesse, Fergus Kerr, Nicholas Lash

Hesse: Christopher, you say there seems 'to be a move in the philosophy of science to a realist conception of science, and arguably realist conceptions are less antipathetic to theology than phenomenalist conceptions'. (p.30). It seems to me that your diagnosis before that, which I would almost entirely go along with, has indicated how the problematic of the subject (or 'the problematic of man' as I would prefer to put it) and the problematic of the object have together led us to a position where there is a danger of the concept of man disappearing in the face of structuralist and other kinds of scientistic attacks and attempts at explanation. I agree with you that this poses a threat to the kind of theology that we have had since the Enlightenment – theology which has presupposed a concept of man as a model for God, so that theology has been essentially man-centred, rather than God-centred in a more traditional way. But this response of yours to this situation would seem to be a reactionary one. Am I right in thinking that you see the way ahead for theology as a return to a more metaphysically-based concept of God, analogous to the return that you think you see in natural science to a more metaphysically-based understanding of the science of nature, that is to the realistic interpretation of theoretical entities and of natural laws as necessary connections?

Harris: It is important to remember that basically what I have been attempting to do is locate sociology and theology (and the relationship between them) in wider movements of thought. What I am drawing attention to is that, as these movements seem to be favouring realism rather more again, the possibility would seem to be open for continuing to view theology in what some people might regard as a rather old-fashioned way. Do I also conceive of theology developing in what, in these terms, would be a reactionary way, that is to say, going back to a metaphysical concept of God? I think, in order to answer this question, one has to ask the question: to whom are theologians going to be talking? If the price of communication between two speakers is to make one's message intelligible to the person with whom one is to communicate, then it seems to me that one might very well speak analogously of God in a metaphysical sense. Having said that, however, I would add that I think it is necessary for those who reflect the character of the Christian faith in any age to attempt to translate that faith into terms which are understandable by those who are most deeply involved in the spirit of that age, and this will be something rather different if we are moving into a structuralist age. It will involve attempting to express the Christian faith in a way intelligible to a structuralist – something which, it seems to me, will constitute a very considerable challenge to theology as it is at present!

Lash: The way you described the theologian's communication problem just then seemed to me to suggest that the Christian has conceptually appropriated his faith, that his only problem is how to put it rather differently when he has to speak to somebody else – a structuralist, for instance – from the way he normally puts it for his fellow-Christians. Now, that seems to me not to describe the condition of Christianity in our culture, because Christian faith and language, experience and inquiry, do not have some prior autonomous area of existence from which we might proceed to go and talk to somebody else. I think I prefer to put the problem in terms of asking: what are the ways in which Christian hope, Christian faith, might find appropriate intellectual expression in our culture?

Kerr: I am a little nervous of saying structuralism is just a passing fashion. So, although I share your doubts, Nicholas, about certain styles of communicating, I am not entirely happy about the way you are articulating these doubts. I don't think we theologians should say we must prepare ourselves for a structuralist epoch, just like that, just because structuralism happens to be the language of the day. I think the first thing we must do is to look at (say) structuralism, and see if it makes any sense at all. If it can be shown to be nonsense, then that's the end of the work. I am still at the stage of wondering whether structuralism, in the way in which it is being practised in France, is more than a lot of incoherent sophistries, but my impression is it need not be resisted immediatley, any more than Aristotle, when he appeared in Paris in the thirteenth century, needed to be resisted immediately. I find stucturalism attractive, myself. You say, Christopher, that 'the true enemy of theology is not necessarily sociology, but any discipline which claims to displace the problematic of the subject, thus leaving room for neither God nor man', (p.29) and you are clearly uneasy about the prevalent man-centred ideology, and I wholeheartedly agree with what you say on this. But I would go further than you. I can't think of a better description of Christian theology than that it is a discipline – an ascesis – that does in fact *itself* claim to displace the problematic of the subject – and I am not displacing it back to 'God', for I want to destroy both 'man' *and* 'God'. More exactly, this is what I believe Christian theology claims to do. For, in saying that I am going 'further' than you, Christopher, all I am saying is that I believe I am merely being orthodox, Chalcedonian, trinitarian, theocentric in a Christian sense! For what constitutes Christian theology in my understanding of it (in contrast to how a lot of theology is taught these days) is that the subject is Jesus Christ, who is neither simply 'man' nor simply 'God'; or, to put things in a slightly different way, the subject is not God in any deistic sense (the sense we usually work with) but the triune God. Theology is the semiotics of a structure of articulated behaviour observable to sociologists (namely, Christian praxis, Christian church and tradition) which discloses the structure of the three-in-one God who has been revealed. (Note that here I am keeping the truth-question completely separate, for this is something on which I think sociology has no bearing at all.) You say yourself, Christopher, that 'in a sense structure has replaced God'. (p. 30) I want to say that, in the Christian revelation *specifically*, structure replaced 'God'. *That* is why I am attracted by structuralism, and can see in it by no stretch of the imagination anything that theologians need fear. Rather the contrary.

Hesse: But there has been terrible confusion about the term 'structure'. Christopher, on the other hand, knows exactly what he means. He means Althusser and Lévi-Strauss, and both of them are very clear – much clearer than most non-natural scientists – about the model and method they are using. This is indebted to linguistic structural studies and communication theory, and has to do with looking for theoretical concepts which can be formally put together in systems and which can yield certain surface structures as epiphenomena. Now, both of them have an ideological position which is not merely anti-theist but anti-humanist. It seems to me that to say a trinitarian Christianity can somehow find the thinking of Lévi-Strauss sympathetic is most confusing. Fergus, are you really wanting to say, in a sense that is genuinely materialistic, that the underlying structure of the material world has to do with theism?

Kerr: I do not see why you think it at all surprising, because it seems to me the whole point of Christianity is that it did destroy a concept of God. Unfortunately it has got to keep on doing so. You see, the doctrine of the trinity is nothing but a structuralist concept of God. I think, incidentally, that Christopher is right in what he says about the influence of Hegel on Lévi-Strauss . . . and at the heart of Hegelianism there clearly is secularized trinitarian christology.

Hesse: But what you are speaking about, Fergus, is a historical church doctrine. You would surely have to strip it of much it has come to be associated with during its history?

Kerr: I agree that, for this reason, a lot of careful work on the meaning-production of the doctrine will have to be done, and here the contribution of sociology and history is going to be extremely important. And not on this doctrine only, for, if Christianity's claims are true, it has also brought to an end a certain notion of man. In this context, I would like to see, for a start, the sort of thing Lévi-Strauss has done for Latin-American mythology being done for Christianity – the sort of work which Edmund Leach has begun on a very very small scale. It is particularly stimulating that it is (as you rightly say, Mary) thinking as materialist as that of Lévi-Strauss which is prompting this reappraisal, because this is in certain ways a repetition of the situation which confronted Thomas Aquinas in the thirteenth century. It looks, you see, to a lot of people as if Plato is the man Christians should make for, and soft-headed Christians continue to make for Plato, but Aristotle was the man Aquinas chose. Why was Aquinas condemned in his age as a heretic? Because he had gone for frank materialism.

Hesse: But Aristotle had a sort of god.

Kerr: Yes, but the wrong god. You can read Aquinas's treatise on the trinity as a destruction of Aristotle's god. I think time and again Christianity will only survive if it goes for the really hard challenge, and today this comes from the positivists, reductionists, the materialists, like Lévi-Strauss. Yet, having said all that I have to repeat what I said at the beginning of my intervention: I personally may be attracted by structuralism, but at this stage we must constantly bear in mind that it may turn out that we will not be able to do with Lévi-Strauss what Aquinas did with Aristotle.

Lash: It seems to me that the attempt to articulate Christian faith in a particular cultural context is always a process heavy with risks, and the risks that I have in mind are not primarily risks of a failure to communicate but rather the risk that we may fail to continue to be able to give Christian expression to human hopes and convictions. I think that these are genuine practical and theoretical risks which Christian theology evades to its cost. The way in which the Aristotelian conception of how reality and experience were to be described did, in the Middle Ages, not only lay siege to but actually threatened the possibility of Christian faith and hope, is, as Fergus has said, not wholly dissimilar to the situation which we face today. Now, I warmly welcome your statement, Christopher, that 'the collapse of a given problematic obviously abolishes that particular conception of God which the problematic has called forth, but the death of a particular God-concept should be no more mistaken for the death of all God concepts than for the death of that of which it is a concept'. (p. 31) My only worry about it is that it could be read as being a little too comforting – as if, never mind, some God-concepts have been perhaps discredited by developments in the social sciences and elsewhere, but don't worry, there are going to be some more around. It might encourage in the theologian an inappropriate complacency. If I combine this statement with the one Fergus has already picked out – 'The true enemy of theology is not necessarily sociology, but any discipline which claims to displace the problematic of the subject, thus leaving room for neither God nor man' – I think I want to know what God-concepts, if any, in your view, are *not* killed off?

Harris: I think this is a difficult question, because in order to answer it one has to think oneself outside what I would call the 'subjectivist problematic' entirely, and start thinking about God in some way other than as subject, and this I don't think I am able to do myself. The answer can only await an attempt to do this. But on this I would like to comment by taking you back to what you rightly said about confrontations being 'heavy with risks', and especially the risk of failing to continue to be able 'to give Christian expression to human hopes and convictions'. I think the difficulty about the structuralist approach, which is also a difficulty that agonizes sociologists, is that the analysis of a human phenomenon which deploys the language of structure cannot be connected up to the language of action. So it would not seem to me that a purely structuralist theology would be any more viable a possibility than a purely structuralist sociology.

Kerr: The problem is the determination of freedom. Lévi-Strauss gives the impression that there is some hidden, ultimate, always receding code which determines all articulate behaviour, so that our lives are dictated by some kind of anonymous non-personal system. And that is frightening. But I don't see that it is any more frightening than the materialism of Aristotle as it appeared in Paris in the thirteenth century.

Hesse: I think the attraction of Lévi-Strauss's approach for me is, in the first place, from the other end – in other words, because of his descriptive concern with people's mythologies. It does seem to me that one way in which current difficulties about the apparently empirical historical claims of Christianity might be met is to re-interpret them as the myth-telling of, say the gospel writers and even the Church councils like Chalcedon. It may even be that they would have understood themselves to be expressing their beliefs mythologically and not necessarily at all in what we would call empirical and historical terms. It is surprising that, at least in English, it is only an agnostic, Edmund Leach, who has in fact attempted to use Lévi-Straussian techniques on this sort of material. As I think he would have to agree himself, since he is an agnostic, Leach has not found it disturbing that his results have come out so formal, so that what you, Nicholas, have just called 'human hopes and convictions' are totally missing. Old Testament mythologies like the Abraham-Isaac story and the Jethro and his daughter story can be interpreted in terms of binary oppositions and structures. The morals are absent, as are the consequences for human religious hopes or human action. For this reason the help that kind of structuralism will give us is very limited, and only its starting point might appeal. But Geoffrey Kirk, in his attempt to apply the techniques to the Greek myths, found himself forced to do something much more contentful, to put back, as it were, the morals into the succession of the mythologies.

Lash: I wonder (and this thought is partly connected with Christopher's use, in his last comment, of the concept of connection between theoretical systems and patterns of action) whether there isn't an important area of problems here concerning, on the one hand, the necessary variety of forms of discourse, and, on the other, concerning the relationships that might obtain between these forms of discourse. Thus, for example, it seems to me inevitable, desirable and appropriate that the primary forms of Christian speech should continue to be narrative in form, and narrative can embody 'in its text' expressions of hope. But what is needed as well as that primary level of narrative discourse (and here I am speaking, as a theologian, of something achieved only with difficulty in the history of theology) is a level of strictly theoretical discourse appropriate to the particular cultural context – in our context maybe a structuralist mode of discourse. That mode of discourse, as formal and theoretical, is not going to embody 'in its text' expressions of hope, desire, interest, conviction. The important thing, then, is that the connections between the modes of discourse are appropriately perceived and constructed. I have the impression that some theologians expect there to be a kind of continuity of logic between theological and religious statement. I fail to see why there should be such a continuity of logic, any more than there is, for instance, between the discourse of a sub-atomic particle physicist and an everyday commonsense description of tables and chairs.

Hesse: But isn't it also the theologian's job to make the connection? It can't be left to the man-in-the-pew to do this, and this is precisely where theologians lose touch with religion in the community.

Lash: I entirely accept the responsibility of the theologian to make the connection, certainly. What I don't accept is the fashionable hostility to theoretical enquiry in theology. I say this partly because it seems to me that the disquiet that you just expressed in respect of structuralist treatment of myths might be appropriate in respect of primary religious language but not necessarily in respect of theoretical theological patterns of enquiry.

Hesse: I feel what we are saying about the problems of varieties of modes of discourse and modes of knowledge takes us back to something at the heart of what Christopher has written. I would like him to go a bit beyond what he has written, into areas which I would dare to call epistemological. It seems to me that the legacy of the distinction between the two types of *Wissenschaft* – *Naturwissenschaften* and *Geisteswissenschaften* – has left us with the object-centred problematic identified with the natural sciences and the subject-centred (or man-centred) problematic identified with the social sciences, whether understood reductively, structurally or not, or whether understood in terms of independent recognition of actions and human intentions. Here are two fairly well-understood cognitive modes. And Christopher is right in saying that hermeneutic methodology is still subjective, because meaning is seen only as brought out of individual human thought or intersubjective dialogue, and hence theology seems to be left out of both scientific and hermeneutic modes. Now, where might one go for some sort of a third mode? Should one see this in terms of a third problematic which will need something as penetrating in the way of epistemological analysis as Kant's in the natural sciences, and as Dilthey's in the hermeneutical sciences? Is this where one is really looking for the new Aquinas, somebody to locate theology as a mode of knowledge?

Harris: I would not identify the problematics of the object with the *Naturwissenschaften* and the problematics of the subject with the *Geisteswissenschaften*. Nor would I equate sociology with the *Geisteswissenschaften*, because I feel that sociology has never as an enterprise been located in either one or the other. It has adopted a positivistic approach and allied itself with the *Naturwissenschaften*, but this has always provoked some revolt in its ranks, forcing it back into the *Geisteswissenschaften*. In fact, we see at least Durkheim and Marx attempting to get out of the opposition between these two types of disciplines. So it seems to me that sociology is essentially an attempt to create the 'third world' to which you refer, and this is reflected in the fact that Marx has been interpreted in a Hegelian or idealistic sense and Durkheim through positivist ideas. I wonder, myself, whether there *is* that 'third world' of discourse which somehow bridges the gulf between these two types of discipline. So I am not clear how to answer the question: where do you see epistemologically one goes from here in sociology and theology?

Hesse: Of course sociology is not uniquely located in one mode. But I think I could agree with Pannenberg that it is not so much that there is a great divide between disciplines, with physics in one box and sociology in another; rather, the divide goes through all the disciplines (here I am exlcuding theology for the moment). So I would not see sociology as a solution in the search for the 'third

world' (not, of course, using this term in Popper's sense), because
the 'third world' is in fact a breaking-free of this problematic which
is either an objectivizing (namely, the external empirical world) or
subjectivizing (in the sense of a hermeneutic discipline): sociology
alternates between these different ways but it does not get outside
them both, and so it cannot be what, in cognitive terms, the word
'theology' designates. Certainly sometimes in the past what a given
society has agreed on calling 'knowledge' has included 'knowledge
of God'. What our society seems to lack is an intellectual unpacking,
not of of other people's beliefs, because sociologists and anthropologists can do this: they can say that for the Nuer there is a god.
But that is not to say, ontologically speaking, I believe there is a god.
What we have now lost in our intellectual culture is any means of
saying there is a theo-logy – a logos of God. I don't know where to
look, and I find very few helpful suggestions anywhere.

Lash: And I am not about to offer one. But your reference there
to Pannenberg might give us some kind of clue as to what possible
direction one might look in. Because isn't it true that the image of
the 'third world' where we can safely locate theology (or maybe
sociology, or maybe both) is a little bit misleading? For one of the
things I take Pannenberg to be saying, and you appear to be agree-
ing with him, is that the construction or inhabiting of the 'third
world' calls in question the assumed dualism and irreconcilability of
the first two worlds. So, with a 'third world' coming into existence,
however awkwardly, the 'first' and 'second' worlds are not
untouched. This is one of the ways by which positivism is undercut.
In other words, what I want to suggest is that, as against the model of
two fundamentally irreconcilable epistemological stances (namely,
those relating to the natural sciences and the hermeneutic sciences),
one has a variety of objects of exploration and enquiry – an irreducible variety of ways in which both positivistic and hermeneutic
elements are to be combined in different patterns of enquiry and
discourse. Now, that's to put it very formally, I grant, but, if the
problem does begin to take on that sort of shape, then it seems to me
to be possible that one might discover a way of talking about the
knowledge of God along these lines. It would be yet another
irreducibly distinct way of combining these elements, and I take it
that something like this is what Pannenberg is trying to do in his
large book *Theology and the Philosophy of Science*. Whether or not
that book works, I think it does point us in a direction.

Kerr: Speaking of this publicly-shared 'knowledge of God' which
we do not seem any more to have, one problem surely is that
precisely by becoming academic, theology has tended to drift away

from religion and from liturgy and from the ordinary people who do most of the believing. And I wonder whether this may not even be a point that you are making, Nicholas, in your Cambridge Inaugural Lecture, where you say 'the vitality and concrete "truthfulness" of Christian speech is a precondition of theology, rather than (as seems often to be supposed) the other way round'. If sustained knowledge of God is anywhere it is in the hearts and the minds of people who actually pray and worship. The academic institution of theology really ought to be rooted back in church, ecclesiastical experience, worship, liturgy and prayer – in what people actually believe. Now here is a task for sociology, not merely at the level of counting heads and deciding what class worshippers fall into, but much along the lines of Robert Towler's investigations of belief – about which he is writing in the Epilogue.

Lash: I think this is absolutely right, and the reasons why it is right are not simply tactical or pragmatic.

Kerr: The faith of the people of God – if there is any faith at all – is carried by the whole congregation.

Lash, Right. And theology comes second, not to coin a phrase. Thus, where the knowledge of God is concerned, it is often assumed, in a situation in which the temper of Christian consciousness is heavily rationalist, that unless the theologian knows God nobody else can. And that seems to me to be precisely the opposite of how the problem ought to be put. Unless these are people who know God, the theologian can't start.

Relevant writings of authors mentioned in this discussion are listed in the Select Bibliography. (pp. 191–9)

Notes

1 Hindess, B. *Philosophy and Methodology in the Social Sciences* (Harvester, Hassocks, 1977) p. 7.
2 Foucault, M. *Les Mots et les choses* (Paris, 1966); English translation: *The Order of Things* (London, 1970) p. 27.
3 Habermas, J. *Erkenntnis und Interesse* (Frankfurt, 1968); English translation: *Knowledge and Human Interests* (London, 1972) p. 308.

Chapter 3

THE SOCIOLOGICAL MODE AND THE THEOLOGICAL VOCABULARY

David Martin

WHAT is theology? It is an attempt to make intellectual sense of a way of life. This does not mean that theology tries to provide the inner rationale for the life style of a stockbroker or a computer technician, or attempts to explain why we should be in a society whose way of life generates brokers and technicians. Those two tasks belong respectively to descriptive and to analytic sociology. It means rather that human existence characteristically engenders ways of living and feeling which try to make comprehensive sense of the human environment and situation. Theology is one of the intellectual disciplines which articulates that comprehensive sense.

But in what sense do I use the word 'sense'? I am clearly not talking about every attempt to elucidate meanings. When I ask a lawyer about the general sense of a legal document his reply is not 'theology'. So I am talking about the articulation of a very particular sort of 'sense', that is, the comprehensive sort. To comprehend is not to grasp this or that, but to hold this and that together. I may grasp a process or note and classify a quality or property, but my cognitive apprehensions concern only finite, delimited sectors of happenings. No doubt those sectors can be linked theoretically and the inner dynamics of one sector compared with those of another sector. This kind of theoretical linkage is no more 'theology' than is a lawyer's account of a legal document.

Theology articulates a 'set' or frame which gathers together into one an approach to our personal and social being, a relation of temporal and eternal, a location or image or focus for harmony and perfection, a meaning which lies beyond our immediate apprehensions and which informs the world of natural and historic process. What is *really* accidental and what is really essential to my health, wholeness and salvation? Where are true joys to be found? Where in the changing scene may a man properly rest his hope? On whay may I – and we – be stayed? What remains? To what do all things in nature and history tend? Where shall we find the secret names of God and the inner story of his purposes? Is the Eternal City being built in time or do its towers lie over the temporal horizon? By what signs and in what signs may we transcend our mortal limitations? What emblems cover and uncover ecstasy? What are the limits that govern even our transcendence of limits?

By what are we bound and how shall we be freed? Who or what can release us?

The queries just listed have not included any reference to God. This is because theological questions overlap the concerns of every systematic and comprehensive quest for meaning and purpose. Nevertheless, within this broad category of concern the theologian does have a peculiar role. He asks his questions in relation to a particular postulate and a special possibility, which is that the concentrated 'image' of meaning and purpose, striving and release, perfection and plenitude, is not merely a subjective construct evoking the energies of men, or an emergent property of the process, but is *there*, objectively present, already meeting the hopes of men, and creatively implicated in the whole from the beginning. So his task is not merely or mainly to explicate the limits and rules under which images are created and translated into social arrangements, but to brood upon the paradox of a plenitude and power which can only express itself creatively within strict limitations and rules, and which only achieves fullness in relation to that which is not itself.

I have pointed to an immense labyrinth of query; and theology is the fumbling attempt to find the connecting thread. In the end there are perhaps only a few basic 'ways' through the labyrinth, each with a specific set of axioms and a characteristic internal logic, including a logic of social relationships. I do not pretend to know exactly how many basic approaches there are, partly because that depends on what principles of categorization you prefer to employ, but I suspect they are strictly limited. The world religions, for example, comprise a very small fundamental set. You can reduce that set even further by proposing more and more comprehensive groupings, as for example the grouping which derives from the common Hebrew root and the grouping which derives from the common Indian root. You can also expand the set by tracing mutations, new combinations and recombinations. And you can even devise formulae for coping with gaps, 'mess' and chaos. What matters in this context is that each ground or frame generates a group of intellectual, aesthetic and social assonances and that these embody certain possibilities at the expense of certain constrictions and limits. They carve an arc out of the spectrum of possibilities. They even embody their own specific dissonances and antitheses. If the point may be put crudely, the labyrinth allows a limited set of connecting threads, and once one or other is grasped you have to accept a particular map of possible paths and close off another map. You can only move along the historic thread by successive acts of closure. The thread itself is not a strict logical progression, but a set of assonances and harmonic relationships springing up from the initial ground.

Theology is the semi-collective enterprise which follows the different threads through the whole labyrinth of query set out above. Normally the theologian works with other people who are bound in and on the same 'Way' and follows through one set of assonances, though he may from time to time compare the costs which attend his own tradition with those which attend another. But whether he follows through his own tradition or compares it with others, he is engaged in a normative discipline. He only describes a particular theo-logic in order to prescribe a Way. Ordinarily he does not amuse himself playing a game with pure internal relationships. He articulates a vision by which he is compelled, and he wishes to show *why* it is compelling. Of course, he will also have to give an account of how his vision relates to the kind of theoretical knowledge which links up the world as grasped empirically. Presumably that is what we are attempting to do now.

So where does the sociologist come in? Surprisingly enough, right at the beginning. First of all, he has to grasp these 'generators' and assonances as a prelude to the task of explanation. He has to understand the underlying structure of world-views. A sociologist who has not grasped the logic of systems cannot see any deviations there may be and has no framework for tracing mutations or showing how a vision is bent and refracted by social realities. He needs at least to grasp the general idea of such a 'logic' to embark even on the task of confuting it. If, for example, he were to maintain that all religions are pure mish-mash or the plausible but *ad hoc* conjunction of chaotic elements, he would need to conceive and construct something systematic against which the chaos and mish-mash might be contrasted.

So far everything I have suggested implies that the roles of theologian and sociologist overlap each other. Both are concerned with the structure of statements and world-views. The theologian concentrates on the idea that the divine image is not merely product but source and ground, and on the normative implications of that idea. However, a peculiar problem emerges with respect to the logic of religious statements in so far as they relate to a socio-logic. Every religious way includes an approved mode of life and implies a particular set of institutional options. Christianity, for example, distinguishes power from truth, and thereby implies a range of options in the relationships between church and state. So long as the theologian broods with normative concern on the implications, say, of the distinction between Caesar and God he is within his *opus proprium*. But he is bound at some point to consider the historical forms in which that distinction has been embodied. This means that he may ask himself *why* the distinction has been minimally observed in medieval Russia and maximally observed in modern America –

and why that maximal observance may be more apparent than real. At this point he leaves his own sphere and enters the spheres of historical and sociological explanation, of sequences of event and motivation and the rules governing man's social constructions.

Of course, this may be an unproblematic change of academic headgear, or at any rate the theologian may treat it as such. One moment he has a normative or metaphysical or theo-logical interest, and at another moment he operates qua historian or qua sociologist. But it is not quite so simple a matter. A theologian changing hats retains the same head, and cannot simply jettison the language in which he usually talks about the world. That language is partly normative and partly descriptive and both the normative and descriptive elements appear to have a problematic carryover into the doing of sociology and history.

Let me give examples which may bring out both the relation of sociology and theology and also highlight a central problem of language and level of description.

The first example contains endless ramifications, so I will state it simplistically. The theologian broods on the norms and images that guide and illumine his particular religious tradition. He observes that these images are embodied in historical reality according to rule-governed orderly processes, which distort or maim them. He observes too that his images of perfection are not merely subject to distortions, but are subject to opportunity costs such that when one fragment of vision is momentarily achieved another fragment is displaced or further distorted. In short he observes the systematic and rule-governed character of the cramps governing this and that human situation.

This will cause difficulties unless he indulges in systematic intellectual schizophrenia, and cuts off his theological from his sociological activity. The first difficulty is a classic one, so classic as to prevent further discussion here. It is that any observation of the ordered character of human social activity and of the systematic cramps governing that activity leads to a question about freedom and responsibility. Given circumstances A and B, and given the opportunity costs attendant on course X as compared with course Y, it begins to look as if the systems of action and interaction are completely determined. And if everything is determined, then moral judgment upon it appears quite inappropriate. However, I do not myself hold a deterministic view, though I do note that *every* comprehensive system of thinking about society runs into a particular variant of the problem of freedom and determinism. Every system says: these things *must* be and these things need not be. Indeed, the most potent systems suggest how men may collude creatively with necessity. The only postulate that sociology qua sociology clearly *requires* is the notion of ordered, rule-governed interrelations. Sociology does not *require* us to accept that every option is already pre-empted by the antecedent concatenation of circumstances. Indeed, my own view is that options are real just because they are very circumscribed. We can choose precisely *because* the range of possibilities is constricted.

The second difficulty is also classic in its way, though less continuously exposed to intellectual scrutiny. I have referred to it before in my 'Political Decision and Ethical Comment'. (*Theology*, October 1973) It is that any perception of the cramps and costs attendant on action leads to a query about the nature of moral and religious prescriptions. No doubt this query arises from the ordinary, ancient and everyday observation that we cannot do what we like and that we nearly always achieve something other than we intended. But the systematic exposure of cramps and costs sharpens the query very considerably. If for example, sociological analysis shows that the conflict of Catholics and Protestants in Ulster is a particular instance in a class of conflicts, so that given the coordinates A to n ... C and P are bound to clash, then ecumenical breastbeating becomes a rather otiose activity. Furthermore if sociological analysis suggests that mediators or intermediate conciliatory groups are likely to be impotent or even to exacerbate the situation, then the search for a mediating role becomes morally very problematic. The moral problem is not solved nor put on one side by such an analysis, but it is set in sharpened perspective. At any rate, the ordinary liberal and (intermittently) Christian assumption that the solution is basically a matter of goodwill is undermined. The situation may at certain previous junctures have been willed, but it is now determined and good-will cannot be relied upon to mend it.

No doubt good-will is required, but the simple willing of the good cannot overcome the structural constraints within which people seek evil. Of course, if everyone were to will the good simultaneously then the structural constraints might be ameliorated or even abolished since everyone would simultaneously desire not only peace and harmony but also justice. But one knows on good sociological grounds, let alone on good theological grounds, that an immediate and universal desire for peace and justice is not humanly or statistically likely. Indeed, a structural constraint is precisely the kind of institutional set which buttresses that statistical impossibility. No doubt the mystery of evil is deeper than an institutional set which inclines the will of men towards evil deeds but the fears and deprivations engendered by institutional arrangements are at least an element in manifestations of 'evil'; and this is unusually clear in Ulster. Evil solidifies; it is more than the mixing of wills.

Contemporary Christians are increasingly aware of how struc-

tural constraints engender activities which are morally reprehensible, at least by the normal canons of reprehensibility. There is a
variety of ways whereby Christians may confront the problem of
structural constraint. One way is to carry on acting charitably in the
knowledge that charity and goodwill are not enough. To love one's
neighbour will not avert tragedy and crucifixion: so much the Christian religion itself ought to make clear. Another way is to down-
grade charitable concern as wrapped in individualistic delusions
about the nature of social arrangements and their supposed respon-
siveness to moral initiative. The new realistic Christian now regards
individual initiative as secondary to structural change; and he may
even conclude that charity is at best ineffective and at worst positively harmful. (Aid to the Third World for example has often had
effects which are economically and morally harmful.) Once the new
Christian has grasped his sociology or his Marxism he expresses his
radical moral and social discontent in a structural terminology. His
prescriptive vocabulary is now composed of analyses of structure
and role and maybe of domination, deprivation and alienation. This
new vocabulary is characteristic of the radical section of the middle
class, and combines fervent righteousness with the espousal of a
semi-deterministic perspective. So sociological sophistication
results in a paradoxical combination of a moralistic critique of
structures with a depersonalized analysis of how they arise and how
they may be dismantled. Indeed, the depersonalized analysis can
deteriorate into a contempt for persons as such: Marxist repression
has often followed this path. The situation alarms sociologists as
well as Christians. The Christians are worried by the query placed
against the language of moral exhortation and against the liberal
and Christian (?) notion that the increase of persons who live and
act in good faith leads to a better society. The sociologists are
worried by the way in which the concept of structure can be reified
and then incorporated in sets of macro-social mechanisms, so giving
rise to fatalism. The sociologists have tried to construct what they
call interactional accounts of people in groups which allow for the
way men jointly construct their social worlds and exercise initiatives
which create as well as reflect the cramps of structure. If these
sociologists are right then Christian (or secular) moral exhortation
remains a valid way of calling for creative initiatives. In other words
if the construction of social reality is a joint enterprise to which all
may make some creative contribution then moral prescriptions and
proscriptions are relevant and viable adjuncts of creativity. Morality is not just a film stretched over fatality.

I wish now to move on to the general problem of the referents of
religious language, in so far as such language seems to cover the
same terrain as sociology at (perhaps) a different level. Let me take

three cases of such language since they are partly concerned with the issues of freedom and necessity already mentioned. The three cases are 'original sin', 'the outpouring of the Spirit' and 'the Virgin Birth'.

The three cases are not only concerned with freedom and necessity but in the most general way with the idea of grace. Original sin belongs to our 'nature' and grace is the power to break into the system of nature so as to transform it. We are formed in sin, in a determinate structure of resistance, and transformed by grace. Grace is the theological term for the transformation whereby divine image and distorted reality are brought into closer conjunction. It lies close to the idea of inspiration, that is, the creative flash which alters the pre-existing pattern and reveals a new potency and potentiality. The question is therefore, how do sociological and theological accounts of resistance and potentiality relate to each other?

I take it that original sin can be discussed as if it has some correspondence to, or relation with the idea of constitutional cramps and resistances. Similarly the work of the Spirit can be discussed in relation to the creative deployment of necessity, while the Virgin Birth at least *prima facie* concerns new mutations or breakthroughs in determinate systems of necessity. If these possible correspondences are not clear perhaps they may become so.

The question is as follows. Does the language of original sin really refer to (or overlap with) the notion of inherent cramps, resistances and limits in the human situation (including, of course, radical concern with the self)? If it does *really* refer to such cramps, is the specifically theological usage undermined or conversely rendered scientifically respectable? If there is an overlap, what is the nature of the conjunction and disjunction? The notion of 'original sin' and the notion of strict sociological limits to the embodiment of divine images are at least linked by one characteristic: they convey necessity. They are concerned with the ineluctable. But are they concerned with one ineluctable or two ineluctables? Man's 'original sin' is a corporate condition: so how does that corporate condition relate to the sociological perception of limits?

It might relate in so far as highly general 'metaphysical' assumptions act as preliminary orientations to material, without themselves being falsifiable or indeed very useful, apart from their capacity to give an orientation. If man really does push against a colossal and complex structure of resistances, embodied *simultaneously* in self and society, then a rather pessimistic Christian might be armed with a useful orientation, and one which gave him an initial advantage, albeit (perhaps) an adventitious one. But here we come to an oddity. Such general orientations like original sin or original innocence are not explanatory. Their lack of falsifiability is part of their incapacity to explain. 'Sin' or 'innocence' explain everything and nothing. And lots of theological concepts are like this: basic orientations which provide a generalized image and cannot be set to work to uncover particular cramps, particular limits, particular resistances. The resistances do, of course, contain elements which are very general, but 'original sin' is too general even to disentangle the general elements of resistance from the localized ones.

The notion of 'the Spirit' raises rather different problems, since it is specifically invoked as a quasi-explanatory category. For example, the Christian Church was born (as Jesus was born) by an infusion or effusion of the Spirit. Individual Christians have vocations which are 'callings' of the Spirit. So what does it mean to say that a new religion is brought into being by the Creator Spirit, the Spirit of freedom? What does it mean to say that men and women at sundry times and places are called of the Spirit? Or that the church is infused by and guided by the Spirit? Is this a characterization alongside our social, historical and psychological characterizations? Is it a form of normative appraisal, an assessment of 'quality'? Is it, for example, like the quality of inspiration which we divine in music or art, but to which we cannot assign a precise causal role? The idea of ecstatic breath entering into and fulfilling human beings is deeply rooted in human language about art and religion, but to what does it refer? Does it refer to the element of freedom in all creation, or to the qualitatively new aspect of a work of art, or to the release and the new perspective which that achievement brings about, or to all these things? Again, this is not just a problem for religion and for religious language but for the relation of scientific descriptions to all language. It would not be so difficult, of course, if theologians restricted themselves to a general defence of the propriety of such language. They could defend the notion that one may use a phrase like the outpouring of the Spirit to cover new, creative, breakthroughs, which lift men from mundane stasis to ex-stasis, that is, to transcendence. In which case the term 'Holy' as applied to 'Spirit' concerns all those instances where the 'Transcendence' embodied a 'wholesome' or genuinely creative and healing possibility, rather than a vision of chaos or evil, not to just those instances for which we have no naturalistic explanation. The trouble is that theologians use the term 'operation of the Spirit' to cover so many doubtful cases. But that can be put down to incautious stupidity, and need not cause us any logical difficulty. It is only necessary to note again the very general character of the religious description. Whereas 'original sin' covered the *general* character of resistance so 'Holy Spirit' designates the *general* possibility of creative breakthrough. (There are, of course, specific Marxist translations for such general terms and indeed most general terms have analogues in other vocabularies or play some functionally or substantially equivalent role in those vocabularies.)

But this brings us to a problem posed by one particular assertion about the Holy Spirit which is fairly central to historic Christianity.

Even generalized references to the action of the Spirit in the 'empirical' Church create intellectual discomfort in those who also use the language of sociological description. The extent of that discomfort depends precisely on how theologians use their terms, and on what doctrine they hold of the relation of 'the Spirit' to the empirical Church.

For example, the Wesleyan revival from 1738 onwards may be characterized as 'a great outpouring of the Spirit'. What does this mean? Such a characterization could be entirely descriptive and entirely unexceptionable. Nobody disputes the existence of extensive 'spiritual' phenomena of a quite dramatic kind leading to changes in life, character and sensibility. But theological language is usually normative as well as descriptive: it pinpoints a happening in order to set it in a context of approval: 'This is the Lord's doing and it is marvellous in our eyes.' Certain classes of events are demarcated as representing the divine activity. Other classes presumably do not represent this activity, or cannot be given a secure theological imprimatur. The 'spirits' have to be tested and some tests yield uncertain results.

What however is indisputable is the rule-governed character of all such spiritual phenomena, whether they pass the theologians' tests or not. The lava of the Spirit runs along the lines of social fault; and the wind of the Spirit blows according to a chart of high and low pressures. It may be, of course, that the theologian merely wishes to say that in all these 'signs' he obscurely discerns the Spirit of God, and does not wish to locate exactly where that Spirit is to be found. It may also be that he suspects a much more complicated operation of spiritual providence which occurs under 'signs' far outside the boundaries of churches and particular religions. He knows it is dangerous to say 'lo here' and 'lo there'. And maybe he also recognizes that in an orderly social universe, as in an orderly universe, the Creator Spirit works within limits, and 'breaks through' according to rules and forms. In which case, the operation of 'the Spirit' may be likened to inspiration in the arts: an act of unveiling, a creative reformulation of pre-existent elements, a fresh fusion, the exploration of a given option, . . . If this is how theologians conceive the activity of the Spirit then maybe there is no tension whatsoever between theological and sociological language.

Jesus was born of the Virgin Mary by the action of the Spirit. I choose this assertion because it is not merely important but also likely to arouse embarrassment. Many contemporary Christians are inclined to dismiss the Virgin Birth as myth, as based on misunderstandings of prophecy and as reflecting views of sexuality they wish to repudiate. Those who think the doctrine physically inconceivable and/or morally reprehensible are also much impressed by the paucity of the historical evidence. So they are not likely to resist a sociological account of the phenomenon. Indeed they may encourage and applaud such an account.

Now a sociological account moves at various levels. I am going to construct an account which shows the *sort* of hypothesis which characterizes sociology without going into its truth or falsehood. Indeed, sceptics may care to note that such a hypothesis as I now put forward is barely susceptible to verification or falsification even in principle. I mean that although the hypothesis refers to the empirical world it is not clear how it may be falsified or verified. One asks whether it 'fits', whether it is intuitively correct or counter-intuitive, whether it belongs to a generally coherent account of processes in the social world and so on, but there is no crucial experiment which might establish it or crucial negative fact which might disestablish it. This is true of most important and insightful sociological theories as well as of minor and stupid ones. All the same, hard-nosed empiricism ignores such theories at the price of ignoring many of the things which matter most.

A sociologist may approach the Virgin Birth in many ways, as for example, by enquiring what correlation might exist between the mythical conceptions of sexuality and divinity and the roles and structures of society at large. He would assume, initially, some loose though complex correspondence. Doctrines, say sociologists, do not land like meteorites from outer space, but grow organically where they have a supporting, fertile social niche or cranny. The only alternatives to this idea of a (very loose) correspondence of signs and structures are randomness, that is, the anarchic intrusion of the Spirit working with a book of random numbers, or a discernible or mysterious Providence, or innate principles or codes which comprise a fairly economic set and generate internal combinations. (Even these notions are not all straight alternatives.)

At any rate let us, for the sake of argument, assume that signs and structures are loosely related and that the sociologist can make sense of the relations. He seeks an appropriate understandable 'natural' relation or correspondence between sign and structure. Actually there are complex reasons as to why this correspondence may be very loose or occluded or express itself in a variety of functionally equivalent forms, but we do not need to explore those reasons here. We do not need to explore them because nothing follows for theology from the assumption of correspondence. God, the theologian may say, reveals himself at sundry times in diverse

manners, and he will be seen in one way by a nomadic desert people
and in another by a settled agricultural people. The 'names' of God
are heard according to a prior resonance within men's social relationships, one with another.

> Adoro devote, latens veritas,
> te qui sub his formis vere latitas . . .

So far no problem, and maybe there will be no problem in what
follows. Suppose that the Roman Empire which united many tribes
and tongues within a single imperium set the stage for a universal
religion. Suppose too that the monotheism of the Jews based on a
covenant relation between Israel and Jehovah, contained a universal possibility. Both these suppositions are *a priori* plausible. What
mutations within the symbol system of Jewry would be necessary to
convert a limited covenant relation, rooted in the ethnic exclusive-
ness of the Jews, into a universal religion?

The biological continuity of the ethnic group would have to be
broken and the particular, localized attachments of the family
would have to be undermined. A universal faith would have to cut
the generational tie and the familial bond. It would have to substitute universal spiritual rebirth for limited continuity. Since the
family is based on a canalization of erotic impulses as well as of
particular local loyalties, a universal religion would need to redirect
to redirect the flow of sexual feeling. Local eros would have to be
converted to catholic agape in that family loyalty became loyalty to
the family of God. The reality of brotherly attachment in the biological family would have to be reformed under the sign of universal
brotherhood in the family of man.

Now, these sociological preconditions of universal faith have
obviously been stated with maximum economy and some crudity.
There may be a variety of ways in which a symbol system might
mutate in order to accommodate them. But it is clear that the figure
of the Virgin and the sign of the Virgin Birth fill complementary
roles in relation to these preconditions. The Virgin Birth signifies a
new genesis in the Spirit which breaks out of the biological continuities of the ethnic group. So it complements the idea of being
born again by the Spirit of God and thereby choosing the universal
community of faith rather than accepting the local community of
origin. It also complements the idea of 'the eunuch for the kingdom
of heaven's sake' since the eunuch and the Virgin together carry the
conception of a universal bond of charity posed against the local
bond of familial attachment. At the same time the figure of the
Virgin has a potential role in relation to that universal brotherhood,
in that the canalized erotic energies may focus themselves on her
rather than on this woman or that woman. There is much else that

might be said since the Virgin stands as an antetype of the temple prostitute and of sacred sex. But this leads into complicated questions of the relationship of ethical monotheism to female deities and sacred sexuality which need not concern us here.

What does concern us is not the precise plausibility of the hypothesis, but the complications of the *type* of theorizing. One implication might be that symbols which claimed an ontological or metaphysical status had a real sociological meaning which underlay and undercut the presumed theological meaning. This is reductionism: theological facade merely glosses the underlying sociological reality. Many people are inclined to contrast the metaphysical form with the sociological substance, to reduce poetic image and theological meaning to the basic socio-logic. Thus one highly intelligent and orthodox Catholic student said to me: 'Are you saying that the figure of Our Lady simply functions as a potent symbol of a set of social changes?'

Perhaps I should try to make clearer what sort of hypothesis I have just put forward. It first of all set out to certain pre-conditions for the birth of a universal religion. Certain attachments and continuities will have to be broken, and the breakage will have to be carried in a more or less coherent code. I then note that the new Christian code persistently contrasts Spirit with flesh, spiritual rebirth with familial loyalty. I also note that the Virgin Birth is by the Spirit, just as all the sons of God are born of the Spirit. So I have set out a possible meaning for one part of a code which is consonant with the rest of the code and with the general preconditions for achieving universality. I have indicated a consonance between a religious image and the sociological requirements of a universal faith. And I have suggested there is an internal consonance within the Christian code between certain key signs: the eunuch, the need for spiritual regeneration, the Virgin Birth.

I have, of course, only touched on a tiny section of the web of signals clustering around the notion of virginity. Varied situations will arouse very varied resonances in that web of signals, so that what at one time carried the concept of breakage may at another time carry a rather different weight of meaning. I am suggesting that one sign and its immediate associated signs lie within the logic of a massive shift from particular to universal. The sign of the Virgin Birth *functions* to reinforce the inner coherence of the code, and to reinforce a certain character structure highly compatible with universality, that is, a character structure in which there is a redirection of sexual affect towards every brother and sister in Christ. I have said nothing about origins. At the birth of a religion all kinds of possibilities will be thrown up but only some will be filtered into the core elements of the faith. My whole emphasis has been on *function*, by which I mean contribution to the broad thrust of a movement, as compared with *origin* and with long-term *consequence*.

If I say that a symbol is consonant with others as part of a system which carries a coded message (say) about universality I do not exclude other kinds of levels of meaning or of 'reality'. Symbols are usually multivalent; and they may 'refer' to a number of levels. In any case if I say that the Virgin Birth codes the signs of universality I am describing how the theological norm of unity is achieved. I am saying how the ontological reality is embodied and how the theological norm is made effective. The embodiment may be partial, the norm may not be fully realized, but that is neither here nor there. I cannot, of course, make any judgment, positive or negative about ontological reality. Signs mediate sociological requirements, social tendencies and human aspirations. That at least is clear. Whether they also mediate a deeper, more deeply interfused 'reality' I cannot say. A sociological analysis does not exclude other meanings or exclude other layers or levels of reference. It may however help the task of theology by exposing a layer of socio-logic which displays inter-relations and dynamic mutations. If a theologian observes the critical paths travelled by socio-logic he may be helped to locate critical paths in the spheres of theo-logic.

So, what in conclusion? Simply that we have to investigate very carefully the relationship between different languages and between the levels of supposed reality to which they refer. We have, for example, to look very carefully at the relationship between the vocabulary of moral exhortation and of structural analysis. We have, for example, to consider the relation between generalized orientations like original sin, and more particular, grounded forms of analysis. We have to expose the socio-logic informing a symbol systems, and consider what light that can throw on the form and development of the theo-logic. But provided we examine these correspondences and connections with care, and do not reduce one level to another, the result may be mutual enrichment rather than mutual destruction.

Chapter 4

THEODICY AND SOCIAL THEORY: AN EXPLORATION OF THE LIMITS OF COLLABORATION BETWEEN SOCIOLOGIST AND THEOLOGIAN

W.S.F. Pickering

Introduction

IN examining the possible or actual relations between theology and sociology as established disciplines, one must begin with a historical base, that is, by placing both sociology and theology in a historical context, and then seeing each as historical processes. What have the terms sociology and theology come to mean with the passing of time?

Such an approach makes it clear that the terms are ambiguous descriptions of certain kinds of intellectual activity. Dr Christopher Harris, in Chapter 2, approaching the subject from a very different angle (the potential conflict between the disciplines) has rightly stressed their diversity of meaning. At various times each has meant something different. The difficulties are compounded by the fact that theology has had a long history; sociology is essentially a product of the nineteenth century. As the disciplines have emerged they have embraced wide areas of thought and each has adopted and used different methods. Sociology, for example, can range from describing changes that occur in a society, such as those in the role of women over a given time-span, to positing hypotheses about the requisites for the existence of a society, and further, to considering epistemological problems about the relation of intellectual categories to social structure. Methods range from the use of statistics to the recording of face-to-face interviews, to the use of historical records, and to rational or *a priori* reasoning. Not surprisingly, there are those who would wish to see the abolition of the term sociology and who would substitute the name social science. And to study theology within the western tradition may range from an exposition of how the soul can communicate with God, to a study of the nature of Christ, to the relations between church and state, and so on. Again, its methods have also been diverse, from the exposition of biblical texts or historical records of the church to metaphysical reasoning, to intuition.

Such vastness of territory and diversity of method on both sides suggests that there can be no simple or direct relation between the two activities. Unqualified connection can give rise to nothing but ambiguity and intellectual confusion. It is like saying: what is the relation between physics and archaeology? No one is so foolish as to suggest there is a simple, general relation, but at least one can point to areas of contact, say in the field of carbon-dating. If there is a relation, it is qualified and restricted to specific, well-defined areas. Admittedly there is probably greater overlapping between sociology and theology than there is between archaeology and physics. However, what is to be stressed is that sociology and theology can only meet at certain points.

It was the purpose of the Symposium from which this book has emerged to discover areas of common meeting or interest between the two disciplines. But these areas have to be carefully determined and selected so that a legitimate type of theological enterprise can be mated with a particular, generally accepted sociological activity, for theology in its totality and sociology in its totality can never be isomorphic activities. And there is another point. It is not sufficient to say where the common field or fields are to be found. To do that and nothing more is to take an easy way out. What is required is to show how each discipline at common points can mutually contribute to particular interests and explorations. Further, if tensions can be said to exist between the disciplines at certain points, those tensions should be spelt out and resolved as far as it is reasonably possible.

I shall delineate one common field where, theoretically at least, a meeting is valid and where there might be mutual development.

This area of meeting was first drawn to my attention as a result of reading a little-known book, published in 1943 in France by Gaston Richard. The book was probably the first of its kind to attempt to deal with the relation between sociology and certain aspects of theology, and was at the same time written by a professional sociologist. There is much that Richard wrote that is irrelevant to the subject today since he was concerned in attacking the positivist sociology of Comte and the rational sociology of Durkheim. But there is also much that is relevant to a modern consideration of the relation between theology and sociology. As is implied by the title of his book, *Sociologie et théodicée: leur conflit et leur accord*, Richard suggests that there is a certain type of theology, namely theodicy, and a certain type of sociology concerned with values that can enter into a fruitful engagement.[1]

In aligning themselves with the achievements and methods of the natural sciences, sociologists have traditionally excluded in their search for truth all references to the supernatural or to God. Such factors are not to be taken into consideration at the level of explanation. The idea of God, or the possibility of divine intervention, stands outside (not above but perhaps below) sociological analysis and discussion. From the time of Comte, the dominant and exclusive supposition has been that social life, solidarity, social institutions, and so on, are capable of explanation without resorting to spiritual factors. Hence sociology is rational and agnostic. Although this was most clearly stated by Auguste Comte, positivism is not the only kind of sociology to take such a stand. All contemporary sociology implicitly or explicitly excludes the divine, or if it does include it, it denies or disregards its operative force in society. Sociology may be and usually is willing to accept the social dynamic of religious institutions, but not their supernatural base.

Many sociologists today would deny even the possibility of a meeting between theology and sociology – and for the moment we will not specify what kind of sociology. All interdisciplinary exercises raise problems for the professional, but none more within the general confines of the human sciences than those which involve the 'science of God' in any shape or form. As Richard wrote: 'Sociology is a science, a branch of the tree of science. Theodicy is a branch of natural theology, an application of the idea of God to the evaluation of the world and its life. Between sociology and theodicy there exists the same opposition, the same incompatibility, as between natural explanation and belief in the supernatural.'[2] Here an attempt will be made to show, along slightly different lines to those of Richard, where the two disciplines are indeed incompatible but also tt demonstrate a compatibility that can be mutually profitable.

The author of *Sociologie et théodicée*

Some knowledge of Gaston Richard's life and work helps us to understand his thought.[3] He was probably never known in the English-speaking world and today even the French have almost forgotten him. Admittedly, his life was relatively uneventful: he became a professor of sociology in Bordeaux in 1902, retired in 1930, and died there in 1945. A benevolent, kindly man, he was not an inspiring or charismatic lecturer, but he was hard-working. He produced a crop of books which, from about 1900 to 1925, were widely read; some went into several editions and were translated into various languages. Today those books, resting in academic libraries, are virtually never opened. Yet behind the apparent ordinariness of his life there are two interesting facets.

First, he was a persistent and searching critic of Durkheim's sociology; indeed, he was often known as 'le vieil adversaire de Durkheim'. What was surprising was that the barrage of attack came from a Frenchman who was also a professional sociologist, but even more unusual, that the critic was once a prominent and senior member of Durkheim's team of scholars, who were as much devoted to sociology as to Durkheim himself, and who helped to produce the journal *L'Année sociologique*. Richard was chosen to follow Durkheim at Bordeaux, when the up-and-coming grand master was appointed to lecture at the Sorbonne in 1902. The two men were contemporaries (born around 1860), both went to the Ecole Normale Supérieure, knew one another, and had very similar intellectual interests. Richard withdrew from the Année Sociologique group in 1907 for a number of reasons, which might be summed up in the excessive claims Durkheim made for sociology and its trespassing into metaphysics. Amongst several points of discord, Richard held that Durkheim adopted a position antagonistic to religion, in so far as his system openly denied the truth-value of religion and also undermined the notion of the freedom of the will. Richard was the only prominent member of the group to desert it, although the team itself never split, which was a remarkable achievement on the part of the Durkheim. The price that Richard had to pay for his action was academic isolation, and despite his abilities and long list of publications he was never given a chair in Paris.

The other facet is not dissociated from the first, namely, his Christian convictions. Richard was born into a devout Catholic family, became an agnostic in his youth, and was then converted to Protestantism while he was at the Ecole Normale Supérieure. To the end of his days he remained a loyal member of the Eglise Réformée, believing that Protestantism was a form of Christianity best suited to the times in which he lived. He alone amongst the Année Sociologique *équipe*, it seems, had a firm religious faith. Most of the members were, like Durkheim, agnostic: many, like him, also were of Jewish background. It was after the death of Durkheim in 1917 that Richard launched his most vigorous attacks, not only against the thought of Durkheim, but also against Durkheimians, whom he accused of manipulating the syllabuses of teacher training colleges so that only Durkheim's type of sociology was taught. It meant an exclusive propagation of Durkheim's *sociologie religieuse*, which Richard scathingly referred to as sociology *dite religieuse*.

Strangely enough, Richard admitted that his main interests were not in the sociology of religion but in discovering the necessary conditions for the existence of society and the effects of social life on beliefs, knowledge and the emotions. He wrote on a large number of sociological topics, and when he dealt with the subject of religion it was usually to attack Durkheim. He felt that the complexity of religious phenomena demanded a cautious approach and a careful use of the comparative method. Only when he was an old man in his eighties did he overcome his fears and wrote the book to which allusion has already been made.

Richard's analysis of social phenomena was essentially evolutionary in the broad sense of the word. Society was gradually becoming 'something better' but such evolution was not inevitable. Almost anticipating Popper's *Poverty of Historicism* and at the same time challenging the liberal optimism of his day, he held that three laws prevented the inevitable progress of humanity. They are:

1. The 'law' of reaction, in redirecting a civilization back to a period of barbarism, as for example, the first centuries of the Middle Ages.
2. The 'law' of arrest, which prevents a civilization making progress, as in India and the Far East. This probably combines with the law of reaction.
3. The 'law' of interference, which is difficult to formulate. It is a contradiction of universal laws. Parallel progress does not occur; for example, value and law proceed step by step, nor does scientific progress necessarily keep pace with industrial progress.[4]

This is not only a good example of the kind of 'laws' that Richard sought to establish for sociology; it also shows why he rejected an optimistic solution to theodician problems resting on historical inevitablility, as in positivism or progressive social reform.

But in order fully to comprehend why this scholar, both dedicated Christian and dedicated sociologist, should have been so insistent that, although sociology and theodicy may speak of the same very fundamental questions, between them there exists 'the same incompatibility as between natural explanation and belief in the supernatural' (and in order also to see why his conclusion is not, at least in an unqualified way, by any means the final one), there is more background that must be filled in. It is necessary – even at the risk of repeating the familiar – to outline the development of the concept of theodicy and of the important contribution some sociologists have made to this development. Only then can we see if this sociological contribution has helped to create common ground for the sociologist and the theologian, or even perhaps confirmed the incompatibility which Richard so insistently stressed.

Theodicy traditionally conceived

Like the terms 'theology' and 'sociology', so the term 'theodicy' should first be seen in its historical setting. Well-known probably is the fact that the term was first coined by Leibniz (1646–1716) and is based on the two Greek words *theos* and *dikē* ('god' and 'justice').

Theodicy is an attempt to defend God's righteousness in the face of evil. Less well-known is the fact that the man whose attacks prompted Leibniz to invent the word was Pierre Bayle. Leibniz was trying to answer Bayle's searching theological criticism that the existence of evil is irreconcilable with the omnipotence of God and his infinite goodness. Using arguments derived from St Augustine and St Thomas Aquinas, he held that evil was necessary in order to bring into relief goodness.[5] For Leibniz, God's world, this world, is the best of all possible worlds, but this idea in turn may have been partly borrowed from Nicholas of Cusa's thesis that all creation is an image of the divine.

The problems that the theodicy of Leibniz covered may have appeared more urgent as theism suffered the assaults of eighteenth-century scepticism, but they were, of course, nothing new.[6] Christian thinkers from the beginning had considered them, and, if one expands the definition, they were also raised by theologians and other thinkers of pre-Christian times. After Leibniz, however, the subject has continued to be one of concern amongst many European thinkers.

Its history is not only long but quite complex. Here all that is possible is to outline the various meanings of the term and the solutions that have been proposed to the problems raised. Briefly, four approaches can be distinguished:

1. A narrow one, where the word theodicy implies little more than apologetics – the defence of the doctrine of God in the face of various kinds of challenge raised by forms of evil.
2. An attempt to tackle philosophically the problem as classically stated by Bayle and responded to by Leibniz – namely, the incongruity between man's suffering on the one hand and God's goodness and infinite greatness on the other.
3. In later developments, the approach wherein theodicy becomes equivalent to natural theology or philosophical theology. This meaning can also be seen in Leibniz.
4. A further widening of the meaning, whereby (partly due to sociology, as we shall show) the word refers to any attempt to deal in a meaningful way with the problem of suffering or evil. In this case, no particular doctrine of God or concept of God is necessarily implied. It is the way any society legitimately attempts to deal with human suffering and misery.

One factor that is exclusively emphasized in the last meaning but which is common to all the others is man's suffering in some form or other. All theodices are based on the jaggedness of human or social experience. Why should I suffer? Why should I die? Why should my family, my society, be afflicted? Why should the world as a whole display such antagonism and hostility? Why is there such inequality amongst men? To these and countless similar questions which have arisen in the history of man's suffering and sense of injustice, theodicy has to supply acceptable answers. In Hinduism there exists a logic which is virtually irrefutable, but in western society the answer has to be given against the background of particular doctrines of God which are summed up in the phrase, ethical monotheism. This particular theological position brings with it very acute problems.

Many of the issues raised by theodicy have not been the exclusive domain of the professional theologian or philosopher. If one takes the term in its wide meaning – questions about the problems of suffering – one can say that, among the philosophers of antiquity, Plato, Aristotle, the Stoics and Plotinus had all dealt with it. But in modern times we find thinkers (the later ones influenced directly or indirectly especially by Kant's critique of traditional theodicy)[7] also proposing, or at least pointing to, practical or historical solutions. Condorcet, Rousseau, Proudhon, Hegel (philosopher in the strict sense, as the word is understood today, but political thinker as well) and Marx, all made suffering partially or completely the springboard of their thought. Evolutionary and revolutionary theories can in their various ways be responses to theodicean problems.

Introducing the names of modern political thinkers who have tried to deal fairly comprehensively with problems raised by theodicy draws attention to the fact that theodicies, defined in the broad sense, can be divided into two general types – those which are primarily concerned with an intellectual solution to the problem of suffering by offering some kind of meaningful acceptance, and those in which the reasoned element is minimal but where emphasis is placed upon action, in the hope that suffering will be reduced by it in the future. The first type is by and large encased within theodicy proper and admits theological or philosophical solutions: the second gives rise to a variety of responses, from science and technology at one extreme, to prayer and ritual at the other; and within the spectrum are various forms of political emancipation, including reform and revolution. In primitive and even advanced religions, response by way of action is to be seen in piacular rites as well as in certain *rites de passage*. However, it is the first type of response, not the second, which is our immediate concern. This is not to deny that a rational or speculative theory legitimately and frequently gives rise to ameliorating action. All theodicies imply an intellectual or meaningful element, even where some form of action forms the solution. Classical Marxism is a modern example of the combination of analysis and action, along with other socialist approaches. Marx actually calls religion theodicy and Marxism is in the last analysis itself a theodicy. However, while most theodicies have components of belief and action, there is frequently the tendency for one or the other to be in the foreground.

Another way of dividing theodicies is to group them into categories according to their general outcome. There are those which are essentially optimistic; that is, the suffering man endures, or the evil to which he is subject, will in the long run be overcome or compensated for. More concretely, the result of suffering may be seen to be beneficial to a man's soul or character: he may be compensated by rewards in a life to come in heaven or through re-incarnation. Again, revolution holds out the hope of material transformation for the better. A contrasting category consists of what might be called pessimistic theodicies, in which it is held that no acceptable solution is possible – man has to bear his suffering for what it is. There is no redemption or final justice. Passive acceptance is the only possible outcome. In one sense this is unsolved theodicy.

Modern theologians and theodicy

Wrestling with matters surrounding theodicy flourishes in times of religious uncertainty. It is true that fashions in philosophy come and go and that schools of philosophy can choose to disregard theodicy in any of its meanings. Philosophy *per se* is not tied to a position or a system. For theologians in the Christian tradition, this is not so. For them there can be no escape, for they are earthed to a certain religious base. Part of their given position is the existence and attributes of God enunciated in the Bible; and central to their study is Christ, who himself suffered. Death is not only an inevitable human event; it has always had great significance for the Christian, whose gospel is a gospel of resurrection implying therefore death. For the theologian, problems raised by theodicy can never be brushed aside: they are permanently present.

Nevertheless, modern theologians of traditional Catholic and Protestant persuasion have largely by-passed theodicy in the narrow sense. Perhaps due to the criticisms of Leibniz by Kant in *Über das Misslingen aller philosophischen Versuche in der Theodicee*[8] and the failure of philosophical theologians of the evolutionary or idealist school such as A.C. Fraser (1819–1914) and F.R. Tennant (1866–1957), the problem of attempting to reconcile rationally God's ultimate goodness with his omnipotence in the face of human suffering has largely been abandoned.

Theodicy in the traditional sense is basically a philosophical activity; hence Richard's assertion that it stands within the realm of metaphysics. Today, many theologians and other thinkers would strongly reject an outcome which is essentially 'mental'. Rational, speculative arguments, which in the end present nothing more than some kind of meaning and imply the acceptance of evil and suffering in the here-and-now, are rejected as being totally unhelpful, and even alienating, even if they are intellectually tenable. Hans Küng sees such argumentation as being as helpful to a sufferer as 'a lecture on the chemistry of foodstuffs to a starving man'.[9] The tendency therefore is to press for an action response to theodicean questions, and within the Christian context this can emerge as political involvement of some kind, or in terms of a christocentric theology as a personal and spiritual leap in identification with the suffering Christ. The first, suggests Küng, is really a question of emancipation and is man-engineered: the second is that of redemption and is God-centred. Küng supports both positions but in the end identifies himself with redemption.[10] In some measure he follows in the footsteps of Karl Barth, who denied the possibility of a natural theology. Küng rejects traditional theodicean arguments and re-solves the problem as a response to the person and action of Christ.[11] Much the same stand is taken by Hick.[12] This approach has strong biblical roots. If it is not a philosophically acceptable solu-tion, it is certainly a spiritual one and borders on the territories of mysticism and practical acceptance.

There is no intention here to expound the other solution which has become increasingly popular: that is, one based on a theology of liberation, which extends into political activity by seeking amelior-ation in the present or immediate future. This to the external eye is little more than social reformation or revolution. Under such cir-cumstances it may be very difficult to differentiate the religious from the political. Its advocates come in the main from South America and are Protestant as well as Catholic, though the roots can be traced to Europe.[13]

Theodicy in the hands of sociologists

Despite its history and meaning, theodicy is a term that is used today by many sociologists. It is found within two contexts, which are not totally dissociated. On the one hand it is employed in a sociological analysis of institutional religion and may be seen as an essential part of religion and even used to define it. On the other hand, it can have a central place within a social theory, and as such is seen to be an integral part of any all-embracing social construction. Crudely con-trasted, the two contexts differ in so far as the first starts with religion, the second with society itself.

Max Weber (1864–1920) was probably the first major sociologist to use the notion of theodicy. For him to do so was a logical step in the development of his distinctive methodology, that of *Verstehen*, which rests on the concept of meaning and especially meaning for the individual.

Within the sociology of religion, which was of particular interest to Weber, his concern was to analyze the practical consequences for human behaviour of certain religious and theological doctrines.[14] For just that reason he focused on the concept of salvation and its application to religions which seemed to him to possess a rational theology. Not surprisingly, his primary interest was in Christianity, Judaism, Islam, Hinduism and Buddhism; in fact the major traditional religions of the world, and to the exclusion of primitive religions. All these gave primary place to salvation in one form or another. The problem he set himself was to analyze the logistics of the salvation path, given certain, assumed preceding doctrines, and also to analyze the consequences of the hope of salvation as they issued in ethical action. In brief, he attempted to explore the rationale of doctrine on the basis of comparing the religions of the major civilizations. Central to his enquiry were the traditional problems raised by theodicy within Christianity and based on the internal conflict of the doctrines of ethical monotheism in the face of human suffering and evil, leading most commonly to a solution which emphasizes doctrines of heaven and hell and the injustices experienced in this world being compensated for in a world to come. But since his milieu was comparative religion, Weber naturally extended the problems and therefore the term to other religions.

The concept of theodicy was thus widened to include criteria which did not specifically relate to ethical monotheism but were centred basically on problems of physical suffering, social inequality and injustice in this world, and how religions dealt with them. For example, he was particularly interested in the theological response of Hinduism in terms of the caste system and doctrine of Karma. He also discerned the variety of responses in a religion. Often there were several theodicies in one religion. And it was in order to classify certain of these that he developed his concept of resentment (the term has its origins in the French word *ressentiment*),[15] namely, a response, exhibited among the disprivileged to the unequal distribution of mundane goods, said to be caused by the sinfulness and illegality of the privileged. The theodicean problem, as Weber saw it, was then resolved by the belief that sooner or later God's wrath would overtake the privileged and the poor would be triumphant, so a theodicy of the underprivileged may give rise to messianism.

It is thus easy to see how Weber's use of theodicy was usefully extended to cover a response in doctrine or action to a situation of suffering or injustice. Weber wanted to find out how within each religious system the doctrines developed in the face of given situations, and the kinds of responses individual devotees were asked to make.[16]

Directly in line with Weber's analysis, some modern sociologists rightly see that a theodicy is a causal factor in creating religious change. Messianic movements are said to emerge in situations of distress which lead to existential crisis. Oppressed peoples find satisfaction in a utopian solution, as for example in their support of millenarian sects. Another clear example of theodicean factors being causal is the emergence of the cargo cults.

Weber's datum-line was religious systems. He was concerned with the logic of their doctrines and their outcome for social action. By adopting a wide definition of theodicy he was able to employ the term on a comparative basis. The merits of this kind of analysis in examining religion are obvious. Whether other thinkers, notably anthropologists, were directly influenced by Weber is difficult to know, but there have been those who have extended ideas similar to his into areas he avoided, namely, primitive religions. Some anthropologists have defined religion in terms of theodicy, thus getting over the old division between a definition of religion in terms of gods or spiritual beings, and one, following Durkheim, in terms of the sacred and the profane, or a similar pair of concepts, the holy and the everyday. Malinowski, for example, saw the experience of suffering at the base of the supernatural.[17] Beattie, more recently, holds to a similar position. In preliterate societies, he has argued, man is 'surrounded by unpredictable and sometimes terrifying hazards'.[18] Where these are not dealt with by empirical and scientific knowledge, men 'must cope with them symbolically and expressively instead'.[19] Hence religion!

Gaston Richard, however, went further. He put forward the theory that every religion constitutes a solution to the problem of evil.[20] He argued that even the most civilized and advanced societies experience moral evil. Historically, ideas of this kind are seen in primitive societies in the concept of taboo. When a taboo is broken social solidarity is threatened, and society is held to be polluted. Expiation is then required. Later religions such as Brahmanism, Mazdaism and Judaism adopt similar doctrines. Religion thus constitutes an early form of consciousness of evil found in society and responds by the institutions of sacrifice and expiation. This is but a brief summary of Richard's theory of religion but it is significant that he makes its starting-point the social recognition of forces that greatly disturb society and man.

But there are sociologists who have preferred to look at the question from a different angle. Their reference point is not religion but society – its structure and composition, the raw material and experiences on which it builds. Talcott Parsons, himself directly influenced by Max Weber, was one such sociologist who began to think along these lines. He holds that social life is never smooth and predictable. Accidents, plagues, and other forms of suffering constantly confront man. To overcome the suffering these cause, man has invented symbolic techniques. By the imposition of non-empirical realities, such as gods and spirits, men are able to resolve their difficulties and to present acceptable meanings.[21] Parsons became a firm exponent of the functionalist approach to religion and this can be seen in many respects to have a theodicean base.

If Parsons began to examine some of the ideas of Weber about theodicy as it were from the other side of the coin, Peter Berger has taken a definitive step, grasped the concept with both hands and developed it to its limits. Through him, it has now assumed an important, if not necessary, place in social theory, and is not to be seen just as an element in a religious system. In *The Sacred Canopy* he held that theodicy is a necessary element in the creation of every society.[22] As religion for Durkheim was a virtual *sine qua non* of society, so for Berger it is a particular facet of religion, its theodicy, without which no society is possible. To outline Berger's theory of society is out of place here, but it might be noted that he visualizes society as a man-made structure which is dependent on a sacred cosmos or nomos. This is a meaningful order imposed on individuals, concerning their knowledge and experience of the world. The structure is, however, fragile. Every social order, once created, is subject to destruction by forces arising out of the human condition. These forces are derived from suffering, evil and death, which are universal and anomic. They have to be contained and integrated within a society or else chaos results. The explanations of suffering, which are usually in terms of religious legitimations, no matter how theoretically simple or sophisticated they may be, constitute for Berger a theodicy. In *The Sacred Canopy* he admits his dependence on Weber for the concept, and relies a great deal on his ideas, but at the same time he develops the concept and employs it within a social theory rather than concentrating on particular theodicies.

This emerges in the universals which Berger states about man, namely, that man cannot accept aloneness and meaninglessness, and therefore in man there exists an inherent urge for the creation of theodicies. Another universal psychological factor is that every society calls for a certain denial of the individual self and of its needs, anxieties and problems. This surrendering of the self to the ordering power of society, which is implicit in all theodicies to some degree. Berger describes as irrational, and indeed masochistic. Masochism is prior to any theodicy.[23] Following Weber, he places various theodicies on a rational-irrational continuum, but includes a generalized statement about primitive religions and, like Weber, sees Hindu theodicy as the most rational. Certain kinds of theodicies also give legitimation to the social conditions of particular groups in society; for example, the underprivileged, where religion is an opiate, or an élite, which has to tolerate the poor and give them alms.

But Berger's contribution to the concept of theodicy is its function in the structure of society, not in the internal coherence of particular theodicies. Every *nomos*, he argues, implies a theodicy. Theodicies directly legitimate a particular institutional order. Not surprisingly, when a theodicy is rejected, the *nomos* can be expected to collapse. Hence, as the Christian way of intellectually and religiously dealing with suffering – a partly rational, partly irrational theodicy – disintegrates, so a revolutionary situation arises, which Berger thinks is happening today. Man must see life meaningfully. If one set of answers is rejected another must be found. Social chaos cannot be of long duration – it is too painful.

We have very briefly outlined Berger's application of the concept of theodicy within his social theory. As such it plays a crucial part. He uses it in a wide Weberian sense of a meaningful socially acceptable response to the universal experience of suffering, inequality and death, set within a number of axioms. Christian theodicy is only one amongst innumerable theodicies, for each society possesses its own. It is a necessary part of social order and as such man will eternally seek it. His theory has a number of weaknesses, not least in empirical verification. But the object is not to raise these but to point to Berger's work to show how the term has become sociologically acceptable despite its theological and metaphysical origins in early eighteenth-century Europe, and ideas behind it well before then.

Dwelling on common ground

Theologians in the past and the present, and of all persuasions and schools, generally acknowledge that somewhere they are forced to take into account the existence of man's suffering. The history of human suffering has limitless forms – death, physical disease, malformation, cruelty to man by man, persecution, social inequalities, anomy, loneliness, guilt, alienation, earthquakes, famines, fear, torture, deprivation, injustice, exploitation, and so on. (And what of cruelty in the animal kingdom?) The history of suffering starts with the history of man himself. It is part of the human condition. And it is a continuing history which shows no signs of abatement. Sufferings may change, but they do not diminish. Dachau, Auschwitz, Nagasaki are irreducible barriers to any optimism that modern society suffers less than earlier societies. To the sensitive person, any degree of suffering, no matter how fleeting, for a day,

for a minute, for a moment, raises the question why. It seems
inevitable and universal and will never go away. It will never go
away because suffering never seems to vanish.

In the classical theodicy of Leibniz, evil or suffering was held to be
of three types:

(a) metaphysical, based on man's finiteness.
(b) moral, associated with man's sinfulness.
(c) natural, that is, physical suffering due to the laws of nature.

The Christian theologian might be happy to accept such a classification. But he would probably want to emphasize the notion of sin
both as a component of suffering and evil, and also as a causal
factor. Sinful actions give rise to suffering.

The sociologist, while he might not be happy to settle for Leibniz's classification, would doubtless accept what is implied by the
categories. However, he would be forced to reject the notion of sin,
other than accepting the acknowledgement of it by religious individuals, or the fact that statements are made about it by theologians.
Sin implies a failure to live up to the demands of a god, the existence
of whom a sociologist cannot openly support. Sin therefore can have
no causal validity unless one reduces sin to immoral action and
nothing more. Even then, for the sociologist an immoral action
would in all likelihood be determined by consequences, and not by
intentions or by a failure to live up to divine standards. In the way in
which theodicy has so far been discussed, little or no mention has
been made of sin, and there have been few references to evil. The
emphasis has been on suffering. For obvious reasons, sociologists
are willing to accept the validity of the concept of suffering for
analytical purposes, as did Max Weber and his successors. Evil as a
concept has to be rejected because of the implication that it is
associated with something metaphysical – the devil or a devilish,
impersonal force which is not contained within this world, and
ultimately is incapable of being controlled by man. Suffering is
universally attested: and it is empircally verifiable.

For any hope of working the common ground of theodicy by both
the theologian and the sociologist, human suffering in its multitud-
inal manifestations will have to be the agreed starting-point, and not
sin or evil. And who will object to this? Strangely enough both the
theologian and the sociologist can and probably will.

Common ground, but common aims?

To ask the theologian to seek out causes of suffering and to analyze
their consequences in society is surely asking him to do something
which is alien to his discipline. Theodicy, as the word implies, has

traditionally been rooted in the doctrine of God, theo-dicy. To ask him to side with the sociologist is surely to turn theodicy into anthropo-dicy (as with Berger). Basically the aims of the theologian and the sociologist even within the realm of theodicy are different, as traditionalists would remind us. The sociologist has no brief to come to the defence of ethical monotheism, nor is he *per se* concerned with problems of natural theology. Sociology cannot assume a particular theological outlook: it has to remain agnostic, and as such it is a secular science. Thus, the sociologist or social theorist has no intention to search for ways of fitting man's misery to God's glory. And at the level of explanation, he can call upon no *deus ex machina* or spirit force. Richard is right in saying that sociology is incompetent to deal with traditional theodicy, such as that of Leibniz.[24]

Theodicy is part of a system of values and ideas. The sociologist would be the first person to state that any type of suffering is mediated through the evaluation of it determined by a society. Sociology legitimately studies the history of moral ideas, and ideas in general – their formation, their development, their influence on society at large.[25] The problem is whether sociology can go beyond the descriptive and deal with the 'ought'. Can it answer the problem of the hierarchy of values, for this is what is posed by all theodicies, not least by traditional theodicies? Richard holds that sociology cannot venture over the scientific border, that is beyond the realm of description and explanation of such phenomena.[26] Ultimate issues of ethics and value judgments are strictly outside its province. It must therefore remain passive in the face of legitimate procedures in this area by philosophy and theology.

Thus, a point of conflict is likely to arise between the secular and religious theodicist in the matter of aim. Is the intention of theodicean studies to reduce suffering? Is a real reduction possible? This is a point of contention indeed not only between sociologists and theologians, but between various types of sociologists, and various kinds of theologians. There are certain social theorists who posit an optimistic outcome of the triumph of good over evil, and the reduction of suffering: others are pessimists. Some, as we have said, are evolutionist, others reformist or revolutinary. The question for the theologian is to ask whether he is satisfied with such a perspective. Whether he is content in working alongside the sociologist to seek only emancipation, or whether his scepticism or perhaps his wider vision causes him to look further afield. He may be able to accept amelioration in the short term but his sights are on redemption, as Küng would wisely remind him.

The possibility of mutual working

From what has just been said it would seem that, traditionally defined, the aims of the sociologist and the theologian even in the common territory of theodicy are so widely different that no mutual influence or cooperation is possible. We should like to examine briefly some of the objections to the possibility of mutality and to suggest the possibility of cooperation. First we must retrace a few steps.

Theologians cannot at some stage fail to come face to face with the problem of suffering, irrespective of how it is defined. Their discipline demands it. Also, it has been indicated that certain sociologists are prepared to examine the issues raised by theodicy, broadly understood, and are ready to introduce the concept into their social theory. However, for sociologists, as for philosophers, theodicean problems are not as pressing as they are for theologians. There is nothing inherent in the discipline of sociology that forces the practitioner to use the concept of suffering. If then there is not the categorical demand, it is legitimate to ask what are the attitudes of sociologists as a whole towards theodicy and suffering?

Indicated in this chapter so far is the fact that theodicy is not a popular concept in sociology, or indeed in social theory. As in contemporary philosophy, it is somewhat outmoded. Two ways of escape are open to those who do not want to use the term. One way is associated with the not unjustifiable fear that theodicy in the hands of theologians smacks of apologetics. However, when used by sociologists, and in its broad meaning, it frequently implies the betterment of the social and human conditions which are analyzed and which are held to be evil or undesirable. It can be associated with evolutionary theory on the one hand, perhaps that of Comte or Spencer; or on the other, commitment to political reform or revolution. In the first case it is implied that the future will be better than the present and thus rests on a particular reading of history, and in the second that the sociologist knows what is good or right or desirable for the human condition. Why should there be a reduction in suffering? There is no sociological reason to support this. It is an assumption based on a particular doctrine of man. Or again, it could be said that some sociologists in their concern for theodicean problems exceed their brief and align themselves with the conclusions of theologians. Witness this longish confession of faith of Robert Bellah in his early academic life. He was much influenced by Parsons, but in terms of religion by Tillich:

Through Tillich . . . I understood existentially the Christian doctrine of sin. I saw that the worst is only a hair's breadth away from the best in any man and any society. I saw that the unbroken commitment to any individual or any group is bound to be demonic. Nothing human can bear such wieght. The totalism of Communism and the totalism of the 'Free World' are equally destructive. And I learned to see darkness within, that we are all assassins in our hearts. If I am not a murderer it is because of the grace I have received through the love and support of others, not through the lack of murderous impulses within me. The only difference between me and the man on death row is that he somehow received less grace. Feeling all this I could no longer hate, or rather justify hatred. Since I participate in the guilt of every man, there is no man I reject or declare unforgivable.[27]

It may well be that an overconcern with theodicy breaks the quest for cold clinicalism to which much sociology aspires, and perhaps to which, in the face of such reflections as those of Bellah and others, it should return. The point is that the task of the sociologist seen traditionally is not commitment to social or human improvement but to description and explanation, in the same way as the geographer describes the terrain, or the geologist explains changes in rock formation. This approach to sociology, often exemplified in the British empirical tradition, or the meta-theory of American sociology just before and just after World War II, rejects any explicit sense of involvement in suffering humanity or the wish to ameliorate it. The claim of scientific objectivity bars such commitment.

The other way of escape is to say that the problems of suffering are methodologically difficult to handle. Suffering is personal, it is impossible to quantify. Given an objective fact, say the death of a loved one, each person suffers in different ways and to different degrees. Similarly, one person can endure great physical suffering but another cannot. And social inequalities, these too can be tolerated more by some individuals, groups, and societies than by others. It is therefore difficult to handle suffering as a key factor. Of course it is true that one can derive certain indicators of suffering such as the number of people unemployed, levels of disease, of infant mortality, and so on, and attempt to show their effect on relevant facets of social life. Seen in the wide sweep, suffering is too big a concept to handle with precision. The aim should be to keep to what is scientifically verifiable. Even indicators of suffering are surrounded by pitfalls.

These ways of escape represent a type of sociology which today is the object of considerable attack. The various arguments used against it need not be rehearsed here. Suffice it to say, however, that science is not value-free. It implies a *représentation* of the world or a *Weltanschauung*. It cannot be said that science as a whole is dedicated to the betterment of mankind. What of atomic bombs? And of even more powerful ways of blasting man off the face of the earth? Or again of new psychological tortures? And if therefore the sociologist, who speaks in the name of science, condemns the theologian for adopting an ideological position, he must see he is not isolated from ideological contamination himself.

While it is true that sociologists together with many social theorists are not sympathetic towards using the concept of theodicy, they do, whether they realize it or not, use the terms and phrases which are akin to those employed in theodicy. They refer to 'structures of resistance', 'limitations', 'cost of change', 'cramps', 'chaos', 'gaps', 'alienation', 'anomy', and so on. Frequently they are not as far removed from the theodicean issues as they often imagine they are.

A basis for mutuality

We have tried to show that the traditional stand of the empirical sociologist with regard to theodicy is not as convincing as he would make it out to be. He is open to the criticism of being indifferent to suffering on the one hand and of using ideas behind theodicy on the other, though he fails to acknowledge them as such. However, social theorists are slowly becoming more interested in theodicy. To those who admit the usefulness of the concept, to Marxists, and to other 'politically motivated' sociologists, the following criteria would seem to be necessary for them and for others to work in the common terrain of theodicy:

1. A sensitivity to suffering in its many forms – a recognition that suffering is a real component of the human experience.
2. A willingness to find a place in sociology for that reality and to find a concept of suffering that is methodologically viable.
3. The acceptance of an 'ought' which seeks a resolution of suffering.
4. That resolution can be of two kinds: (a) the pursuit of amelioration through the elimination of those conditions which give rise to suffering, or (b) the offering of an acceptable meaning to suffering, where it cannot be eliminated, for example, in cases of death or natural disasters, such as earthquakes.
5. It is not the task of the social theorist or the theologian just to describe the theodicies of the past. They must attempt to create new theodicies or reinterpret the old.

On the other hand, it must be borne in mind that the sociologist is not primarily concerned with the individual and the unique, but rather with the general and the social. His concern is therefore with (a) social inequalities and injustices, (b) institutional limitations and sufferings, and (c) widespread suffering – crudely stated, socially significant suffering. As we have indicated, the sociologist should be sensitive to suffering. Often statistics and a concern for large-scale suffering blunt his sensitivity just as much as may the goal of scientific objectivity.

Thus, what the sociologist can legitimately tackle are questions of generality about suffering in its many forms, about causes of suffering, and the consequences of suffering viewed within the ideology of a given society. He cannot answer questions of particularity about suffering. 'Why was it I happened to be on the pavement when the car crashed into me?' This is a possible question for the religious theodicist: it cannot be answered by science or by sociology. To this question there would appear to be only two solutions. One is that which says the event occurred according to chance, and which may be acceptable to the scientist. The other comes from the theologian who could offer a solution by suggesting that it was caused by the will of God. This is not to say that the modern theologian would make such a statement, but that such statements stand legitimately within his field.

But it is not the sociologist who has to make all the running to remain in the common territory. The theologian cannot expect to have it all his own way and to concede nothing. By a strange contradiction, theologians may often appear as indifferent to suffering as sociologists. The reason is that in practice they have approached the problem of theodicy only intellectually and rationally in an attempt to reconcile suffering with the attributes of God. This has meant in practice that they have wrestled with abstract doctrine rather than with analyzing various forms and categories of suffering and misery – metaphysical, moral, natural – which have not been clearly differentiated and are often held to be manifestations of some universal principle, for example, evil. The result has been that all suffering is seen to be one and of a kind. Thus, the theologian working in theodicy is quick to generalize about suffering *in toto*.[28] Theological theodicy has the inbuilt weakness of all too readily ignoring the details of the life of human societies and their struggle for existence. Admittedly Hick attempts to examine various kinds of suffering and evil, but he does so purely through the eyes of the philosopher. Rational understanding is the only outcome here.

Whilst working within the common territory, it is legitimate to call on theologians to consider more carefully the nature of suffering, not so much in individual psychological terms but in social ones. In short, the theologian is asked to analyze more conscientiously the problem of causation of suffering and the consequences of it. Both the theologian and the sociologist (where applicable) should avoid seeing suffering in any 'absolutist' terms as if it were an overall unified entity, emanating, for the theologian, from an evil superhuman being, from the 'mere fact' of sin, or from some blind metaphysical force. What is required is that both the theologian and the sociologist must select some specific area of suffering, for example, social deprivation, political persecution, physical disease, and make whatever contribution they can to an understanding of it, and hopefully point to ways of amelioration. If their task is in another direction, in examining contemporary and historical theodicies, their search should be to discover the basic value assumptions and ideological content of such theodicies and their relation to the state of various kinds of suffering in the society in which the theodicy is found.

These are some of the projects which both the sociologist and the theologian can tackle together. And they are certainly big enough and difficult enough! Mutuality, it is hoped, will mean that each can learn from the other, and that the theologian can make as much a positive contribution as the sociologist, and vice-versa. Of course the 'natural' fear of the theologian will be that he will find himself being 'reduced' to the human and sociological level and will thus follow in the footsteps of the sociologist rather than making a unique contribution based on assumptions about God and the spiritual. This fear can become minimized in two ways – by a careful working out of the boundaries and basic suppositions involved in working in the area of theodicies, religious and secular. And in the realization that in the last analysis both the theologian and the sociologist will each have to make a leap of faith in trying to work together and seeing practically how far they can cooperate and mutually support each other.

Notes

1 Richard, G. *Sociologie et théodicée: leur conflit et leur accord* (Paris, 1943).
2 *Ibid.* p. xix.
3 See Pickering, W.S.F. *Durkheim on Religion* (London and Boston, 1975) pp. 343–59; and Pickering, W.S.F. 'Gaston Richard: collaborateur et adversaire', *Revue française de sociologie*, XX, 1979, pp. 163–82.
4 Richard, *op.cit.* p. 265.
5 Leibniz, G.W. *Essais de théodicée sur la bonté de Deiu, la liberté de l'homme et l'origine de mal* (1710).
6 See Hick, J. *Evil and the Love of God* (London, 1966).
7 Kant, I. *Über das Misslingen aller philosophischen Versuche in der Theodicee* (1791).
8 *Ibid.*
9 Küng, H. *Christ sein* (Munich, 1974); English translation E. Quinn: *On Being a Christian* (London and New York, 1976) p. 429.
10 *Ibid.* p. 430.
11 *Ibid.* p. 432 ff.
12 Hick, *op. cit.* p. 388 ff.
13 See, for example, Segundo, J.L. *Liberation of Theology* (Dublin, 1977).
14 Weber, M. *Religionssoziologie* (Tünbingen, 1922). English Translation Ephraim Fischoff, *The Sociology of Religion* (Boston, 1963) Chap. IX. See also Weber, M. 'The Social Psychology of World Religions' and 'Religious Rejections of the World and their Directions', English Translation H.H. Gerth and C.W. Mills in *Essays from Max Weber,* (London and Boston, 1948).

15 *Ibid. The Sociology of Religion*, p. 110 ff.
16 For an analysis of Weber on theodicy, see Obeyesekere, G. 'Theodicy, sin and salvation in a Sociology of Buddhism', in E.R. Leach (ed.) *Dialectic in Practical Religion* (London, 1968) pp. 7–40.
17 See Malinowski, B. 'Magic, Science and Religion', in J. Needham (ed.) *Science, Religion and Reality* (London, 1925) p. 39.
18 Beattie, J. *Other Cultures* (London, 1964) p. 227.
19 *Ibid.*
20 See for example Richard, G. 'Sur les lois de la solidarité', *Revue philosophique*, LX, 1905, pp. 441–71; and Richard, G. *Sociologie et théodicée, op. cit.*
21 Parsons, T. *The Social System* (London, 1952) p. 375.
22 Berger, P.L. *The Sacred Canopy* (New York, 1967); and *The Social Reality of Religion* (London, 1969) see Chap. 3.
23 *Ibid.* p. 57.
24 Richard, *Sociologie et théodicée, op. cit.* p. 198
25 *Ibid.* p. 199.
26 *Ibid.*
27 Bellah, R.N. *Beyond Belief* (New York, 1970) pp. xv–xvi.
28 See, for example, Küng, *op. cit.* p. 428 ff. (see n. 11).

Chapter 5

THE RATIONAL SYSTEM OF BELIEFS

W. Donald Hudson

THERE is a certain point at which the concerns of theologians, sociologists and philosophers meet. My name for this point of convergence will be 'the rational system of beliefs' (or 'the rational system' for short). First, I will say as clearly as I can what I mean by this expression. Then, in the second part of the chapter, I will try to show how that to which it refers concerns theologians, sociologists and philosophers respectively.

I The Nature of the Rational System of Beliefs

Criteria of Rationality

When we call a belief 'rational', what we normally intend to say, and are taken to mean, is that it fulfils some of a range of criteria. If I were required to give examples of such criteria, I would offer the following: the belief in question must not be self-contradictory; it must be supported by the relevant evidence; and the person who holds it must be prepared to surrender it, if he finds what appears to him to be good reason to do so.

To say that these three are criteria of rationality is not to say that, in every instance of rational belief, they must all be fulfilled. We might call them, to adopt an expression of Wittgenstein's, 'family resemblances' of rational belief. He was speaking of general terms; and 'rational belief' would be an instance of what he meant by a general term, though his own example at the place referred to was 'game'.[1] According to Wittgenstein, we cannot list the necessary and sufficient conditions for the correct use of a general term on any and every occasion, but only point out 'family resemblances' be-tween how it is employed on the various occasions of its correct use. His point in using the expression 'family resemblances' was this. All the members of a family may not possess every one of the family resemblances (build, features, colour of eyes, gait, temperament, etc.) in common. Similarly, two rational beliefs may not possess all the criteria of rationality in common. One may be self-consistent and open-minded whilst the other is supported by relevant evidence and is open-minded. It may happen, of course, that two members of a human family both possess some of the family resemblances although they do not have any of them in common. John, for instance, may have the family's fair curly hair and clear blue eyes, but his cousin, Mary, poor girl, only have its snub nose and flat feet. Similarly, again, two beliefs may both be rational, although the one is so because it is self-consistent, whilst the other is so because it is held open-mindedly.

I do not want to say that my list of three criteria of rationality exhausts the 'family resemblances' of rational belief. Indeed, the main point, which I am going to try to make in the first half of this chapter, is that there is another criterion of rationality besides these three, namely, 'conformity to the rational system of beliefs'. In distinguishing this fourth criterion from the other criteria of rationality I shall speak only of the three that I have mentioned above, namely, self-consistency, evidential corroboration, and being held open-mindedly. But this does not mean that I deny the possibility of other criteria of rationality besides these three. If there are others, then all I want to say is that I would make out the same distinctions and connections between them and the criterion which I call 'conformity with the rational system of beliefs' as I make out below between that criterion and the three which I have mentioned.

The Rational System

What then have I in mind when I speak of 'the rational system of beliefs' (or 'the rational system' for short)? The answer is twofold, in that I am thinking of a system which consists both of beliefs about what *is the case,* and about what it *is appropriate to do* (or to choose). In a couple of words, this system consists of certain *propositions* and certain *principles*. These propositions and principles have two features in virtue of which they belong to the rational system. First, they regulate what it makes sense to say or do, and second, general assent is given to them in our society. When any given, particular belief is said to be rational one thing which may be meant is that it conforms to the system of beliefs, which these generally-held, regulative propositions and principles constitute.

Is it rational, for example, to believe that life exists on other planets besides the earth? If we say 'Yes', we are thereby normally taken to imply that this belief is in accordance with such-and-such generally-held beliefs about the nature of life and of the universe. Again, for example, is it rational to make the means of contraception readily available to schoolchildren? If we say that it is, we shall be taken to imply that we think doing so would be in accordance with such-and-such commonly held beliefs about what ought to be done, or chosen, for young people of school age. Of course, we may be in a minority in holding that particular beliefs, such as those which I have just mentioned, are rational. But that does not affect the point. By claiming that they are rational (as 'rational' is commonly used) we are saying, in effect, that they are in accordance with certain generally-held, regulative beliefs about what is the case, or what it is appropriate to do, if only people had the wit to see that this is so. If anyone doubts that 'X is rational' is often taken to imply 'X is in conformity with the rational system of beliefs' (as I have defined this latter expression), he has only to consider what people would do who did not think it rational to believe in extra-terrestrial life or contraceptive pills for schoolgirls. Such people would try to show that, if only we think about these matters carefully enough, we shall see that the former belief contravenes certain facts of nature which are not in dispute and the latter goes against certain norms of conduct to which most people in our society subscribe.

I must now give a more specific indication of the kinds of belief which I take to be comprehended within this rational system of beliefs. But, before doing so, let me emphasize once again that when I call the system 'rational', I do not mean to say that it *fulfils* certain criteria of rationality, but rather that being in conformity with it *constitutes* one such criterion.

The Content of the Rational System of Beliefs

I said earlier that there are two main classes of generally-held, regulative beliefs in the rational system, namely those which are about what is the case (propositions) and those which are about what it is appropriate to do (principles).

As for those about what *is the case*, I do not think we can do better than follow the lead which Wittgenstein gave in his last writings, called *On Certainty*.[2] G.E. Moore had maintained that there are certain propositions which we all know for certain to be true and which together form what Moore called 'the common sense view of the world'.[3] Wittgenstein thought that Moore was mistaken in concluding that we *know* such propositions to be true, because all Moore had to go on was the fact that we feel certain of them and these two things are different. (§137) Nevertheless, he recognized that Moore had called attention to a special kind of proposition which plays a 'peculiar logical role' in our thinking. (§136) Propositions of this kind, said Wittgenstein, are 'anchored in all my *questions* and *answers*, so anchored that I cannot touch' them. (§103) He meant that they determine what counts for us as a reasonable question to ask or a sensible answer to give. The examples of such propositions, which he took from Moore or propounded himself, can be seen, I think, to fall into the following three classes, although Wittgenstein for his part did not so classify them.

First, there are propositions which are so fundamental to our world-view that we cannot form a conception of what would count as evidence against – or even for – them. One example of such propositions which Wittgenstein gave is that things do not disappear when no one is observing them. (§119)

Second, there are propositions which are fundamental to certain specific disciplines. Two examples from *On Certainty* are 'Nature is uniform', (p. 315) which is fundamental to physical science, and 'The earth existed long before I was born', (§233) which is fundamental to history. The uniformity of nature is presupposed in everything which counts as a question or answer peculiar to physical science; and belief in the past is implicit in everything which we would classify as a historical inquiry or discovery. Rudolf Carnap's distinction between 'internal' and 'external' questions is relevant here.[4] There may be some context external to science or history, in which nature's uniformity or the past's existence can be questioned; but neither can be doubted *within* the respective disciplines which they constitute. There are universes of discourse – such as science or history – in which it is at the present time definitive of a rational man to engage, though of course different individuals do so with differing degrees of sophistication. The propositions which are fundamental to these disciplines constitute the second kind of propositional beliefs within the rational system.

Third, there are propositions which are not, like the first kind, such that we cannot conceive what would count as evidence for or against them; nor yet, like the second kind, such that they are severally fundamental to certain disciplines of thought or universes of discourse. Propositions of this third kind are simply ones which are very widely and consistently taken for granted in our society. An example which Wittgenstein gave was the proposition that no one has been to the moon. (§111) Now, of course, that is no longer true. But, at the time when Wittgenstein wrote, if anyone had said, 'When were you last on the moon?' this would have been considered an irrational thing to say (except of course, in a joke, a futuristic play, or some such special context). Even now, if anyone, apart from a few famous astronauts, said that he had been on the moon, no one would believe him.

I am not concerned to defend Wittgenstein's particular examples but only to point out that there are propositions of these three kinds, which can be seen as widely and generally regulative in our society of what it makes sense to say or is considered rational to believe.

The second main class of beliefs within the rational system I described above as principles concerning what it *is appropriate to do* (or to choose). A simple example will make clear what is in mind. Suppose we were to ask a man if he thought that the Trades Unions should accept a five per cent limit for wage increases at the behest of the Government; and suppose he answered 'No'. In reply to our further question 'Why not?', suppose two alternative replies came from this man. First, the reply, 'Because one in four of the members of the Trades Unions is under twenty-five years of age.' Then the reply, 'Because the Unions can't rely on the Government to keep its promise to hold dividends down to a like five per cent.' Why does this latter reply seem to us a rational thing to say, but not the former reply? The reason is simply that we are at home with the belief that it is appropriate to make agreements with those who can be relied upon to keep their side of the bargain, as we are not with the belief that it is appropriate to refrain from entering agreements if one in four of those entering with you is under twenty-five. There are many such generally-accepted principles of action within what I call the rational system of beliefs; and when we say that a particular belief about what should be done is rational, we often mean that it is in accordance with one or more of them.

A distinction should, no doubt, be drawn – within this class of generally-held, regulative beliefs about what it is appropriate to do (or to choose) – between *logical* and *practical* principles. Between, for example, a rule such as the law of non-contradiction and a maxim such as 'Honesty is the best policy'. Moreover, within *practical* principles, a distinction can be made between those of *expediency* and those of *morality*. Some philosophers, like Kant, have seen this latter distinction as that between hypothetical and categorical imperatives. Others like Mill have seen it as the distinction between action for the sake of the *summum bonum* and for the sake of other ends. But it is enough for our purposes simply to note that there is a distinction between moral and non-moral principles of action and that the rational system of belief includes both kinds. We have already seen that principles of expediency – such as the appropriateness of making agreements with those who can be relied upon to keep their side of the bargain – are included in the rational system. But so also are moral principles. Why does it sound rational to say – using a moral 'ought' – that we ought to help the weak, but not that we ought to help people just because they have red hair? Simply because the former, but not the latter, accords with a belief about what it is morally appropriate to do to which people in our society generally subscribe.

I hope that I have now said enough to give a clear picture of the various *kinds* of belief which I take to constitute the rational system. But so far I have said nothing about the possibility of change within this system. So, to this I turn.

Change within the Rational System of Beliefs

Wittgenstein puts it neatly when he says in *On Certainty* that fundamental propositions form 'the riverbed of thoughts'. (§97) He adds: 'the bank of that river consists partly of hard rock, subject to no alteration or only to an imperceptible one, partly of sand, which now in one place, now in another gets washed away, or deposited'. (§99) In other words, the 'riverbed of thoughts may shift'. (§97)

Changes certainly do occur within the rational system. This is so, whether we are thinking simply of beliefs about what is the case, like Wittgenstein's fundamental propositions, or about principles concerning what it is appropriate to do (or to choose). That which men take for granted on both counts will differ from age to age. The interesting question is: what are the dynamics of change within the rational system?

I emphasized earlier (p. 82) that, when I speak of the system of beliefs as 'rational', I do not mean to say that it meets certain criteria of rationality, but rather that conformity with it is one such criterion. However, even whilst holding firmly to that view, we may recognize that changes within the rational system frequently result from the application to its constituent elements of the other criteria of rationality. Where beliefs, which have been generally held and regulative in our society, are discovered to be self-contradictory, or contrary to the relevant evidence, or such as cannot be held open-mindedly, these beliefs lose their hold, first on a few people, and then, in the course of time, upon the majority. This process of change is, of course, somewhat erratic and patchy; but it does go on.

As an example of the kind of thing I mean, take the belief that the way to get the best out of your children or work-people is to be very strict with them. I think we can say this was once a generally-held, regulative belief in our society. Particular acts, which accorded with it, were deemed sensible, and those which did not, foolish. Though it was a principle of action, this belief rested upon a claim as to fact: namely, that 'the best' (by which was meant effort, honesty, obedience, etc.) could in fact be got out of juveniles and employees by severe, rather than kindly, treatment. This claim is vulnerable to the criterion of relevant evidence. Do the facts confirm it? I think most people in our society have come to the conclusion that they do not. And that is why the belief that the way to get the best out of your children and work-people is to treat them very strictly no longer forms part of the rational system. This illustrates how change within the system may be due to the application of other criteria of rationality to elements within it.

Changes, as I say, are often due to the application of these other criteria. But not always. They sometimes occur within the rational system *to all appearance* quite fortuitously – people in general simply stop believing something and so it ceases to regulate between sense and nonsense as it once did. To take a simple example of such outmoded propositional beliefs, think how people used to believe that a man's family background determined to a great extent the kind of man he is. Again, to take examples of beliefs about ends of action which it is appropriate to pursue, think of such things as education, independence, community spirit, etc. They can suddenly loom large in people's estimation and determine what it is considered appropriate to do, as they never did before. The quite uncritical assumption, for example, in our society, that one should secure for one's children the fullest possible academic education was not always characteristic of well-disposed parents.

What I wish to say about changes in the rational system, such as those to which I have just been very sketchily referring, is that they do not come about because someone 'proves' that (for example) beliefs about family background are against the relevant evidence, or that education and independence are consistent, open-minded ends to pursue. It is not my task to explore the total subtle and highly complex range of possible associated factors. The point I am making is merely that it is not *through the application of these other criteria of rationality* that the changes I referred to have come about – or not exclusively. People can just (so it seems) lose interest in something, as I think they have in family background. And they can simply (so it seems) stop caring about certain ends of action and come to value others very highly, as I think they have come to value education. Considerations of consistency, relevant evidence and open-mindedness may have a marginal effect on such changes. But the case for total determinism is now – nearly everybody agrees – almost impossible to defend, and I would contend that we have to recognize that people have at least some freedom of choice as to what they will believe to be the case, or to be appropriate as ends of action. And from time to time, I contend, they exercise this freedom of choice upon the content of the rational system.

So, in my view, the dynamics of change within the rational system is two-fold in origin. It operates through normative and fortuitous factors. Normative, in so far as the changes are due to criteria of rationality. Fortuitous, in so far as they are due to this 'freedom of choice' of which I have just spoken.

The Logical Distinctiveness of Conformity with the Rational System

The rational system, I have already said repeatedly, is so called not because it conforms to criteria of rationality, but because conformity with it is one such criterion. Nevertheless, the question may be raised as to whether this criterion can be reduced to the others. Does not conformity with the rational system, someone may say, amount in the end to conformity with criteria such as self-consistency, etc.? The answer is that it does not. But some considerations may seem at first enounter to suggest that it does.

One thing which may be pointed out in favour of the view that it does is the fact that the other criteria are themselves undoubtedly *part* of the content of the rational system. Amongst those beliefs within it which concern what it is appropriate to do we must include the principles that we should not contradict ourselves in what we say, that we should take account of the relevant evidence in deciding matters of putative fact, and that we should always be prepared to change our beliefs if we come upon good reasons for doing so. Part of what we may mean in calling beliefs or beings rational is that they conform to these principles. But, of course, there is *more* to the rational system than criteria of rationality such as those to which I have just referred. They are part, but not the whole of it. As we saw above, in addition it contains at least three different kinds of propositional belief and also principles of expediency and morality.

Nevertheless, someone may persist, is not this additional content of the rational system *subject to* the other criteria of rationality in a way which means, in the long run, that it is really they with which a belief has to be in conformity in order to be rational? We have already seen (p. 85) that changes in the content of the rational system may occur because of the application of these other criteria of rationality to elements within it. This may suggest that the rational system is really just a deposit of human self-criticism, the fruit of man's continued efforts to re-evaluate his ideas of how things are and how life ought to be lived. And it is a short step from thinking of the system in this way to the conclusion that conformity with it is really conformity with these other criteria of rationality. But, of course, what this conclusion does not allow for is what I called above (p. 86) the fortuitous factor in the changing content of the rational system. That content is not simply the product of the normative operation of the other criteria of rationality. It is, in part, the product of man's free choice of beliefs to hold and of ends to pursue. So we cannot accept the claim that conformity with the rational system is reducible to conformity with the other criteria of rationality.

A further consideration against such reductionism is as follows. A particular belief may have been in conformity with the rational system at the time when it was held, even though we would now judge it by one or more of what I have called the 'other criteria' to be irrational. In such case, we might hesitate between calling the belief in question rational or irrational. Suppose, for example, that we were discussing a Victorian father who had been very strict with his children about their behaviour at meals. He had banished them to cold bedrooms on bread and water for failing to eat up their porridge, or something of that sort. We might well say that this Victorian's belief that what he was doing would get the best out of his children was not irrational, given the rational system of beliefs as it was in his day, whilst considering it highly irrational in the light of what we would now regard as relevant evidence. Such a case further establishes that the criterion of conformity with the rational system cannot simply be equated with what I have called the 'other criteria'.

The Dialectic of the Rational System

An important point about the rational system, which has been coming into focus throughout our discussion, is what may be called – without implying any of the metaphysical overtones of the word – its dialectical character. There is within it a perpetual tension between its established and its emergent content. We noted the dynamism created within it by normative and fortuitous factors. (p. 86) Conformity to it is not a matter so much of accepting certain beliefs and abiding by them; but rather, of being committed to that dialectic between conformity and criticism which is characteristic of any rational enterprise. Learning to be rational[5] is in part a matter of acquiring certain accepted norms and learning how to operate within them; but it is also a matter of learning how to subject these norms to experiment and re-evaluation. Nothing which has been said about conformity with the rational system is at variance with this conception of rationality. Conforming to the rational system involves conforming to those normative principles which make for change within it; and allowing for those fortuitous choices which point us to new beliefs or ends of action. Room is allowed not only for self-criticism, but also for flights of fancy, both of which have been essential to the expanding intellectual life of mankind.

II The Rational System as a Point of Convergence

Theologians, sociologists and philosophers are concerned with the rational system of beliefs in different ways. Nevertheless, it serves as a point of convergence for them. It is often said that the three disciplines have much to do with one another; and, more specifically, that sociology and philosophy can assist the theologian in his work. But I do not think that those who say this kind of thing are always as clear as they might be about exactly how the concerns of the three disciplines come together. What I wish to say is that they do so with regard to rationality; and, in particular, with regard to the criterion of rationality which I have called conformity with the rational system of beliefs. I will try to show, first, that theologians have to satisfy this criterion in their formulations of Christian doctrine. Then, I will say how I think sociologists and philosophers respectively can enable them to do so more effectively. I bring philosophy into the picture because I do not think that there can be any fruitful relationship between sociology and theology without, so to say, the services of philosophy as midwife. I will discuss the three disciplines in turn.

Theology and the Rational System

In their work, theologians necessarily have to satisfy some criteria (or criterion) of rationality. I take their aim, as theologians, to be two-fold: namely, that of *explaining* and *defending* Christian belief. The two aims are logically distinct from one another, though in practice they usually, perhaps invariably, go together. In explaining a belief, the theologian is normally seeking to defend it, and, in defending it, to say what it really means. Neither of the theologian's aims – explanation or defence – can (logically) be achieved without fulfilling some criteria (or criterion) of rationality.

Take, as an example of theological *explanation*, the contention that the belief that Christ died for us really means that in his death he paid a penalty which we had incurred by our sins. It does not seem irrational to suppose that this is what the belief in question really means, as it would seem irrational, for instance, to suppose that what it really means is that Christ jumped over the moon. Now, why? Because, given the relevant evidence, that is, the ordinary meanings of the words used, the notion *paying a penalty which we have incurred* is consistent with the notion *dying for us*, as the notion *jumping over the moon* is not. Paying a penalty incurred by us is *conceivable* as an explanation of Christ dying for us; and to say that it is 'conceivable' is simply to say that it fulfils certain criteria of rationality, such as self-consistency, support by relevant evidence, or whatever.

Again, take, as an example of theological *defence*, the kind of reasons which have sometimes been put forward in defence of the belief that Christ died for us. It has been said that we were in the kind of plight through our sins where only someone's death in our place could save us; and that, since God's nature is love, nothing could be more credible than that he should therefore send his Son to get us out of trouble. The aim of such a defence is clearly to show that Christ's death for us is something in which we can believe because it meets certain criteria of rationality. For one thing, it is self-consistent: God, being love, would wish to save us. For another, the relevant evidence of the kind of plight we were in is invoked to show that someone had to die for us. And so on. This defence is an argument and so it serves its purpose only when it is tied in by criteria of rationality with the belief which it purports to defend. If anyone said, for instance, that we can believe that Christ died for us because he had fair hair, what would we make of that? It would not be recognizable as a defence because there is nothing in our conception of what makes a belief rational onto which it would latch.

I am not, of course, suggesting that the particular explanation of Christ's saving death, to which I have referred, is correct; nor the defence of belief in it, triumphant. All I have been trying to show by these simplistic illustrations is that theologians necessarily invoke criteria of rationality in their hermeneutical and apologetic labours. It is logically impossible for them to explain or defend Christian belief without doing so.

It may be of interest to note in passing that this is true, even when what the theologian is attempting to explain or defend is declared to be itself logically impossible. Tertullian,[6] for instance, held that certain Christian beliefs are logically impossible. But he argued that this is the very reason why we should believe them. God, being infinite, is different from everything else. The fact that a belief about anything else was logically impossible would be a good reason for rejecting it; but the fact that a belief about God is logically impossible is a good reason for accepting it. This follows, according to Tertullian, from the premise that God is different from everything else. No doubt, there are lots of things wrong with this argument. But my point is simply that it *is* an argument; and so proceeds by appeal to criteria of rationality. Even the most 'anti-rationalistic' of theologians cannot detach himself from criteria of rationality. His inescapable concerns are explanation and defence. And neither is logically possible apart from an appeal to criteria of rationality.

Among such criteria is the one about which I have been speaking at length in the first part of this chapter, viz. conformity to the rational system of beliefs. In the remainder of my remarks about theology, I want to show how determinative for the work of the theologian this criterion of conformity with the rational system is. The best way of doing so is probably by continuing to think about the belief that Christ died for our sins.

Christians have from earliest times held this belief. A lot of Christian theology down the ages has been designed to explain what it means and to show that it is credible. Three main ways of achieving these objectives have been adopted. They are commonly called 'theories of the Atonement'. According to the first, the death of Christ was a device whereby God delivered men from the power of the Devil. According to the second, it was a penalty for sin paid by Christ on our behalf. And according to the third, it was a means whereby love for God was kindled in the hearts of men through the revelation of his love for them. To say that these three theories comprehend all thought about the Atonement would, of course, be a gross over-simplification. They have in fact passed through many subtle and complicated permutations and combinations in the history of doctrine. But for our purposes that does not matter. The point I wish to bring out about theology can be adequately illustrated from simple versions of the three theories. Each of these purports to show the intelligibility and credibility of the belief that Christ died for our sins by invoking generally-held, regulative beliefs, both about what is the case and about what it is appropriate to do. That is to say, they do so by reference to the rational system of beliefs, as it prevailed at the time when they were propounded.

An example of the first kind of theory is found in Origen. He wrote: 'he (sc. the Devil) had us in his power, until the ransom for us should be given to him, even the life of Jesus, since he (the evil one) had been deceived, and led to suppose that he was capable of mastering that soul, and he did not see that to hold Him involved a trial of strength greater than he was equal to'.[7] This seems to mean that God tricked the Devil into accepting Christ, whom he (that is, the Devil) would not be able to destroy, in exchange for men whom he could destroy. This theory explains and defends the belief that Christ died for our sins, but only for those who believe (i) that the Devil exists and (ii) that when someone is doing evil, it is appropriate to defeat him by deception.

Anselm provides an example of the second kind of theory. Influenced no doubt by feudal notions of the *wergild*, or honour-price (that is, an institution whereby the greater the person injured, the greater the penal satisfaction required) Anselm argued that, since men's sins were an offence against God, no satisfaction for them is possible 'unless there be someone to pay to God in compensation for the sin of man something greater than everything that exists except God'. He drew the conclusion that 'no one, therefore, . . . can make this satisfaction except God Himself'.[8] From which he then inferred that it was necessary for someone to die who was both God and man: who, as man, could pay the price for disobeying God and, as God, was able to pay a sufficiently high price. Once again, all this is only illuminating, given certain beliefs. It makes sense of the Atonement, but only for those who share Anselm's beliefs (i) that God is related to men in something like a feudal manner, and (ii) that the appropriate way to atone for an offence is by paying the *wergild*.

Abailard is the most celebrated exponent of the third kind of theory. His own account of Christ's death was, to some degree, parasitic on the second kind of theory because it assumed that a penalty for our sins had to be paid; but Abailard nevertheless had his own distinctive view of the purpose of the Atonement. He describes it as follows: 'that . . . by the exhibition of such grace (sc. in Christ's death on our behalf) (He) . . . might draw our minds away from the will to sin and incline them to the fullest love of Himself'. [9] This theory, in its turn, makes sense of the Atonement, given two beliefs (i) that it is psychologically possible for human wills to be redeemed from evil by an exhibition of grace, and (ii) that the best way of dealing with those who have done you wrong is to make them into better people if you can.

In each of these three examples, I have called attention to (i) a propositional belief about something which is the case, and (ii) a principle concerning something which it is deemed appropriate to do in certain circumstances. My intention has been to show that each theory presupposes such beliefs on the part both of its proponent and of all those – namely, people in general at the time – to whom it is addressed. Of course, each theory presupposes a host of other such propositions and principles besides the ones which I have specifically mentioned. Most of these others are common to all three theories. They are propositions about God, man, this world and the next world; and principles of logic, of expediency and of morality. But what I have tried to show by these simple illustrations is that the rational system, at the time when each theory was propounded, contained elements which made *that* particular theory intelligible and credible.

This, then, is what the rational system has to do with theology. Without a background of generally-held, regulative beliefs, with which it is in conformity, no piece of theology would be intelligible or credible for those to whom it is addressed.

There has, of course, been a great deal of change and development within theology through the ages; and the dynamics of all this can, in fact, be seen as provided by the need for conformity with the rational system.

Some changes have been due to what I have called the other criteria of rationality (self-consistency, evidential corroboration, open-mindedness), but, it will be recalled that these are included within the content of the rational system. Simple examples of their effects in theology are as follows. The need for self-consistency led some theologians to abandon the penal theory of the Atonement because they came to think it self-contradictory to conceive of God as one who is both loving by nature and yet demands a penalty for sin. Again, the criterion of evidential corroboration led some theologians to modify their Abailardian theology in the light of their own experience of forgiving people who had wronged them. They deemed this experience to be relevant evidence for an understanding of the Atonement and it led them to the conclusion that not even God can put an end to sin simply by saying 'I forgive'. As one of them expressed it: it is 'the common exigent of life' that propitiation is 'the necessary precondition of forgiveness'.[10] Open-mindedness is not a quality for which theologians have been remarkable in times past. But they have always recognized that there is more to Christianity than they have understood and, in recent times, the essentially tentative nature of all theological formulations is a point upon which many theologians have become insistent. In such ways, conformity with that part of the rational system which consists of these other criteria has produced change.

But what is more interesting, perhaps, from our point of view, is those developments within theology which have been due to changes in that part of the content of the rational system which is additional to the other criteria. I have tried to show that Origen's, Anselm's and Abailard's theories of the Atonement respectively presupposed certain beliefs about what is the case and what it is appropriate to do. Such beliefs were held at the time. But changes came. In so far as men have ceased to believe in the Devil or in the appropriateness of God deceiving him, they have ceased to take Origen's view of Christ's death; in so far as they have ceased to think of God as feudally related to men or to see any obligation in the *wergild*, they have ceased to take Anselm's; and in so far as they may have had doubts about its psychological and moral presuppositions, to take Abailard's.

The point to grasp is that the operative, fundamental changes here have all been in the content of the rational system. Every piece of theology presupposes certain beliefs – as Origen's presupposes the existence of the Devil, and so on – and where these presupposed beliefs cease to be part of the content of the rational system, the theology which rests on them has to be changed, if it is to continue to be intelligible and credible to reasonable men. In sum, then, the rational system bears upon theology both because the task of the theologian in explaining and defending Christian belief cannot be fulfilled without reference to it; and because developments in theology cannot be explained apart from the persistent demand that theology should conform in its explanation and defence of Christian belief to the changing content of the rational system.

Sociology and the Rational System

Sociologists study group behaviour. One aspect of any given group's behaviour is the beliefs which its members hold: and another is the changes which have taken, or are taking, place within these beliefs. If we are thinking of generally-held, regulative beliefs, then we may say that it is the sociologist's task, among other things, to describe the rational system of beliefs in any given society and to trace the developments which have recently taken place within it. In studying these things, so far as our own society is concerned, sociologists are certainly lighting up the theologian's task. For, as we said, the theologian's objectives, of explaining and defending Christian beliefs, can only be fulfilled in so far as theology brings these beliefs into line with the rational system. Therefore, when sociologists make clear the empirical content of, and the recent developments within that system as it prevails in our society, in effect they are setting the theologian his task. Given these generally-held, regulative beliefs, can Christianity be explained and defended in conformity with them? If not, it will be neither intelligible nor credible to our contemporaries.

Arguing that it is in fact neither of these things, A.C. MacIntyre,[11] in a much discussed paper, held that Christianity has now lost the 'social context' which once gave it meaning. He unpacks this notion of a 'social context' in terms of 'norms of intelligibility'; and I think that by both expressions he means something similar to what I have meant throughout this chapter by 'the rational system of beliefs'. There are generally-held, regulative beliefs, common to believers and unbelievers alike in our society, says MacIntyre, but Christianity does not conform to them. Therefore, what a believer has to do, in order to make his religion believable, is 'to supply a social context which is now lacking and abstract a social context which is now present'. In other words, he has to suppose the rational system to be other than it really is. To suppose, for example, the belief that everything must have a cause in order to make sense of the belief that God is first cause; or to suppose the belief that submissiveness is an appropriate attitude for some human beings to adopt towards others in order to make sense, for example, of St Paul's injunctions (*Ephesians* 5: 22) about wives submitting to husbands, etc. On this view, Christianity demands an out-of-date physics and an out-of-date ethics to make it credible. But this very fact makes it incredible. For the rational system of beliefs cannot be tinkered with just to suit the convenience of believers.

That is true enough, but is the *basic* assumption here correct, namely that the rational system in our society at the present time is hostile to religion in general and Christianity in particular? This is a question of empirical fact and it is one to which sociologists can help to supply the answer. They can do so in three ways.

First, by making clear what the content of the rational system actually is at those points where Christianity presupposes it to have a certain content so far as physics, history, ethics or whatever, is concerned. When theologians have said what they think Christianity requires its adherents to believe, the question always arises as to whether or not these beliefs conform to relevant propositional and practical beliefs within the rational system. Is the conception of nature presupposed, for example, by a Christianity which includes belief in miracles compatible with generally-held, regulative beliefs about the natural world? Is what Christianity takes to be right or wrong concerning war, sex, race relations, etc. compatible with generally-held, regulative principles of morality or expediency? These questions are crucial so far as the intelligibility and credibility of Christianity are concerned. Obviously they can only be answered when we are quite clear what these generally-held, regulative beliefs are with which Christianity needs to be compatible. Sociologists can tell us what they are.

Second, sociologists can answer the question as to how far religious belief itself is part of the content of the rational system. There are at least two ways in which they can do this. One is by setting up investigations to discover what religious beliefs, if any, are still generally-held and regulative in our society. The other is by finding out what is widely taken for granted in our society where religion is concerned. On both counts, of course, the evidence may not be conclusive one way or the other.

In 1968 for example, the Independent Television Authority commissioned a survey of popular attitudes to religion. The staff of Opinion Research Centre interviewed a random sample of 1071 adults and came up with results which showed that belief and unbelief are fairly equally distributed in our society, though with more belief among the elderly and the female members of the population than the young and the male. Fifty-six per cent of all age groups taken together professed certainty that God exists and forty-six per cent professed that they were strongly influenced by this belief.

A safer guide to what people believe than what they profess is what they take for granted. In our society, do people assent to any religious beliefs in the undoubting way that they assent to the fundamental constitutive propositions of, say, science or history? Wittgenstein imagines a schoolboy who keeps questioning fundamental propositions. In the science class he asks, 'But is nature uniform?'; in the history class, 'But did the earth really exist long before I was born?', and, in general, 'But do things really stay there when no one observes them?' And so on. His teacher grows impatient and says 'Stop interrupting me and do as I tell you. So far your doubts don't make sense at all.' (§310) And quite rightly, says Wittgenstein. (§315) For if the boy goes on like this, he will learn nothing. He is wasting his own time and that of the class. This illustration is intended to show the extent to which the propositions which the schoolboy questions are taken for granted in our society. But now, suppose this boy had asked in the Religious Education class, 'But does God exist?' Would that question have struck his teacher – does it strike us – as equally otiose? The answer we give is about what we take for granted in the case of religion. Sociologists can tell us how this question would be generally answered in our society.

By these two kinds of empirical observation – finding out the religious beliefs which people profess and finding out what they take for granted where religion is concerned – sociologists can tell us to what extent, if any, religion is, in our society, still part of the rational system, as it has been in past ages and other societies.

There is a third kind of discovery which sociologists could conceivably make and which would inform us as to the content of the rational system. Suppose, as seems not unlikely, their investigations show that religious beliefs are no longer part of the rational system. Will it follow that to hold such beliefs is irrational? Not necessarily. Particular religious beliefs could still be in conformity with the rational system, even though they were *not part* of it. Whether or not any particular religious belief *is* in conformity with the rational system is, as we shall see in the next section, a philosophical, rather than a sociological, question. But sociologists can show us whether or not particular religious beliefs *are regarded* as irrational in our society. And in showing this they can add to our understanding of the content of the rational system. What are the generally-held, regulative beliefs which prevail in our society? People's estimate of religious belief will carry implications which help to answer that question. Many people in our society who count themselves unbelievers, would not, I think, wish to call religious belief irrational. They would be inclined to say simply that it is hard to show what counts as evidence in the case of religion – or to see the evidence as pointing conclusively in any one direction – but they would hesitate to dismiss religious belief as irrational by the criterion of relevant evidence. Even though they themselves think it unlikely that there is a God, who watches over us, they can see the point of people who believe this, praying to him, trusting him etc. Even though they consider that Christianity over-simplifies moral issues, they tend to admire those who take it seriously and try to put it into practice. Where a belief clearly fails to conform to generally-held, regulative beliefs about what is the case, or what it is appropriate to do, the attitude which people adopt to that belief seems far more condemnatory than the attitude which most people in our society seem to adopt to religion. If I am right about this, our understanding of the content of the rational system needs to take account of that fact. But whether I am right or not, sociologists, in helping us to see clearly whether or not people in general in our society regard particular religious beliefs as irrational, are inevitably making the content of the rational system clearer to us.

In these three ways, then, and perhaps others also, sociology concerns – or could concern – itself with the rational system. In so doing it will make clearer for the theologians what it is with which their explanations and defences of Christian belief have to conform if they are to be credible and intelligible.

Philosophy and the Rational System

Practically everything which has been said in this chapter so far illustrates how the rational system of beliefs comes within the range of a philosopher's concerns. In our analysis of what it means for a belief to be rational, we were led to the notion of conformity with the rational system of beliefs; and having been led there, we were constrained to attempt a classification of the different kinds of belief comprehended within this system and to differentiate conformity with it from other criteria of rationality. These endeavours – to discover the role which the rational system plays in our thinking, and to analyze its constituents so that we might discern that role more clearly – are typical examples of philosophy at work. Similarly, our discussion of the aims and development of theology and the extent to which the achievement of the former, and the course of the latter, may be said to depend upon the criterion of conformity with the rational system, was an exercise in philosophical analysis. As was also our attempt to work out the ways in which sociology could conceivably extend our knowledge of the rational system's content.

In addition to such descriptive analysis, however, philosophy exists to make critical judgments. These are about, amongst other things, the *implications* of what is said, and the validity of the *moves* which are made in argument. With regard to the theologian's task of explaining and defending Christian belief in conformity with the rational system, there are two respects at least in which philosophers can shed light for him to work by. For one, they can show where, in particular, the *implications* of any piece of theology are vulnerable to the criterion of conformity with the rational system. For another, they can assess the extent to which *moves*,

which attempt to develop theology in order to meet the demands of
that criterion, are legitimate. Let us look more closely at these two
critical functions in turn.

To take the former; in propounding, or assessing, any piece of
theology, it is necessary to discern the precise points at which the
question of its conformity with the rational system arises. I said
earlier that sociologists set theologians their task by showing what is
the content of the rational system with which the theologian has to
come to terms. But merely to describe the content of that system is
not enough. It is necessary to discern the points at which any piece
of theology is crucially related to that content. In its belief in a Devil,
or in miracles, or in certain possibilities of human nature, etc., a
given theological doctrine may, or may not, be compatible with the
rational system. It is at these points that the tensions arise, which
render theology intelligible or unintelligible, credible or incredible,
congruent as it is or in need of change. To discern where these points
of tension are, to see what the crucial implications of any given piece
of theology must be so far as its conformity with the rational system
is concerned, is work for the philosopher rather than the sociologist.
Sometimes it is obvious what these crucial implications are. The
belief that God tricked the Devil, for example, presupposes the
Devil's existence. When that belief was first put forward, it was in
conformity with the rational system because nearly everybody
believed in the Devil's existence. But if anyone put it forward today,
it would be obvious that here was a point at which the belief in
question did not conform with the rational system. Sometimes,
however, things are not so obvious. Take belief in miracles. Two
questions, amongst others, arise about this belief. Does it imply that
nature is not uniform? And, if it does, is this implied belief incompatible with the rational system or not? Very complicated and
far-reaching considerations, concerning the implications of the concept of miracle and of recent developments in natural science, are
raised by these questions. It is for the philosopher to discern what
these implications are and how they relate to one another. In so
doing, he will be pinpointing the task of the theologian, who wishes
to make belief in miracles intelligible and credible. And, similarly,
for other doctrines.

But philosophy does not simply light up for the theologian what is
required of him. It assesses the extent to which he achieves this. It
answers this question: in formulating – and particularly in re-
formulating – Christian belief, has the theologian *successfully*
brought it into conformity with the rational system? Two questions
are really comprehended within this one question. The first is: does
any given theological formulation conform with the rational system? And the second: is this formulation which it gives to Christian

belief recognizable *as* Christian belief? Let me show more precisely
what I mean by these two questions, by taking two recent examples
of the re-formulation of Christian beliefs. They concern the doctrines of resurrection and eternal life, in which Christians have
traditionally believed, but to which the two authors whom I shall
mention have given very radical reformulation.

Paul van Buren in his *The Secular Meaning of the Gospel* (Lon-
.don, 1963) states the question which he is trying to answer thus:
'How can the Christian who is himself a secular man understand his
faith in a secular way?' (p. 2) He considers belief in Christ's resurrection as a case in point. Jesus was, throughout his life, quite
unconcerned about physical safety, material security, having a good
name, etc.; and when he came to die, he did so with a complete
freedom from fear or anxiety. Things which other men worry about
so much did not trouble him at all. (p. 123) This is the content which
van Buren gives to the doctrine of the resurrection. Knowing Christ
in the power of his resurrection is taken by him to mean being
'caught up in something like the freedom of Jesus' by accepting his
teaching and following his example. Believing that God raised Jesus
he interprets as a matter of making this freedom from anxiety
'fundamental to one's life and thought' and taking it as 'the point
from which one sees the world and lives in it'. (p. 133) In a somewhat similar vein D.Z. Phillips says in his *Death and Immortality*
(London, 1970) that eternal life 'is not *more* life but this life seen
under certain moral and religious modes of thought'. (p. 49) We
should think of it as 'participation in the life of God'. (pp. 54–55) If
we ask what this amounts to, Phillips' answer is that 'in learning by
contemplation, attention, renunciation, what forgiving, thanking,
loving, etc. mean . . ., the believer is participating in the reality of
God'. (p. 55)

Now, first, do these reformations of Christian doctrine conform
to the rational system? If authors such as Harvey Cox are right in
their view that 'profanity',[12] that is, being bounded by purely terrestrial horizons, is characteristic of our society, then it would seem so.
For the accounts of resurrection and eternal life which we have just
noted are thoroughly terrestrial. They demand belief in nothing
except the possibility of certain psychological states in Jesus and
those who strive to be like him. They restrict resurrection and
eternal life to this world and this life.

But now to the more troublesome question: is what they leave us
with recognizable as Christian belief at all? It seems clearly to be the
intention of van Buren and Phillips to explain to us what the
traditional doctrines of resurrection and eternal life really mean and
to show that they are credible. But it is hard to avoid the conclusion
that their arguments to this effect proceed by fallacious equivo-

cation. The word 'resurrection' can be used figuratively to mean 'rising above anxiety, fear, etc.' (Sense 2) as well as literally to mean 'coming back to life' (Sense 1). Van Buren's argument is, in effect, that Christian belief in resurrection (Sense 1) can be accepted because resurrection (Sense 2) is an historical fact. Again, the expression 'eternal' can be used to mean 'unconditioned by spatial or temporal considerations' (in which sense, logical, moral or spiritual truths may be eternal) and also to mean 'going on for ever'. Phillips' argument is, in effect, that belief in life which goes on for ever is possible because belief in life subject to moral or spiritual criteria is possible. The equivocation in both cases is the harder to spot because it is certainly *part* of the Christian concept of resurrection that it is a victory over sin and death and so over the anxiety consequent upon them; and *part* of the Christian concept of eternal life, that such life is not subject to the change and decay which we see all around us in this world. But unless 'resurrection' and 'eternal life' are taken to mean that individuals continue their lives after death, then these words are not being used in the sense in which they are normally used in Christian contexts. If van Buren or Phillips had affirmed that they were proposing beliefs with which to *replace* Christian ones, there would be no equivocation in their argument. But that is not what they affirm.

Whether my particular criticisms of van Buren and Phillips are accepted or not, they illustrate the kind of thing I mean when I speak of philosophy critically assessing the extent to which the moves made by theologians, in their attempts to bring Christian belief into conformity with the rational system, are successful.

III Conclusion

To recall the title of this book, I have tried to show that theology and sociology can be in alliance, rather than conflict, because of their mutual concern with the rational system of beliefs. Regarding theology, my argument has been that theologians can render Christian belief intelligible and credible only by bringing it into conformity with certain propositional beliefs and principles of action (or choice) which are generally held in our society and are regulative of what it makes sense to believe. Being in conformity with this rational system is a criterion of rationality logically distinct from other criteria, such as being self-consistent, being supported by relevant evidence, or being believed open-mindedly. These other criteria are undoubtedly comprehended within the rational system as principles concerning what it is appropriate to believe, but they are not its whole content. As for sociology, I have argued that its proper task is to make clear the empirical facts concerning the actual content of the rational system and any developments which have recently taken place within it. Thereby it can light up for theologians that with which they must bring their explanation and defence of Christian belief into conformity.

But I have claimed that, left to themselves, so to speak, theology and sociology cannot fruitfully interact. They need the services of philosophy to make their alliance productive. For it is philosophers who must, on the one hand, show precisely where the implications of any piece of theology are crucial so far as conformity with the rational system is concerned; and, on the other, judge whether any development within theology brings Christian belief into conformity with that system at the cost of changing such belief into something else.

Notes

1 Cf. Wittgenstein, L. *Philosophical Investigations* (Oxford, 1958) I. 66–67.
2 Wittgenstein, L. *On Certainty* ed. G.E.M. Anscombe and G.H. von Wright, trans. D. Paul and G.E.M. Anscombe, parallel English and German (Oxford, 1974).
3 See Moore's 'A Defence of Common Sense' and other papers in his *Philosophical Papers* (London, 1959).
4 See his 'Empiricism, Semantics and Ontology' in *Revue internationale de philosophie* (Bruxelles, 1950).
5 Cf. my 'Learning to be Rational' in *Proceedings of the Philosophy of Education Society of Great Britain,* XI, 1977, pp. 39–56.
6 *De Carni Christi.*
7 Origen on Matthew 16:8. There is some difference of opinion about the correct interpretation of this passage (cf. Cave, S. *The Doctrine of the Work of Christ* (London, 1937) p. 97.)
8 *Cur Deus Homo?* (quoted in Cave, *op. cit.* p. 127).
9 Abailard on Romans 4:25 (quoted in Cave, *op. cit.* p. 135).
10 Bushnell, R. *Forgiveness and Law* (1874) (quoted in Cave, *op. cit.* p. 223).
11 'Is Understanding Religion compatible with Believing?' in John Hick (ed.) *Faith and the Philosophers* (London, 1964).
12 Cf. his *The Secular City* (London, 1965).

Chapter 6

FROM SOCIOLOGY TO THEOLOGY

Robin Gill

THE time has come to ask whether current attempts to explore the relation between theology and the social sciences allow the theologian to construct a viable theological system on their basis.

This is an ambitious question! It is quite possible to see what a systematic *sociological* account of theology would entail. Whatever else it is, theology is a socially constructed reality and theologians are fellow human beings existing in particular cultures and societies. But it is not nearly so clear what a 'theological account of sociology' might be – despite a few important attempts to provide one. Here I will try to outline a possible solution to this problem.

For well over a century first Protestant and latterly Catholic theologians have accepted the need for rigorous, critical scholarship. Although biblical and doctrinal fundamentalisms still exist, even within academic circles, there is now very widespread agreement that the critical tools provided by the philosopher and the historian are prerequisites of satisfactory theology. Naturally churchmen may not always be happy with the results of much scholarship, since they regard them as at times excessively iconoclastic. Nevertheless, theologians themselves show no signs of abandoning them. Rather, they are likely to claim that they constitute essential features of rigorous, academic, honest theology.

There is, of course, nothing new about historical or philosophical theology. New Testament theology is itself historical theology in so far as it was written only after the death of Jesus and yet depends upon his life for its *raison d'être*. And philosophical theology may be thought to have started with the Hellenization of Christianity – itself a biblical phenomenon – when Christian theology was adapted to the philosophical terms of Greek culture. Certainly by the Fathers theology was both historical and philosophical.

The new element within the contemporary theology is that is is, or at least should be, rigorously self-critical. The tools of the contemporary historian or philosopher are used not simply to translate, adapt or spread the gospel, but to call it into question. Essential to critical theology is an insistence upon self-examination. In biblical studies this has caused major changes – some of which are only now impinging upon the Catholic world. In doctrinal studies it is already evident within both Protestant and Catholic worlds that assumptions and dogmas of the past are being increasingly questioned. Both biblical and doctrinal criticisms are widely accepted and require little justification amongst academics.

One of the dangers of this situation is that historical and philosophical means of assessing the validity of theological notions may gain a virtual monopoly within universities. Indeed, the problems posed for theology by these two disciplines seem to provide the theologian with more than enough difficulties. Not surprisingly, it has become hard to distinguish academic theology as it is currently taught in the West from general courses in the philosophy of religion or the history of religious ideas. The tools provided by philosophy and history appear thoroughly incisive and rigorous in contrast to other methods of assessing the validity of theological notions.

Nonetheless, it is more than a little surprising that the social sciences have been so largely overlooked in this desire of contemporary theology for rigorous self-criticism. Of course, there are sharp divisions amongst social scientists – both between and even within its various sub-disciplines and specialities. These divisions in turn may have served to baffle those outside the discipline and make them distrustful of its incisiveness and rigour. Yet similar divisions can be found amongst historians and philosophers, and comparatively few deny their claim to be incisive and rigorous. It remains something of a mystery why theology has been so slow to examine itself in the light of the social sciences.

As a theologian I believe that it is essential for theology to continue this rigorous self-criticism. For me, theology is essentially a dynamic discipline in which concepts are tested and re-tested afresh in each age and culture. In our own age and culture the social sciences should be playing a more important role, alongside philosophical and historical methods, in this dynamic process of discovery and re-discovery.

Once this point is conceded, fresh possibilities arise for theology. Instead of concentrating upon the purely cognitive aspects of theology, as the philosopher is inclined to do, the theologian may be encouraged to explore the dynamic between faith and practice. I shall return to this point in more detail, but for the moment I am suggesting that if the theologian resorts to the social sciences in his task of rigorous self-criticism he may eventually be encouraged to undertake a theology of practice, as well as the current more formally cognitive type of theology. For convenience I will refer to this possibility as 'praxis theology'.

There are two basic features of praxis theology. Most contentiously, it would maintain that sociological techniques and theories (and perhaps psychological techniques and theories too, but I must leave that to other specialists) can be used actually to arbitrate on the validity of differing theological notions – or, at the very least, on the validity of particular interpretations of theological notions. Clearly this notion of arbitration takes me considerably beyond the three sociological approaches to theology on which I have written elsewhere (and will summarize briefly below). It will need careful qualification later, but it obviously belongs specifically to theology rather than sociology. Precisely because it is contentious I will be devoting most of this chapter to it.

The other major aspect of a praxis theology would be this. Such a theology would attempt systematically to unpack the social implications of particular theological positions and notions. As I will be indicating later, this too raises numerous problems for theologians. Nonetheless, there is much wider agreement amongst them on this aspect of a praxis theology. Thus, although individual theologians might differ with each other on the exact social implications of their veiws, most might agree broadly (with one or two important exceptions) that their views do indeed have social implications. Certainly most contemporary theologians are not 'political theologians'. However, most would still agree that their theological views are relevant to such social issues as abortion and euthanasia. On the other hand, few might concede that the social effects of their theological positions are actually relevant to the validity of these positions.

Already I have introduced a distinction between the social effects and the social implications of theological positions. For the sake of clarity I will confine the first to largely unconscious consequences of theological positions and the second to deliberate, intended or conscious consequences of such positions. Specifically sociological techniques and theories are more relevant to a study of the first than the second. It is appropriate for the interested sociologist to investigate the way particular theological positions have, or even could have, particular effects upon society. The theologian can then, I will contend, use such investigations to become more self-critical. However, the intended social implications of a particular theologian's positions are not so subject to sociological investigation. They belong much more fully to the specific task of the theologian himself. Here there are much better established areas of conflict and methods of procedure actually within theology itself.

Before seeking to justify my claim that a praxis theology would in part be concerned with assessing the validity of theological notions in the light of their social effects, I must indicate how such a study differs from my more specifically sociological attempt to analyze theology. I have suggested three distinct approaches.[1]

Three sociological approaches to theology

A. *A study of the social context of theology*

This approach depends upon the assumption that theology does not work in a vacuum, but that theologians tend to make claims about the society or culture within which they operate and then incorporate these claims into their theology. Precisely because the theologian is concerned to communicate with his contemporaries, he is obliged to respond (sometimes critically) to contemporary plausibility structures. This was most evident in the secular theology movement, in which theologians deliberately wrote in a response to a supposed process of secularization within society at large. However, it is also apparent in contemporary liberation theology, particularly in its conscious espousal of social and political models from the Third World. Sociological analysis could provide incisive and rigorous tools for the theologian to understand better the social context within which he operates.

B. *A study of the social determinants of theology*

The focus here is less upon the task of the theologian than upon theology itself. This approach assumes that as a human enterprise theology is socially determined. It suggests a correlation between social structures and theology, regarding the latter as a product of the former. Theology, like all other ideologies and explications of beliefs, is viewed as a human product or as a social construction – whatever else it might be. On the basis of this approach it becomes possible to use techniques developed in the sociology of knowledge to study the ways in which differing theological positions are correlated with differing social structures.

C. *A study of the social significance[2] of theology*

Here the possibility is explored that theology, even as a product of society, may in turn have an influence upon that society. If the previous approach regards theology as a dependent variable within society, this one allows for the possibility that theology may also act as an independent variable. Overall, theology is seen as a socially constructed reality – that is, as something that is both socially constructed *and* a social reality. To give a single example, certain forms of Marxist theory would suggest that theology is the product and expression of certain socio-economic divisions within society, and in particular the expression of the rulers over-and-against the ruled. In these terms theology is seen as a social construction. But there is also a possibility that Marx and Engels were themselves unwittingly influenced by the prevailing Hegelian theologies[3] of their day, and an even stronger possibility that certain versions of liberation theology, having incorporated a Marxist critique actually into their discipline, are proving influential within parts of the Third World. An extraordinarily complex web of interactions between theology and society emerges from this example; Hegelian theological ideas may have influenced Marx and Engels' critique of theology, which in turn has been adopted by certain influential versions of liberation theology. A combination of approaches B and C, then presents a view of the role of theology within society which the sociology of knowledge can do much to clarify.

All this is ground that I have covered and argued at length elsewhere. Taken together these three sociological approaches to theology seek to offer the theologian a relatively unexplored, but nonetheless incisive and rigorously academic, means of examining his discipline.

It is important not to overstate the 'newness' of these three approaches to theology. Implicitly and sometimes even explicitly critical theologians have often alluded to their particular social context and shown an awareness of the social determinants and significance of their discipline. It is a commonplace of theological polemics to demonstrate how opponents' views are inadequate responses to their social context, products of certain social factors, or lead to undesirable social consequences. Further, various forms of existentialist theology have made systematic use of the concept of *Sitz im Leben* or social context – arguing that contemporary theology must respond directly to contemporary thought-forms and not to those of first century Christians. In addition, both biblical and doctrinal criticism have shown a considerable awareness of the relation between ideas and beliefs on the one hand and social or cultural factors on the other. Finally, church historians have frequently emphasized the role of specifically theological elements in the shaping of religious and political events. A combination of hermeneutics, historical research, apologetics and even theological polemics has already made considerable use of these three sociological approaches to theology. What theologians have seldom done, though, is use these approaches systematically or with any reference to the obvious fund of scholarship provided by the discipline of sociology itself. Too much has been just too amateur.

Once these three approaches are studied systematically and rigorously, each raises rather different problems for the theologian. Whilst the latter has come to accept a variety of philosophical and historical means of assessing the validity of theological notions, he has yet to adopt more specifically sociological ones. Thus he has faced the criticisms of the logical positivists, the functional analysts, those requiring evidence of meaningfulness and clarity, those checking christological claims against the shadows of the 'historical Jesus' or the beliefs of the Early Church, and so forth. What he has yet to realize is that these three sociological approaches themselves raise crucial problems for Christian theology.

The first approach, based on a study of the social context of theology, raises problems more of communication and plausibility than of validity as such. 'True' theology may indeed be able to ignore its social context, either by expressing 'timeless' truths or by using terms designed for other social contexts. Whilst it may not thereby be rendered invalid, it might be regarded by many as largely irrelevant. The consequence of ignoring contemporary plausibility structures is for theologians to produce work which may appear increasingly anachronistic. Clearly this was a matter which concerned Bultmann deeply, even if we might dissent from the analysis of actual plausibility structures that he provided. Clearly too this is a matter which currently concerns those attempting to develop 'indigenous' theologies in non-Western contexts. In fact, while it is perfectly possible for theologians to ignore totally the social context in which they operate, few have actually done so in the past or do so in the present.

The second approach, based on a study of the social determinants of theology, does at first appear to raise the problem of validity in a critical way. The systematic attempt to explain all theological ideas and beliefs as products of particular social structures does seem to be an attempt by the sociologist to falsify them or at least to support a relativist position. Even when a distinction is made between 'explaining' something and 'explaining it away' and a further distinction between the 'origins' and 'validity' of ideas, a problem of validation remains – if not for the sociologist, at least for the theologian. As Mannheim argued, the social source of ideas *is* usually construed to be relevant to their truth or falsity, whether a formal logical relationship exists or not.[4] Thus, as I maintained at length in *The Social Context of Theology*, if we successfully demonstrate a disreputable source for something, we usually distrust it thereafter – genetic fallacy or no genetic fallacy.

On the other hand, there is a somewhat disconcerting element within Christian theology which almost glories in disreputable origins. For Paul the *skandalon* created for Jews and Gentiles by the origins of Christianity was almost something to boast about. And for theologians like Kierkegaard, Christianity was considered to be both outrageous and nevertheless true. Further, various types of mystical theology have delighted in paradoxes verging on outright inconsistencies.

Yet there is still an aspect to this sociological approach to the-

ology which does concern its validity. If, for example, a Marxist
critique of the discipline is adopted, whereby it is seen as an expression of the ruling class, and contemporary confirmation for this
is gathered from the middle-class bias of most Western churches,
then it might become more difficult to trust its 'universality'. Or
again, if, as I argued in *Theology and Social Structure*, it is evident
that the Churches' pronouncements on ethical issues such as abortion tend to follow rather than lead public opinion, it might become
more difficult wholly to trust them in the future.

In this last situation the theologian is faced with a number of
options. He may question either the particular findings or the
methodological bias of the sociologist. Alternatively, he may return
to a complete separation between origins and validity, claiming that
whatever the social source of his theological notions they are still
valid. However, if he resorts to none of these options he may have to
revise his claims or his ideas. In the process he would be affording
sociological analysis a more central role than hitherto in the validation of theological notions, since it is such analysis which provides
him with the initial suspicion of the invalidity of the notions. This is
certainly not to claim that sociological analysis can directly discredit
particular theological positions. Such a claim would result in the sort
of confusion of sociological and theological concepts that has unfortunately characterized several previous attempts to correlate the
two disciplines. Rather, it is to claim more modestly that sociological analysis may at times raise theological suspicions – suspicions
which must then be investigated, not in the light of further sociological analysis, but in the light of the claims of the gospel as a whole.

However, it is the third approach, based on a study of the social
significance of theology, which offers the theologians the most
serious problems of validation. What appears to the sociologist as
the social significance of theology, appears to the theologian as its
social importance. There is an inescapable evaluative element in the
latter's response to this phenomenon which the former usually
attempts to avoid. The claim that I will develop now, from the
theological (emphatically not the sociological) perspective, is that
an adequate assessment of the validity of particular theological
notions must take into account their potential or actual social
effects. Further, if these effects appear to be at variance with the
gospel as a whole, the theologian is given *a priori* grounds for
distrusting their validity. If accepted, this peculiarly social criterion
for assessing the validity of theological notions has radical implications for theology at large. It could serve to break the current virtual
monopoly of philosophical and historical criteria in the discipline.

Before attempting to substantiate these claims, two initial points must be made to avoid confusion. First, it is important to recognize that there has always been some concern about the social effects of theology. It has been a commonplace of theological polemics to maintain that 'heretical' beliefs tend to lead to wrong and often 'immoral' actions. 'Orthodoxy' and 'orthopraxis' have frequently been seen as inseparably correlated. Nevertheless, outside these one-sided, and often unself-critical, accounts, attention to the social effects of differing theological positions is rare and rigorous study of them rarer still. In short, this is largely unexplored territory. And second, I do not believe that it is a part of the task of theology to call into question the validity of the gospel as a whole. Certainly it belongs to the task of the philosophy of religion. But theology as theology assumes the overall validity of Christianity: it operates 'as if' the Christian gospel is fundamentally valid and seeks a critical explication of it, not a critique of its foundations. This position accords with my definition of theology as 'the written and critical explication of the "sequelae" of individual religious beliefs and of the correlations and interactions between religious beliefs in general'.[5] Accordingly the problems of validation with which I am concerned here are always partial ones. It is the validity of particular theological notions and positions which are under inspection, not the claims of the gospel as a whole. This point is crucial if confusion with the philosophy of religion is to be avoided. My concern is primarily with the 'inner coherence' of the social effects of particular theological positions with the whole gospel.

Faith tested by practice

The claim that the potential or actual social effects of particular theological notions are relevant to their validity points to a deep rift within intellectual thought over the last hundred years. The prevailing wisdom within the West suggests that the study of 'ideas' as 'ideas' belongs largely to the discipline of philosophy and that the study of human behaviour belongs to the social sciences. In general, social scientists have tended to avoid epistemological questions, whereas philosophers have maintained a largely cognitive orientation. For the latter, and indeed for most theologians too, 'ideas' can be studied in isolation from 'behaviour' and 'behaviour' is to be considered only derivatively and incidently. Given this sharp division between the study of 'ideas' and the study of 'behaviour', immediate hostility must be expected to any attempt to suggest a relationship between the social effects and validity of theological notions.

There is, however, a radical alternative to this prevailing wisdom suggested by Marxist thinkers. In various ways they have tended to reject the study of 'ideas' simply as 'ideas' and unrelated to empirical 'behaviour', and to offer instead a synthesis of the two. Amongst Marxist writers the division between philosophers and social scientists is not nearly so apparent as it is amongst non-Marxist intellectuals. Further, although there are very sharp divisions amongst Marxists themselves, there might be widespread agreement that 'ideas' can be fully understood only in relation to 'behaviour' and vice versa. For the Marxist the problem with Western philosophy is that it is overly cognitive and all too often chooses to ignore empirical factors and determinants such as class, power-structures and economic structures. The problem with the Western social scientist, on the other hand, is that from the perspective of the Marxist he tries (and fails) to be 'value free' and ignores the moral and political context within which he operates and devises his research. So a Marxist philosopher will tend to carry a concern for socio-political structures actually into his philosophy and the Marxist social scientist will filter his empirical research through a self-conscious philosophical/ideological commitment.

The germ of this radically different orientation can be traced back at least to Karl Marx and Frederick Engels' *The German Ideology* of 1844. In this extended polemic against the prevailing Hegelian and Young Hegelian forms of theology and philosophy, the two authors sought to show the connection between 'ideas' and consciousness on the one hand and class structures and material behaviour on the other. They contended that Hegelianism was to be identified as 'ideology', itself reflecting a spurious division between mental and material behaviour and in turn an equally spurious division between the privileged rulers and the disprivileged ruled. There is much debate, of course, about the exact import of their term 'ideology' and whether or not they explained its origins solely in terms of economic substructures. What is interesting here, though, is that they contended that 'ideas' which are left unrelated to 'actions' are vacuous.

The following quotation from *The German Ideology* well illustrates the opposing perspectives of the Hegelians and Marx and Engels:

In direct contrast to German philosophy which descends from heaven to earth, here we ascend from earth to heaven. That is to say, we do not set out from what men say, imagine, conceive, nor from men as narrated, thought of, imagined, conceived, in order to arrive at men in the flesh. We set out from real, active men, and on the basis of their real life-process we demonstrate the development of the ideological reflexes and echoes of this life-process. The phantoms formed in the human brain are also, necessarily, sublimates of their material life-process, which is empirically verifiable and bound to material premises.[6]

The blend of empirical and philosophical elements and the correlation between 'actions' and the validity of 'ideas' evident in this passage, are quite alien to much contemporary Western thought.

Not surprisingly they are also alien to much contemporary theology. The cognitive orientation of contemporary philosophy has proved too attractive for most recent systematic theologians. Doubtless through a desire to produce theological/philosophical correlations which appear plausible to twentieth-century man, the theologian has often been happy to consider 'faith' in isolation from 'practice'. Encouraged by the apparent relevance to theology of continental philosophy, he has concentrated upon 'faith' and upon the grounds for faith and not upon 'faith' as it relates to and is tested and made intelligible by 'practice'.

Of course there have been a few theologians who have been concerned to relate 'faith' and 'practice'. Since the rise of liberation theology they have become more plentiful. Some have adopted the Marxist critique of knowledge and society *in toto* into their theologies: some have even used this critique to assess the validity of particular theological positions. Nevertheless, for most Western theologians (as distinct from Third World theologians) this critique is no longer thought to supply a relevant analysis of the societies within which they operate. Although a correlation between Marxist and Christian thought would have undoubted usefulness in certain contexts – indeed it has been attempted on several occasions over the last thirty years – it is doubtful if it could prove so useful in the present Western context.

Whatever the merits or demerits of the Marxist perspective within philosophy or the social sciences, it is arguable that its insistence upon the inseparability of 'ideas' and 'actions' is peculiarly pertinent to Christianity. Without any overall commitment to the Marxist critique of society, it is possible to maintain that 'faith' and 'practice' will be badly misunderstood within Christian theology if they are treated separately. For Christians, 'beliefs' are not usually statements merely about 'the way things are', that is, they are not simply cognitive. Credal statements, for example, are not just recitations of religious knowledge or opinion: when used within the liturgical context they are expressions of religious commitment. As Talcott Parsons observes, 'acceptance of a religious belief is . . . a commitment to its implementation in action in a sense in which acceptance of a philosophical belief is not . . . religious ideas may be speculative in the philosophical sense, but the attitude towards them is not speculative in the sense that "well, I wonder if it would make sense to look at it this way?"'[7] At the very least, some degree of correlation between 'faith' and 'practice' would appear essential within Christian theology in a way that it might not be elsewhere. Indeed, I prefer to use the term 'faith' in this context to 'belief' precisely because an element of commitment is implicit within it. In addition it avoids some of the philosophical and sociological difficulties attached to the concept of 'belief'. The term 'practice', on the other hand, is intentionally wide – covering both intended and unintended modes of behaviour.

Once the possibility is allowed that the social effects of theological notions might be relevant to their validity, then the reason for much of the polemic within the history of Christian theology becomes evident. The christological and trinitarian controversies that took place within the Early Church were certainly not fired by a desire for correct 'religious knowledge'. In part the struggles before Chalcedon were politically and culturally based, reflecting the balance of power and difference of milieu between East and West. But in part they were also fired by the fear that distorted Christian faith would lead to distorted practice. If this were not the case then the extraordinary degree of bitterness caused over a single Greek letter in the *homoousios/homoiousios* debate would be without adequate explanation. At the heart of this debate and many another between Docetists, Arians, Apollinarians and so forth, lay the fear that if Christ was only 'like' God or only 'like' man, then he could not have effected man's redemption and in turn man's sinful nature could not have been changed. A christology that expressed anything less than the incarnation of God in the world was thought at Chalcedon to be socially ineffective. A Docetic christology denied that Christ ever became man, whereas an adoptionist christology denied that he was ever fully God. The result of either was thought to be the same; the incarnation would have been ineffective and mankind would have been left unredeemed.

A double link, then, can be seen in the Early Church's correlation of faith and practice. Wrong faith was to be feared both because it had the immediate social effect of 'anarchy' and 'immorality' and because it had the eschatological effect of eternal damnation. Just as orthodoxy and orthopraxis were deemed to go hand-in-hand, so conversely did 'heresy', 'anarchy', 'immorality' and 'damnation'. In the Medieval Church, too, and in the bitter controversies engendered by the Reformation, the same correlations are to be found. Religious tolerance regarded as a desirable virtue is a comparatively modern phenomenon and is possible only when 'heresy' is no longer widely feared. In ages of religious intolerance much depended upon accurate theology!

Even within some of the more radical contemporary sects 'heresy' is still perceived in part as a challenge to their authority.

Movements like those of the Jehovah's Witnesses and the Scientologists go to great lengths to devise social mechanisms for controlling 'heretical' views. In the case of the Scientologists this meant changing from a somewhat diffuse counselling movement or cult to a strictly controlled, bureaucratic sect. For the Jehovah's Witnesses, 'orthodoxy' is only maintained at the expense of a high loss of members. Yet in either movement 'heresy', if allowed, would entail not just a change of faith but also a change of practice. Once dissuaded from his ardent millenarianism the Jehovah's Witness might lose much of his enthusiasm for proselytism, and once allowed to experiment with differing counselling techniques the Scientologist might lose much of his commitment to the techniques and metaphysical beliefs of the movement as a whole. In both sects the social effects of 'heresy' are to be feared: a rigid orthodoxy is offered as the means to control these effects.

A stress upon the social effects of faith is also to be found in certain types of contemporary existentialist theology. Here the emphasis is less on the evil effects of 'heresy' than upon the beneficial effects of the gospel. The gospel is to be trusted, not because the events it describes are historically accurate, even less because the Church claims that they are to be trusted, but rather because it still has the power to change people. It is the gospel itself, regarded as proclamation, which is seen as salvific, not the events portrayed in the gospel. Various theologians have held this position in the last hundred years – ranging from the proponents of 'symbolic christology', through followers of Bultmann, to some present-day exponents of the gospel as 'story'. They have in common a disinterest in the 'historical Jesus' as in any way affecting the gospel today, a distrust of metaphysics and an emphasis upon the social effects of the gospel.

A rather different stress upon the social effects of faith is to be found in some of the current versions of liberation theology, whose exponents, more in common with the traditional understanding of 'heresy' than the emphasis of existentialist theology, tend to point to the harmful social effects of opposing view-points. Thus, they have suggested a close correlation between Western theology and Western imperialism and colonialism, or sometimes just between Western theology and Western male chauvinism. This is usually linked to a positive stress on the 'liberating' social effects of liberation theology itself, but the more negative emphasis frequently predominates. Whilst a Marxist critique of society is by no means essential to this approach to theology, it is in fact often adopted within it.

Of course, the fact that a correlation between faith and practice has often been made within Christian theology (even if it is largely absent from recent systematic theology), does not itself demonstrate that it ought to be made. Still less does it demonstrate that the social effects of theological notions are relevant to their validity. This is especially the case when it is admitted that so much of this correlation has been made on a now thoroughly unfashionable understanding of 'heresy'. Few may wish to return to the attacks against 'heresy' and the fiery theological polemics that have bedevilled so much Christian history in the past. Most, I suppose, would regard past correlations of opposing theological convictions with 'anarchy', 'immorality' and 'eternal damnation' as distortions of the gospel. It is nonetheless still possible that previous attempts to link faith and practice (however distorted) were pointing to a correlation which has been wrongly ignored by contemporary systematic theology.

This possibility is further strengthened by a study of the New Testament. The mysterious, eschatological parable of the sheep and the goats lays stress upon both the positive and the negative social effects of faith: 'anything you did for one of my brothers here, however humble, you did for me' and 'anything you did not do for one of these, you did not do for me'. (*Matthew* 25: 40, 45) The parable denies neither the importance of faith nor its eschatological consequences, yet it makes a clear connection between it and practice. Again, there is the frequent mention by Paul of the 'fruits of the Spirit' and the changes effected by our life 'in Christ' – all of which are discernible *ante mortem*. And the Johannine Epistles constantly connect faith with its social effects: 'love must not be a matter of words or talk; it must be genuine, and show itself in action' and 'if a man says, "I love God", while hating his brother, he is a liar'. (*1 John* 3: 18; 4: 20) James 2 is clearly not alone in connecting faith with practice.

This connection is again supported by those interpretations of the Synoptic gospels which hold Jesus's parables and miracles together. Just as the Synoptic parables are not generally advanced as moral tales, so the miracles are not presented as *ad hoc* acts of human kindness. Instead both find a common purpose as proclamations and even demonstrations of the Kingdom of God: 'If it is by the finger of God that I drive out the devils, then be sure the Kingdom of God has already come upon you.' (*Luke* 11: 20) Further, the whole Passion story in these gospels becomes not just an expression of Jesus' faith but a demonstration of this faith. For Matthew in particular, as his constant use of Old Testament 'proof texts' indicates, the Passion events served to verify the faith that lay behind them. Here faith was tested and indeed vindicated by practice.

The specific connection between the social effects and validity of particular theological notions that I am suggesting must be qualified in a number of ways. First, it should be stressed again that this is a specifically theological, not sociological, claim. From the perspective of the sociologist of religion there can be no legitimate jump from the social effects of faith to the validity of that faith. In the framework of the type of sociology of religion that I sought to defend in *The Social Context of Theology*, there can be no concern for theological validity at all. Durkheim's celebrated claim that 'there are no religions which are false . . . all are true in their own fashion'[8] was, it is important to note, a specifically sociological claim. It expressed his conviction that 'it is inadmissible that systems of ideas like religions, which have so considerable a place in history, and to which, in all times, men have come to receive the energy which they must have to live, should be made up of a tissue of illusions'.[9] For Durkheim, religious belief and ritual were 'true', not because he himself was a religious believer (he was not), but because as a sociologist he observed that it was a social reality exercising a crucial social function. Similarly the sociological identification of theology with theodicy affords theology a crucial social function: since theodicy is an omnipresent cultural phenomenon, theology is by definition an omnipresent social reality. Nevertheless, in neither instance does the sociologist as a sociologist wish to claim that religion or theology really reflect 'the way things are', or that particular expressions of faith 'do justice to God'. The claim is only that religion is a genuine human response to genuine human problems. The theological claim, in contrast, obviously does wish to go further: the Christian theologian *is* concerned to assess how far particular theological notions adequately reflect the object of Christian worship and the claims of the gospel,

Second, my proposal does not replace more traditional methods of assessing the validity of theological notions. One of the criticisms frequently made of Bultmann's theology is that despite his prodigious biblical scholarship, the whole emphasis in his theology is upon the contemporary effects of the gospel. He shows no interest in historical 'checks' for these effects and leaves us little reason to believe that they are the same today as they always have been. In contrast, my own position does not question the admissibility of historical and philosophical means of assessing particular theological positions. It claims only that social means have been wrongly neglected.

Third, only provisional validation or falsification can be gleaned from a study of the social effects of theological positions. There are two sides to this crucial claim, a negative one and a positive one.

Negatively, if it can be shown that certain theological notions as they are perceived by others lead to social effects that appear inconsistent with the claims of the gospel as a whole, then the theologian is given provisional warning that either they or the way they are understood may be false. Naturally particular theological notions may have different social effects in different social contexts. For example Matthew 27: 26 (the so-called Christ-Killer text) has quite different connotations, and possibly effects, today after the Nazi holocaust to those intended by the gospel writer. Theological notions may indeed have several effects upon societies. Again, it may not always be easy to be sure of the 'claims of the gospel' in any particular situation. Modern understandings of the pluriformity of the gospel make this particularly difficult. Nonetheless, without having to resort to even more arbitrary external criteria or values, a concern for inner coherence is usually thought to be a proper part of the theologian's task.

Positively, it is tempting to verify theological notions by the simple pragmatic principle of whether or not they 'work'. Indeed, most people may validate their particular expressions of faith by some such principle, not by their supposed 'empirical fit' or by the additional belief that they will be 'eschatologically verified'. Such a straightforward theological (as distinct from general philosophical) pragmatism has obvious attractions: the social effects of theological notions which accord with the gospel and with general Christian practice (and in this sense 'work') would act as 'proof of these notions' validity. Unfortunately, expressions of faith that 'work' may still be false. So, the faith of the Jehovah's Witness that God is to bring the world to an end in the next few years has undoubted benefits. The individual thus persuaded is given a clear incentive to strive hard for the gospel, to concentrate exclusively upon the Kingdom of God and to live a devoted and faithful life. All of these effects seem to accord thoroughly with the claims of the gospel and with general Christian practice. An exclusive use of social effects to assess the validity of theological notions – without a parallel philosophical analysis of the grounds on which they are held and an historical analysis of the way God is thought to act by past Christian thinkers – may lead to some curious results. Social means of assessing theological notions can offer only provisional validation or falsification.

Fourth, an obvious objection to my proposals is that theologians cannot be held responsible for the social effects of their notions. Thus, if Weber is correct and there really was a connection between the theological notions of Calvin as popularly perceived and the moral ideas necessary for the spirit of Capitalism at its inception in the West, Calvin cannot himself be held accountable. According to this view a theologian should only be held accountable for the ideas he in fact proposes and not for the ideas he is perceived to propose by others. Thus, the fact that some particularistic expressions of christology and soteriology appear to be strongly correlated with anti-semitism in places, would not of itself necessarily worry their exponents.

Naturally it may be difficult at times actually to demonstrate a link between certain types of practice and particular expressions of faith. From a sociological perspective, measuring the social significance of particular theological positions is undoubtedly difficult – though by no means impossible, as I tried to demonstrate in *Theology and Social Structure*. From a theological perspective, however, the concept of 'accountability' involved in this objection involves more ethical than theological considerations. Nevertheless, if it were to be sustained it might place the theologian in an even more isolated role than at present. I have already maintained that he is concerned with communication and that on this account he must take seriously the social context within which he operates. What I am now claiming is that in future his concern for this context might also lead him to study the ways in which his notions are perceived by others and with the potential and actual effects these notions might then have upon them. An essential part of the theological task in the future, if it is to be rigorous and self-critical, may well be a systematic attempt to assess the possible social effects of *all* our theological ideas.

The scope of praxis theology

It is now possible to offer the outline of a theological system using the perspective offered by social criteria. Unlike other works, it would not be possible to study the three components of faith in systematic theology – namely, creation, redemption and sanctification – without a continuous reference to practice. In the context of these three components such a system would in fact present a thoroughgoing theological analysis of the relation between faith and practice as it appears in Christianity. In terms of the foregoing argument it would be based upon a complex interactionist model, supposing that (a) Christian faith inevitably involves practice, and (b) that practice should in turn remould faith.

It is, of course, a matter of considerable theological debate whether and to what extent faith does necessarily involve practice. Some, like Brunner, have suggested that fairly detailed social and political implications can be derived from the Christian doctrine of creation. Others, like Barth, have remained comparatively apolitical in their theological writings (even if Barth himself was politically active in his personal life). A praxis theology would be forced to look at this debate afresh, involving as it does the religious/secular issue at the level of the individual and the church/state issue at that of society. Unlike previous attempts, though, it would seek to examine theoretical positions on the relation between faith and practice alongside empirical data of the way people do relate notions such as that of creation to moral or political occasions.

It is clear that the social implications of theology will depend very much on the type of theology that one adopts. It is not simply that different theologians have different ideas about the extent to which theology is directly relevant to social and political issues. Rather it is that, both theoretically and empirically, theologians obviously differ considerably amongst themselves on almost every theological issue and that as a result one would expect the social effects and implications of their varying notions to be correspondingly diverse. This is not intended to be a judgmental observation. It is an admission of theological pluralism. Indeed, from the sociological perspective, Christianity throughout history must appear as a highly pluralistic phenomenon. Accordingly, a praxis theology might acknowledge this pluralism by tracing the social effects and implications of diverse theological traditions and notions – not in an attempt to produce a sociology of theology, but rather in an attempt to produce a self-critical theology which was conscious of the complex interaction between faith and practice.

Contemporary political and liberation theology is in part already engaging in such a theological programme. It is generally concerned to unpack the social implications of theological notions and, at times, it is even conscious of some of the unconscious social effects of particular types of theology. Nonetheless, only recent exponents like Fierro and Bonino have been seriously self-critical. It is arguable that some of the inter-war theologians were distinctly more aware of the methodological problems confronting those concerned with the social implications of the gospel. In other words, the social implications of one's own theology and the defective social effects of other people's theology have sometimes been arrived at too hastily. A genuinely self-critical and scholarly praxis theology would need to be much more careful than this.

A fundamental issue in a praxis theology would be to distinguish carefully between the social effects and the social implications of particular theological notions and then to trace the connections between the two. To return to this difficult distinction, it is evident that there is at times a radical difference between the supposed implications of particular notions on the part of the theologian himself and the actual effects these notions might have upon society. In *Theology and Social Structure* I attempted to trace the effects of *Honest to God* upon various sections of society. I suspect that John Robinson himself intended few if any of these effects, for, judging from his later theological writings, there was a very great discrepancy between the intended social implications of *Honest to God* and its actual social effects. The two are certainly not identical, but are nonetheless not unconnected with each other.

Given that the two are distinct and that a praxis theology would have to be responsive to both, it might typically proceed as follows. Taking into account the various methodological problems involved, it might seek to unpack the social implications of varying theological notions. This would be primarily a theoretical and theological task. It might then seek to use sociological data, techniques and theories to compile a picture of the actual, possible and potential social effects of the same notions. This would, of course, be primarily a sociological undertaking. Once assembled, this picture could then be compared with the claims of the gospel as a whole and then used to assess the actual theological validity of these notions (along with philosophical and historical means of assessment). This again would be primarily a theological task – as would the final stage of re-assessing the social implications of these notions.

Inevitably such a praxis theology would need to be a painstaking and laborious exercise. This would be the case particularly if it was attempted in the context of all three components of systematic theology – creation, redemption and sanctification. Nevertheless, I am convinced that it is necessary if the current cognitive bias of much Western theology and the lack of critical precision of early liberation theology is to be overcome. An adequate understanding of the relation between faith and practice within Christianity demands nothing less.

Notes

1 See further, Gill, R. *The Social Context of Theology* (London, 1975) and *Theology and Social Structure* (London, 1977).
2 Whenever I use the term 'significance' I have the strictly *sociological* sense in mind – i.e. something is considered 'significant' because it has an effect upon society and not because it is thought to be important by that society.
3 See Martin, R. 'Sociology and Theology', in D.E.H. Whiteley and R. Martin (ed.) *Sociology, Theology and Conflict* (Oxford, 1969).
4 See Mannheim, K. *Ideology and Utopia* (London, 1936).
5 See Gill, *Theology and Social Structure, op. cit.* pp. 2–5.
6 Marx, K. and Engels, F. *The German Ideology*, ed. C.J. Arthur (London, 1970) p. 47.
7 Parsons, T. *The Social System* (London, 1951) p. 367.
8 Durkheim, E. *The Elementary Forms of the Religious Life* (London, 1915) p. 3.
9 *Ibid.* p. 69.

Chapter 7

THE SOCIOLOGY OF ROMAN CATHOLIC THEOLOGY

Gregory Baum

MY eyes were bigger than my stomach when I chose as the topic for a case-study of theological activity seen sociologically 'the sociology of Roman Catholic theology'. My interest in the topic is intense, but its scope is far too extensive to be adequately treated here. What I am presenting is better thought of as the outline of a research project.

At one time Catholic theology was highly uniform, defined almost exclusively in terms of the official Scholasticism. We shall look at this period in the first section of this chapter. Fortunately, as we shall see, we can rely here on an important monograph dealing with the political source of the imposed theological conformity. Since that time, especially through Vatican Council II, Catholic theology has entered upon a fertile and pluralistic phase, the social foundations of which no sociologist or political scientist has as yet studied in any depth. I will not be able to hide the admiration I myself have for the achievment of Catholic theology over the last decades. In the second section, the major part of this chapter, I shall specify four social factors that affect the style of theology, and relate these factors, by way of illustration, to recent developments in Catholic theology. In this context I shall defend the thesis that despite a certain modern trend that estranges theology from the life of the Church, Catholic theology, with all its pluralism, has been able to preserve an intense pastoral concern.

I

Let me first make some remarks on the uniformity of Catholic theology between the Vatican Councils I and II. In the nineteenth century, more especially under the reign of Pope Pius IX, the Catholic Church repudiated and condemned the new liberal, civil society that was then being created through growing industrialization and the establishment of republican and democratic governments. The Catholic Church feared that the new bourgeois civilization – which Toennies was to call *Gesellschaft* – undermined the spiritual and material cohesion of the inherited social order. The liberal spirit introduced a new and previously unheard-of individualism; it encouraged rationalism in its various forms and promoted a new secularism. Liberalism weakened the inherited sense of authority and threatened the hierarchical order of traditional society. The *Syllabus of Errors*, published in 1864, was the great manifesto of defiance Pope Pius hurled at modern society.

In this context the Church also rejected modern nationalism, associated as it was with the bourgeois state. The bourgeoisie promoted nationalism as a social movement that would inspire ordinary people, including the workers, to participate in the struggle against the remnants of feudalism and the building of a new society that would possess the freedom and independence appropriate to the bourgeoisie's commercial and intellectual interests. Since the nationalist movement in Italy threatened the survival of the papal territory, a remnant of the feudal age, the Holy See felt the pressure of liberalism, secularism and nationalism in a very concrete way. Pius IX decided to make the retention of his secular possession a symbol of fidelity to the Catholic tradition. After the March on Rome and the creation of the kingdom of Italy, Pius IX moved from his repudiation of modern society to a stance of non-cooperation.

It was only with the accession of Leo XIII to the papal throne that the Holy See adopted a more open approach to society. What was necessary for the well-being of the Christian people and the strength of the Christian Church, Leo believed, was the building of a new Christian social order. To this aim he dedicated his pontificate. While he continued to denounce modern liberal society, Leo also disassociated himself from *l'ancien régime*, characterized by absolute kingship and privileged aristocracy, that was directly attacked by the liberals. The ideal for a new Christian social order was drawn from the Church's mediaeval experience, the organic society, united by a common faith, in which all estates, ranks and classes accepted a common set of values and understood themselves without envy, as part of a universally recognized social hierarchy. Could this idealized image of society be introduced in the late nineteenth century? Leo XIII thought so. One of the major instruments for the creation of this new Christian social order was his intellectual and educational policy, namely the restoration of Thomism as the Church's official philosophy.

The political function of the Thomistic revival in the nineteenth century and its adoption on the part of the Holy See has been studied in a major monograph by Pierre Thibault, *Savoir et pouvoir: Philosophie thomiste et politique cléricale au XIXe siècle* (Quebec, 1972). This book is a masterful study on the politics of knowledge. It presents a detailed analysis of the intellectual and educational policy of the Holy See and its effect on theological life in the Catholic Church. At the end of the eighteenth century, Thomism, and more generally Scholasticism, had disappeared from the Catholic centres of learning. Thomism was revived in the early part of the nineteenth century by a few Jesuits in the southern part of Italy, was then welcomed at a few universities in Italy, and was eventually recognized by the ecclesiastical government as the philosophy that best responded to the intellectual, social and political needs of the Church at that time. The restoration of Thomism culminated in Leo XIII's encyclical, *Aeternae Patris* (1879), which made Thomism the official philosophy of the Church, to be taught, developed and defended at all Catholic schools and university faculties. Thomism was henceforth the sole sound philosophical approach to be followed in Catholic theology. The restored Thomism determined (1) the Church's response to modern science and its truth claims, (2) the Church's social message in the face of the contemporary upheaval, and (3) the Church's political stance vis-à-vis the new political order.

(1) Thomism enabled the Church to affirm the dignity and coherence of natural reason and thus approve of the principal orientation of the scientific age. But since Thomism is empirically based and hence more humble and cautious in regard to the philosopher's power to penetrate the *ratio* or *logos* operative in the world, it provided a philosophical base from which to argue against French rationalism and German idealism. Thomism recognized the limitations of reason and defended its openness to the supernatural. Thomism thus created intellectuals who pursued their investigations in a highly rational way and at the same time were willing to submit themselves to divine revelation as mediated and defined by the ecclesiastical magisterium. Thomism also defended the objective character of truth against the new philosophies that attached cognitive value to personal feelings and religious experience and thereby undermined the role of authority in religion. Thomism, moreover, protected the abiding nature of truth against the evolutionary theories of the nineteenth century and became the Church's bulwark against historicism and the emergence of the historical consciousness that threatened to relativize the ancient creeds.

(2) In the midst of modern social upheaval, Thomism provided the Catholic Church with the vision of an organic society derived from 'the age of faith', which generated a critique of both liberalism and socialism. Against a liberalism that fostered individualism and blessed the competitive economic order, the Church affirmed the social, cooperative nature of society and demanded that governments promote the common good, stand above the interests of the ruling class, and protect the poor from exploitation by the rich. Against a socialism that advocated class struggle and the radical reconstruction of society, the Church affirmed the mutual dependence of the ranks and classes of society and insisted that social

justice could be brought about only through the acceptance by all of common norms and values. Ultimately it is religion, the Christian religion, that assures social peace and social justice.

(3) Of greatest importance in Thibault's analysis is the political role of Thomism. The Church was in danger of being pushed to the margin of society. It no longer had a clear point of entry into the making of society. For not only was liberalism wedded to secularism, even *l'ancien régime*, based on the divine rights of kings, thought itself superior to the Church and tried to use it for its own purposes. The Church had never accepted the theory of the divine right of kings: the divine right to rule was attached to the Church of Christ alone. In this dilemma Thomism provided a new perspective. What was it? In Thomism the hisotrical human reality is divided into two spheres, the natural and the supernatural. While Thomism protects the integrity and relative independence of the world and its secular status, it subordinates the world to the supernatural as revealed in Christ and mediated by the Church. There is, then, in Thomism the recognition of the world as world and the relative autonomy of the natural order – and hence the Church has no 'direct power' over the state – but since this world is both wounded by sin and called to the supernatural order, its autonomy is limited. The Church, as the organ of the supernatural in history, thus exercizes 'indirect power' over society and its government. The Church continues to guide the state by clarifying the meaning of the common good for the social order. Despite the new emphasis on secular developments and scientific achievements, the Church retains an essential role in the making of society.

Thibault readily admits that the great Thomistic philosophers of the twentieth century regarded the promotion of Thomism simply as a matter of truth: they paid little attention to the political meaning it had for the ecclesiastical government and in many instances may not even have been aware of it. They were, however, ill at ease with the curious contradiction that a philosophy that presented itself as rationally demonstrable and hence as independent of divine revelation was at the same time imposed on Catholic schools and their teachers by ecclesiastical legislation.

Thibault gives an account of the success of the ecclesiastical policy in suppressing the theological trends existing in the Catholic Church of the nineteenth century. The theologies that emphasized religious feeling and the personal meaning of faith, as we find it in Baader and the young Moehler in Germany or in Bautain in France, were not allowed to develop. The new theological interpretations of history as the unfolding of a divine *logos*, inspired by German idealism, were rejected as irreconcilable with Catholic truth. Even the conservative thought of John Henry Newman found no lasting echo in the Catholic Church: it was too empirically oriented, too nominalistic, too attentive to religious consciousness, too much imbued with developmentalism to be in harmony with the official philosophy. The same Thomistic orthodoxy undermined the Tübingen school of theology which combined speculation and historical research since it, too, advocated a concept of truth that was too dynamic. At the end of the nineteenth century a single philosophy and, based on it, a single theology reigned in Catholic schools and seminaries.

Why was this Roman intellectual and educational policy so successful? Why did all the schools follow the Roman directives? Since Thibault wrote a politics, not a sociology of knowledge, he was content to answer this question in terms of the power exerted by the Holy See on bishops and Catholic faculties. Because of the fear and trembling experienced by the Catholic Church in the face of Enlightenment and modernity, the Catholic people and their bishops looked towards the papacy as the defender of the faith and gladly submitted to the Roman laws and directives. But Thibault does not examine the social conditions of the regional churches to understand the functions Thomism actually exercised in various parts of Europe and America. Thus he does not even consider the possibility that a philosophy which was an ideology of ecclesiastical rule for the papacy might have a different, in fact a critical meaning in a particular local church. In the Antigonish Movement, a cooperative movement of the 1930s in Eastern Nova Scotia, Canada – to give a single instance – Thomistic anthropology was actually used to contrast what society was with what it ought to be, and thus provided a starting point for a theory of alienation produced by modern capitalism.[1]

II

How did Catholic theology move into its present pluralistic phase? Only the barest outline of this interesting story can be told here. The attempt of the so-called modernist scholars to react to the Enlightenment in a more positive way was crushed by the ecclesiastical government under Pope Pius X. The papal action greatly increased the uniformity of Catholic theology. It was really only in the 1940s that a significant dent was made in the reigning Thomistic orthodoxy. Catholic scholars who then were allowed to apply the critical method to biblical research produced influential works on biblical theology that burst the framework of Scholasticism. The biblical concepts revealed themselves as far too rich to be fitted into an antecedently constructed theological synthesis. It became clear that Thomism was simply one great theological system and not the sum and substance of Catholic wisdom.

By the 1950s Catholic theologians were turning to modern philosophies for help. They did this cautiously, usually following the hints of previous Catholic scholars. Often they pretended that they were simply expanding the as yet unexplored aspects of Thomism. Most important here was the neo-Kantian philosophy of Karl Rahner and a group of kindred spirits who, following the philosophical work of Maréchal, developed an original philosophical approach, often referred to as 'Transcendental Method', that integrated into Catholic theology the characteristics of modern thought, namely 'the turn to the subject' and 'the historicity of consciousness'. Another line of innovation was the introduction of process thought into Catholic theology. Blondel's early work, *L'Action*, which had put him under a cloud during the modernist crisis, became a book that inspired a new, vitalist trend in French Catholic theology. Life itself was understood as the organ of the supernatural. While it may be necessary to distinguish between creation and redemption, they are in fact combined in a single historical reality. God is creatively and redemptively operative in the self-constitution of humankind. Teilhard de Chardin extended this processive perspective to the cosmic scale and introduced the evolutionary theory into Catholic theology. These attempts at innovation were often frowned upon by the ecclesiastical magisterium. Pius XII had to intervene in punitive actions several times to protect the established orthodoxy of ecclesiastical Thomism.

It was only at Vatican Council II that Catholic theology was allowed to pass into greater freedom. Some of the theologians who had had difficulties with the Roman authorities were now the very ones who inspired and helped compose the conciliar documents. At this Council the Catholic Church was willing to acknowledge its own pluralistic structure, understand itself as a union of many local and regional churches, each with its own tradition, its own language, its own theological wisdom, each responsible for building up the unity of the Church in the midst of its plural manifestations. We are told:

From the beginning of her history the Church has learned to express the message of Christ with the help of ideas and terminology of various peoples, and has tried to clarify it with the wisdom of philosophers. The Church's purpose has been to adapt the Gospel to the grasp of ordinary people as well as to the needs of the learned as appropriate. Indeed, this accommodation of the revealed Word ought to remain the law of all evangelization. Each nation then develops the ability to express Christ's message in its own way. (*Gaudium et Spes*, No. 44)

What were the social foundations of this theological development? A complete answer to this question would be a major project of sociological research. The Catholic Church, which before the Council had closed itself off from modern society and modern thought, was now willing to do what the Anglican and Protestant Churches had done decades earlier, namely to be open to modernity and Enlightenment. At Vatican II, the Church recognized a more historical self-understanding, and reached out for a process metaphysics that would correspond to this more historicist understanding of the human reality.

We note that the bishops and the influential thinkers responsible for church renewal at Vatican II belonged to the more industrialized nations – at least to those industrialized nations where Catholics represented either a majority or a significant minority with great cultural confidence. France, Belgium, Germany and Holland provided the leaders at Vatican II, while England and the USA, though industrialized, did not. In France, Belgium, Germany and Holland there was an influential Catholic middle class which demanded that theology take seriously the Enlightenment and its own cultural aspirations. France and Belgium were what used to be called Catholic countries: there a substantial section of the bourgeoisie, still committed to faith, had reconciled itself to the secular world. In Germany and Holland Catholics had long been in socially inferior positions. The ruling class was Protestant, and so was the dominant culture. Even the secular outlook in these countries had a Protestant air. After World War II, however, the Catholic communities achieved new prominence in these countries. After the division of Germany, the Catholics of the *Bundesrepublik* made up more than half the population and assumed a correspondingly wider role in the national culture. In Holland the Catholics of the south, disadvantaged at one time, had made major educational advances and began to understand themselves as equal partners in a common social enterprise. At this point Dutch Catholics combined the fervour of a minority with the cultural confidence of those who have just arrived, a combination that proved to be fruitful for theology.

Thanks to this leadership from the industrialized countries, Vatican II decided to open itself in a critical way to the Enlightenment and elevated many views and values derived from liberalism into the Church's own self-understanding. The famous conciliar constitution, *Gaudium et Spes*, spelled out the Church's relationship to the modern world and constituted a dramatic counter-statement to Pius IX's *Syllabus of Errors* of a century ago. At Vatican II the Catholic Church was willing to accept the modern world, albeit in a critical way, to regard the world religions and the various cultural movements in modern society as partners in a dialogue, and possibly, if agreement on certain principles were possible, to greet them as collaborators in the building of a more humane society.

The Catholic Church has now joined the modern world, in terms defined by the more successful industrialized nations. A few years after the Council, as we shall see further on, the Latin American Church clearly recognized the extent to which Vatican II had permitted itself to look upon the world through the eyes of the Western bourgeoisie.

Although study in depth of the social foundations of the conciliar renewal and the subsequent theological pluralism is a project for the future, this is the place and the moment to introduce a few sociological considerations that may be helpful in the study of theological pluralism – whether Catholic, Anglican or Protestant. Theology, I propose, is a function of several social factors. There is, of course, a creative element in theology that defies explanation. This, I take it, can be taken for granted in 'the sociology of knowledge'. I defend the position that theology varies in accordance with (1) the social location of the Christian community, (2) the dominant culture to which it belongs, (3) the academic institution in which it is taught, and (4) the socio-economic class with which it is identified.

Let me illustrate the usefulness of these four categories by applying them to well-known aspects of Catholic church life and contemporary theological pluralism.

(1) That the social location of the Christian community affects the theology it produces was alluded to in my remarks on the contribution made by German and Dutch Catholics to Vatican II. The fact that England and the USA did not produce bishops and theologians who affected Vatican II in the same way must be related to the social location of the Catholic Church in these countries. In the Anglo-Saxon world Catholics have been a minority, often a disadvantaged and despised one, exposed to a special kind of bigotry. Catholics were a people apart, a poor but happy tribe, constituting a distinct subculture. In the USA this subculture was at one time largely working-class people of recent immigrant stock. In England the Catholic community was also to a large extent made up of working-class families of Irish background, but there was also a significant community of educated Catholics, often derived from middle-class converts to Roman Catholicism, who produced a culture of their own, a kind of counter-culture that attracted Englishmen at odds with the dominant ethos of their society. Because of the Anglican Establishment, one might add, English Catholics adopted an attitude of indifference and aloofness vis-à-vis the Reformation churches that even the ecumenical movement of the sixties was unable to melt completely. Both in the USA and in England, despite significant differences, Catholic theology prior to Vatican II remained unenterprising, tied to the old Scholastic orthodoxy, an academic subject that was taught at the seminaries to prepare young men for the priesthood, not a field of inquiry for Christians wrestling with the ambiguities of their culture.

In the late fifties and early sixties, the social location of American
Catholics underwent a significant change. Andrew Greeley has
shown that during this period Catholics joined the mainstream of
American life. Catholics were successful in education; they had
become as socially mobile as Protestants; they assumed leadership
positions in business, at universities and in politics. The election of
John Kennedy to the presidency was a symbol that American
Catholics had arrived. From being the church of the immigrants the
Catholic Church now became the church of the middle class, supporting its members in their desire to become good Christians in the
mainstream of American life. We have here the unusual combination of the fervour of a minority with the confidence of those who
have arrived, similar to the one noted in connection with Dutch
Catholicism a decade or so earlier. Greeley held the view that
American Catholicism would have undergone profound changes
even if Vatican II had not taken place. In his book, *The New Agenda*
(New York, 1973), Greeley tries to show in considerable detail how
this shift in social location has affected Catholic theological understanding and the preaching of the gospel.

For Greeley, one might add, not only theology but religious
experience itself is largely a function of people's socially defined
existence. Religion fulfils certain needs in society and its individual
members: as this society changes and people's problems and needs
are accordingly modified, their religious experience will also
change. Greeley thinks that bishops and theologians have an exaggerated view of the power they wield over the religion of ordinary
people. The norms provided by the bishops and the ideas proposed
by theologians have power only if they tie into and clarify people's
religious experiences. Thus Greeley regards it as the task of bishops
and theologians to discern the religious experiences actually taking
place in the community, to provide norms that clarify the meaning
of these experiences, introduce rites and symbols that intensify
these experiences, and offer interpretations that relate these
experiences to the self-understanding of the universal Church of
past and present.

English Catholicism did not undergo the same transformation as
the American Catholic Church. English Catholics have also been
upwardly mobile, and many middle-class church-goers are unhappy
with the present style of ecclesiastical teaching and preaching; but
the social factors that define the position of the Catholic community
are significantly different – sufficiently so to warrant a different kind
of ecclesiastical and theological development.

(2) That theology is also a function of the dominant culture to
which it belongs is a commonplace. This is an aspect that must be
attended to in any sociology of theology. I am always impressed by

the difference between Anglo-American and German theology, whether it be Catholic or Protestant. There is a tendency in the Anglo-American world to regard science as the most reliable and most certain form of knowledge, and hence to make scientific knowledge the model for other forms of cognition, even if these cannot fully come up to this standard. The dominant intellectual trend tries to reduce complex forms of knowledge to more simple ones. Similarly there is a tendency to look upon development and evolution in terms that are derived from a branch of the natural sciences, for instance, biology, mechanics or cybernetics. In Germany there is also great respect for the natural sciences, but from the early nineteenth century on, German thinkers have reacted against the rational Enlightenment by emphasizing that the really important things, such as human history and personal life, can be known and understood only through modes of cognition quite different from those operative in the natural sciences. (The social foundations of the German reaction to the Enlightenment have been studied by Karl Mannheim.)[2] The privileged model of knowledge is here self-knowledge. The knowledge of human life and history will always include the exploration of consciousness. In this context the model for development and evolution tends to be drawn from the study of history, in which the transformation of consciousness and the role of ideas are taken very seriously. Evolution, in the German context, always seems to be some sort of unfolding of hidden meaning and power. It is my impression that these distinct mainstream patterns of Anglo-American and German thought are reflected in Christian thought.

In Catholic theology the differences between these two styles of thought might be illustrated by comparing the theology of the two neo-Kantians, the early Bernard Lonergan and Karl Rahner. A similar difference exists, I believe, between Anglo-American process theology inspired largely by the scientist-philosopher Alfred North Whitehead, and German process thought, always based on some dialectics of unfolding consciousness.

(3) That theology also depends on the academic institutions in which it is taught is a consideration that gives rise to a micro-sociology of theology. Theologians often tell the joke that one difference between German and French theology can be accounted for in terms of their different sources of revenue. The German theologian is a well-paid professor at the public university: when he writes his theological treatises, believing the professors of philosophy and of history are looking over his shoulder, he wants to demonstrate that his own exercise of *Wissenschaft* conforms to their standards. But in France no government funds are available for theological education and research. Theology is taught at sem-

inaries financed by the contributions from the faithful. Hence the
French theologian writing his books has the fervent Christians
looking over his shoulder and so wants to demonstrate that theology, however abstract and learned, remains spiritual, sounds
edifying, and nourishes religious sentiment. This is a joke, but it is
also more than a joke. It suggests that the institutional base of
theology, and this includes its economic connection, has an effect on
the style of theological thinking.

Open dialogue with Enlightenment thought has moved the
institutional home of theology closer to the university. I believe this
could be demonstrated from developments in theological education
in most of the industrialized countries. In the United States and
Canada prior to the 1960s, Catholic theology was taught at isolated
institutions, the seminaries, and had very little contact with the
public universities. This has changed drastically since Vatican II.
Many Catholic seminaries have moved closer to university cam-
puses; some have united with Protestant divinity schools to form
larger academic institutions with a certain university connection;
others again have located themselves right on the university cam-
pus. Many secular universities which in the past, for a variety of
reasons, refused to offer courses in theology and the history of
religions have since the 1960s opened departments of religious
studies in which there is room for comparative religion as well as
theology properly so-called. Today there are many theologians in
North America, Catholic and Protestant, who are university professors, paid by secular agencies, with no institutional link to the
churches whatever. Will this shift in institutional base change the
style of theological thinking?

I regard the estrangement of theology from the life of the Church
as a contemporary danger. This danger is caused by a variety of
factors, one of them the institutional factor mentioned here – the
teaching of theology in a context no longer defined by Christian
faith. Still, I wish to defend the thesis that until now contemporary
Catholic theology, despite its pluralistic form, is characterized by a
strong pastoral orientation. A certain link between theology and
church life is of course intrinsic to the theological enterprise and
hence is found to some extent in all forms of Christian theology,
Catholic or Protestant. Moreover, the impact on contemporary
theology of existentialism and developmental psychology on the
one hand and political reflection and 'ideology critique' on the
other, has given a strong pastoral (therapeutic and/or emancipatory) orientation to Christian theology. Still, the danger of theology's estrangement from the Church persists. There is, however,
one reason connected with recent Catholic history that makes contemporary Catholic theologians resist this danger and focus on the

pastoral meaning of their theological task: I am referring here to the role of Vatican II in the contemporary Catholic renewal.

The opposition to the imposed Thomistic orthodoxy in the years prior to Vatican II was usually inspired by pastoral concerns. Priests involved in various forms of ministry found that the official theology was too far removed from the problems and the experiences of ordinary people. It did not offer much help to preaching; it made little contribution to pastoral counselling; it did not relate the intellectual life of the educated to the inherited wisdom of the Church, etc. Growing numbers of theologians resisted abstract, non-historical Scholasticism because it pretended to be independent of historical circumstances and hence appropriate for all parts of the Church – the homeland and the mission field. The modernist protest against the offical theology had failed very largely because it was promoted by a small group of intellectuals without backing from ordinary church-going Catholics. The magisterium crushed it without difficulties. The critical theological movements of the forties and fifties, however, were carried by significant sections of the Catholic people. What the theologians were writing dealt with the concerns of these people: the new theological approaches clarified their religious experiences and confirmed them in their intuitions regarding the contemporary meaning of Christianity. The demands for renewal made by bishops and their theologians at Vatican II were enthusiastically supported by large numbers of Catholics back home. It was not because of an abstract idea of truth but because of promised pastoral effectiveness that the bishops at the Council, conservative men on the whole, finally decided to promulgate conciliar documents that broke with many views and stances defended by the Catholic Church in the past. The breakthrough to theological pluralism in the Catholic Church was not the result of a purely intellectual development; it was an expression of a religious renewal, it was based on new religious experiences and the new orientations these experiences demanded from the pastors of the Church. Ever since Vatican II, I hold, Catholic theology has remained in touch with actual Catholic movements in the Church.

Perhaps I judge the present situation too much from the North American perspective. In North America, theology has not reached the level of scholarship, specialization and systematization that we find in Germany and Holland; yet in North America theology reaches out to vast numbers of people, to teachers, social workers, community organizers, to committed Catholics of all sorts, who follow the results of new research and theological developments in the hundreds of summer schools, evening classes, week-end workshops, and study groups organized across the country. Though the Catholic Church is somewhat divided between those who affirm the contemporary renewal and others who have canonized the Catholicism of yesterday, Catholic theologians (today both men and women) do not find themselves isolated. They do not feel that they simply speak for themselves; they are aware that they represent a significant group of people, that they verbalize the religious concerns of vast numbers and that in their theological work they remain in conversation with them. Since in the present situation some Catholic theologians are again under a certain ecclesiastical pressure, more gentle and more subtle than the heavy-handed strictures of the past, it is especially important for theologians to be deeply rooted in significant sections of the Catholic people. The tension with the ecclesiastical magisterium makes them more pastoral in their theological work. They realize that if they defend themselves against the magisterium in purely academic terms they will not be heard, but if they can show that their thought is pastorally significant and actually corresponds to the Christian life of the community, then – they trust – they will be able to keep their theological approach alive in the Church.

(4) Finally the relation of theology and economic class, all too often overlooked, must be given adequate attention in any sociology of theology. The celebrated acknowledgement of this principle is the teaching document published by the Latin American Bishops' Conference, the so-called Medellin 'Conclusions', of 1968.[3]

In order to forumlate the meaning of the gospel for the present day, the Latin American bishops examined the modern world with its contradictions and possibilities, the same modern world that had been studied by Vatican II – but they arrived at a very different perception of it. The perception of Vatican II had been worked out by Western theologians largely identified with bourgeois culture: they shared the optimism of the sixties, they hoped that the growing cooperation between nations and the ever wider coordination of efforts on a global scale would promote the development, the human development, of all sections of humanity, including the less developed peoples; and they saw in this extended human development the trend of history that was divinely favoured and hence to be supported by the Church. The Church at Vatican II spelled out a religious ethos that fostered development! Yet the Latin American bishops looked at the same world of growing cooperation and coordination from the perspective of their own countries. The new world system that seemed to be in the making was not a sign of hope to them: on the contrary, they recognized it as a world-wide economic network produced and directed by the highly industrialized Western nations, in which they, the Latin Americans, had a subordinate and peripheral place. The growing world system was such that the centre inevitably enriched itself at the expense of the periphery.

The Latin American bishops considered that what was needed for a sound Catholic theology was a more careful and critical analysis of the economic system that determined the material conditions of life on their continent. Preachers had to be aware of the structures of oppression that pushed vast numbers of people into misery and dehumanization. The bishops did not want the Christian religion to be the consolation offered to people for the damage done to them by an unjust society. They introduced the notion of social sin and insisted that the redemption wrought by Jesus Christ implied the liberation of the people from man-made structural evil. This emancipatory orientation was admittedly only one line of thought in the Medellin Conference, one line among several pastoral approaches to the Latin American reality; but it was this emancipatory orientation that called forth the most extensive theological literature.

Thanks to the influence of the Latin American bishops on the Third Synod of Bishops held at Rome in 1971, the Synod published a startling teaching document, entitled 'Justice in the World', which adopted the notion of social sin, claimed that the Christian notion of divine salvation included the liberation of men and women from all the oppressive conditions of life, and asserted that active involvement in social change was a constitutive part of the Christian life. What emerged here, even at the highest ecclesiastical level, was a new orientation in theology, one which holds that the gospel can only be understood (and theology can only do its proper task) *after* a person has identified himself or herself with the oppressed, the marginalized, the crucified in this world. This new trend recognizes that religion and theology always fulfil some sort of political role and insists that unless Christians engage themselves in the emancipation of humankind, their religion and their theology, however learned, will actually be an ideology legitimating the existing unjust power relations.

This type of theology has been made familiar in the Catholic Church through a considerable body of theological literature produced by Latin Americans, summed up under the title of 'liberation theology'. This literature has been made available to the English reader by Orbis Books, the publishing company of the Maryknoll Missionary Fathers in the USA. The same type of theology is found in a more traditional vein, taking up the thought of Hegel and Marx, in the 'political theology' of German Catholic and Protestant thinkers. It is also found in various liberation theologies produced by Christian groups suffering from institutionalized oppression, for example, by the Black Americans or the native peoples of North America. The same trend is found in the theology associated with the Catholic Left in the so-called Catholic countries like Italy, France, Spain and Quebec. Even the small Catholic Left in the English-speaking world is attempting to formulate the Christian faith with a sense of concrete political responsibility.

The tensions in the Catholic Church at this time include the gap between renewal-minded Catholics, actually the mainstream, who welcome the reforms of Vatican II, and the minorities who, for a variety of reasons, still cling to their pre-conciliar religion. There is however a much more fruitful tension between two distinct groups of progressive theologians: (1) 'the liberals' – the majority, I believe, who understand divine salvation as the source of personal conversion, personal growth and personal holiness and hope that present society will be improved so that more people will be able to live out the full implications of God's salvific power, and (2) 'the radicals' – who, following the model of Medellin, understand divine salvation in terms of social transformation (and in this context only, also in terms of personal transformation) and who give priority to the analysis of the concrete forms of structural evil and demand a corresponding commitment to social change. The first group tends to consider the theological enterprise as unrelated to an economic base; they hold that human existence is essentially the same among rich and poor, and since the gospel addresses itself to this universal human condition it has identical meaning for all. The second group denies this. They hold that 'liberal theology', while interesting, learned, and even inspiring, is ultimately linked to a very particular social experience, namely that of the middle class, and hence makes Christians insensitive to the history of human suffering in past and present. The tension between these two trends, may I add, gives rise to important theological debates, of great benefit to 'liberals' and 'radicals' alike.

The new political theology, I wish to stress, is based on new religious experience. It expresses a religious yearning for the fulfilment of the divine promises: that God's will be done on earth as it is in heaven. The social base for this new religious experience has been small communities of activist Christians, the so-called *communautées de base*, as well as other networks of small groups. Some of these social configurations have received the attention of sociologists.[4]

The point I wish to make at the end of this contribution is that religious experience itself is affected by the social context in which it is situated. The sacred is not a fixed category, it does not have an identical structure in all societies and all social locations. Religious experience varies in accordance with a variety of social factors. This ought to be obvious to sociologists. Curiously enough, despite the research of great scholars like Max Weber, there are sociologists who think they can tie themselves to a single definition of the sacred and regard as of inferior value religious experiences that do not live up to this definition. Peter Berger, for instance, thinks that Rudolf Otto's descriptive definition of the sacred has normative value for sociologists and, according to some of his remarks, even for theologians. In a recent article, this well-known American sociologist accuses certain trends in modern theology of being devoid of an authentic sense of the transcendent because they reflect religious experiences that do not live up to Rudolf Otto's definition of the sacred.[5] This is unsatisfactory reasoning. There is no easily available normative definition of the sacred. Theologians in particular are very much aware that in the biblical literature a great many religious experiences are recorded. In many of these the sense of God's majesty, Otto's *tremendum et fascinans*, is inextricably linked to the sense of God's justice and holiness. Here the sacred becomes the bearer of a judgment on human life and society and of a promise for the righting of present ills. Religious experience had to do with human transformation. The Early Church believed that God's ultimate self-revelation took place not in a startling theophany but in a human being, the man Jesus Christ.

There is, therefore, no reason to suppose that the humanistic bent of contemporary Catholic theology, whether personalist or socialist, is due to some sort of betrayal of the spiritual, of transcendence, of the sacred, of otherness, as some traditional Christians have argued. These theological trends are grounded in actual religious movements within Catholicism: they reflect new kinds of religious experiences such as prophesy, fellowship, turning points in life-orientation, the raising of consciousness, compassionate identification with the exploited, and others – all religious experiences of humanization. To the believing community they manifest God's redemptive presence in human life, as the hidden dynamics carrying history forward to the fulfilment of the divine promises.

Notes

1 McDonald, D.J. 'The Philosophy of the Antigonish Movement' pamphlet. (Antigonish, 1942).
2 Mannheim, K. 'Conservative Thought' in *Essays on Sociology and Social Psychology* (London, 1953) pp. 74–164.
3 The 'Conclusions' of the Medellin Conference are published in English by the United States Catholic Conference (USCC), Washington, D.C. For an interpretation of the Medellin Conference and its impact, see Berryman, P.E. 'Latin American Liberation Theology' in S. Torres ed. *Theology in the Americas* (New York, 1976) pp. 20–83.
4 Cf. Paiment, G. *Groupes libres et foi chrétienne* (Montreal, 1972).
5 Berger, P. 'For a World with Windows' in *Against the World for the World* ed. P. Berger and R. Neuhaus (New York, 1976) p. 10.

Chapter 8

GOD, MAN AND MEDIA: ON A PROBLEM ARISING WHEN THEOLOGIANS SPEAK OF THE MODERN WORLD

John Orme Mills

'Epistemological imperialism'?

LIKE politicians and journalists, theologians (including drafters of
ecclesiastical statements) are getting a reputation for only too easily
assuming the role of amateur sociologist, that is, for making quasi-
scientific observations on the character, function and constitution of
society based on unscientifically controlled and analyzed data.

Robin Gill, for one, has very recently discussed this tendency,[1]
and it demands much wider attention among theologians than it has
at present. Politicians and even journalists might be forgiven, but
theology claims the status of a serious academic discipline and
arguably what we have here is a brand of 'epistemological imperialism' (to coin a phrase) which could undermine its claim to that
status. By 'epistemological imperialism' I mean arbitrary appropri-
ation by the practitioner of one specialism of another specialism's
vocabulary and specific areas of concern without a corresponding
taking-over or critical adaptation of the frames in which these were
located, or the presuppositions in which they were rooted, or the
governing criteria of the specialism in which they had become
defined.

Instances of this apparent 'imperialism' cannot, however, always
be ascribed simply to unawareness or disregard of the rigours of a
different discipline.

The Latin American theologian J.L. Segundo has recently sum-
marized a critique of modern sociology by the Argentinian sociologist E. Verón.[2] Verón, in his paper,[3] argues that present-day sociology 'is retreating from realms of human social life that are of
increasing importance and simply refusing to deal with them', and
Segundo claims that these are 'the very realms which are the most
important in any collaborative effort between sociology and theology'.[4] He concludes his analysis by saying:

There is no valid reason why we must resign ourselves to an irrational separation of
the two disciplines, even in the framework of the most up-to-date scientific canons.
But neither can we twist history to our purpose and allege a cooperation that is not
there in fact.[5]

Assuming what he is saying is correct, because of certain shortcomings (or shifts of interest) in recent sociological theory, sometimes theologians have to choose between (a) making sociological observations themselves, unaided by the sociologist, and (b) on certain crucially important issues staying silent.

Prominent among those theologians who are aware of the dangers and temptations of making speculations about society that could turn out to be mere exercises in 'epistemological imperialism', and who have opted for silence, is the Roman Catholic, Karl Rahner. He has been uneasy about Church statements on the nature of society that are not directly founded on revelation and are open to refutation by sociologists, now or in the future. (An obvious example is the Medellin Document on the future of Latin America, produced by the Conference of Latin American Bishops in 1968 and written about by Gregory Baum in Chapter 7.)[6] But Rahner's caution has made him critical not solely of the 'politically radical' element in the Roman Catholic Church. In 1969 he said in a report to the International Papal Commission of Theologians, which was also indirectly addressed to the Roman Sacred Congregation for the Doctrine of the Faith (the successor of the 'Holy Office'):

We [namely 'the Church and her official doctrinal authorities'] interpret the situation of today and tomorrow in terms of the situation of the yesterday to which we have been accustomed . . . The first step to be taken is the recognition in all honesty that we do not know the situation in which we ourselves stand in terms of sociology and human ideas.[7]

Let us, however, suppose that all these deficiencies (but *only* these deficiencies) had been rectified. Let us suppose:

(a) that theologians and churchmen *did* know the situation in which they themselves stood 'in terms of sociology and human ideas'.

(b) that the state of sociological theory and practice *was* such that it could assist and order the theologian's understanding of society's structures and symbols as effectively as other sciences have assisted and ordered his understanding of the structures and symbols of ancient sacred texts.

(c) that sociologists and theologians, whenever working in each other's disciplines, *did* all subject themselves to the rigour of that other discipline.

Would this Elysian state of affairs totally eradicate this 'imperialism' I have been writing about?

It would, of course, lead to the eradication of much of it. Nevertheless, as I shall attempt to make clear, there are reasons for thinking that:

(a) unless the churches and their theologians were going to stay mute about a range of matters of urgent concern, theologians would (in spite of these major advances) almost certainly still occasionally be making statements that would at least *appear* to be unsubstantiated sociological utterances.

(b) and the eradication of these particular instances of 'imperialism' (if instances of 'imperialism' they actually are) would be the consequence of a change more profound and far-reaching than anything mentioned here so far.

Unity and the media

The intractability of the problem (and an indication why an easy solution is not likely to be close at hand) can, I think, be discerned particularly well by looking at one sentence in a modern Roman Catholic offical document on the mass media.

This document, the Pastoral Instruction on the Means of Social Communication published in 1971 by the Pontifical Council for the Instruments of Social Communication and commonly referred to as *Communio et Progressio*,[8] is in many ways admirable, and here I am not making a critique of its general aims and proposals but examining questions raised by this one specific statement with which it opens: *'The unity and advancement of men living in society: these are the chief aims of social communication and of all the means it uses.'* (n.1)

This claim that the media are 'unifying' is repeated elsewhere in the document: the media 'unite men in brotherhood' (n.2); they are 'indispensable to the smooth functioning of modern society' (n.6); they 'can contribute a great deal to human unity' (n.9), providing 'some of the most effective methods of cultivating that charity among men which is at once the cause and the expression of fellowship' (n.12); they should bring about 'a deeper understanding and a greater sympathy between men' (n.18); they are, in short, 'powerful instruments for progress'. (n.21)

It looks as if we have here a sociological statement: a statement about the function in society of the mass media. We are told, so it seems, that (a) the media increase social cohesion, and (b) this greater cohesion is beneficial.

But what foundation is there in sociological research for this statement? The brief answer is that there is very little, and what evidence we have could possibly more easily be used to support a conflicting statement. The second proposition contained in the statement need not be examined, for it is dependent on the first – the 'unifying' claim for the media – and this would be questioned by many media sociologists.

Sociologizing on the media

Media sociology has had a chequered history. This is partly, perhaps, because some of the most influential research of the past has been financed by commercial and political organizations with a material interest in the results published, and partly because it has incorporated a lot of unexamined popular ideology. But, primarily, it is because its theoretical basis has been weak.[9] Until the late 1930s it was taken for granted that the media had an enormous manipulative influence on society. From about 1940 (when controlled surveys began to be made) until roughly the mid-1960s the opposite conclusion prevailed; it was thought that the effects of the media were marginal, and that they merely mirrored society. Klapper,[10] notably, argued (or was said to argue) that the power of the media had to be located within existing structures of social relationship and systems of culture and belief. But since around the time of Klapper's study there has been another shift of opinion. It has increasingly been recognized that the place of the media in society *can* be very much more than marginal and that they *can* be an instrument of social power; but this thinking has been the outcome of a change and refinement in methodology which significantly qualifies the revised conclusion. There has been a shift away from the traditional research formula 'who says what in which channel to whom with what effect',[11] which presupposes that the interaction of media and audience can be satisfactorily analyzed out of their total social context. The media are certainly important, but the nature and extent of their importance can only be reliably assessed within the context of society *as a whole*. This is what is now being stressed, and so far not much has been done to examine the media within that total context.[12] There is, however, growing consensus among media sociologists that 'modes of communication . . . are determined by the structure of social relations', not the reverse,[13] and more attention is being given by researchers to examining the role of media organizations,[14] the utilization of the media by economically dominant interests,[15] and exploitation of the media by the audience.[16]

It is doubtful, therefore, that according to acceptable sociological criteria the media can be seen as an independent formative influence that can be employed *directly* to transform society, however important those media may be. They are important because means of disseminating communications on such a scale, means rightly or wrongly feared or bought by such a range of dominant power groups, cannot fail to be important in a society of our type. But it cannot hereby be assumed that the instantaneous reception of identical messages, images and assumptions by a great number and variety of people with no comparable opportunities for feed-back is likely to have a *cohesive* effect on those people. It may uniformize the society, but not necessarily increase unity and understanding in it. The opposite has frequently been feared by sociologists. It has been thought that exposure to the media, if only because of the character of these media, may actually *separate* men. It can inhibit change sometimes; it might favour the spread of authoritarianism; it can probably indirectly confirm prejudice.[17] It might actually increase inchoate, irrational and extremely privatized attitudes and mediate experiences of rootlessness and anomie.[18]

The one prominent modern author on this subject whose theories support the 'unifying claim' for the media found in *Communio et Progressio* is the widely influential but highly controversial Marshall McLuhan (himself currently a member of Rome's Pontifical Commission on the media).[19] Some of McLuhan's insights are important as well as exciting, but informed critics agree that, whatever truth there may be in some of them, it is impossible to build soundly and directly on the kind of foundations he has chosen to lay.[20] They lack the necessary firm factual content.

Yet does all this imply that what we have here, in *Communio et Progressio*, is merely an instance of careless and maybe misguided thinking, a sociological claim which would not withstand examination by serious sociologists and so would be better abandoned?

The media and the Church

No truth-claim exists as an isolated proposition, but above all utterances appearing in Church documents have a history and must be read within the context of that history, whatever may be their apparent content and in whatever kind of vocabulary they may be couched.

The official attitude of the Roman Catholic Church towards the mass media was always ambiguous. In 1936 Pope Pius XI published an encyclical on the cinema, *Vigilanti Cura*,[21] and in 1957 Pope Pius XII published an encyclical on the cinema, sound broadcasting and television. *Miranda Prorsus.*[22] Both of these (following traditional Catholic teaching on human invention) called the new media 'true gifts of God'. Pius XI founded Vatican Radio. Pius XII furthermore declared:

God is the sovereign good . . . God has chosen man to be the mirror of His own perfection. He wills him, therefore, to share in this divine generosity, to be associated with Him in His work of giving . . . So from time immemorial man has always of his very nature, instinctively, sought to share with others his own spiritual possessions. This he does by means of signs borrowed from material things, signs which he has continually striven to render more and more perfect. (n.18, 19)

The line of argument here is explicitly theological and, in the following lines of this text, the idea that the media *themselves* are unifying is carefully avoided; but here we see the nucleus of ideas that clearly were to be taken up and developed in *Communio et Progressio*.

But the general tone of these two encyclicals is cautious and protective. Pius XII, especially, stressed the potentially corrupting influences of the media. Civil as well as ecclesiastical authorities were urged to exercise strict censorship, and it was recommended that national offices should be set up to act in a watch-dog capacity. It was, at least initially, primarily for negative (namely, defensive) reasons rather than positive (namely, apostolic) reasons that the remarkably extensive network of Roman Catholic organizations concerned with the media – a network begun in the 1920s and still expanding – came to be.

The decree on the mass media published by the Second Vatican Council in 1963, *Inter Mirifica*, [23] was considerably more positive and more nuanced than the papal documents which had preceded it. It asserted freedom of information to be one of man's rights, but it did not consider more than cursorily the question of the *positive* role of the media in the Church's life. Instead, it proposed that another document should be drafted after the Council 'to ensure that all the principles and rules of the Council on the means of social communication be put into effect' . . . the document *Communio et Progressio*, from which comes the statement under discussion. And by 1971, when this finally appeared, much had happened as a result of the Roman Catholic Church's major shift in its understanding of its relationship to the world, as reflected in its official teaching both at the Council and afterwards (see what Gregory Baum says in Chapter 7). [24] Symbolically, in 1966, the Index of Prohibited Books ceased to have legal force in the Church. Pius XII's *Miranda Prorsus* and the Pontifical Council's *Communio et Progressio* are products of culturally different worlds. In the later document we see a remarkable switch of emphasis: the media are no longer viewed primarily as potential menaces but as beneficial forces. But *theologically* there is equally remarkable continuity. And this fact is very pertinent to the heart of our discussion.

In *Miranda Prorsus* Pius XII had repeated the classical Catholic teaching that sharing is of man's very nature, as child of God called to participate in God's work, to mirror God's own self-giving. And this idea is echoed in passages of the important Council document on the Church in the Modern World, *Gaudium et Spes* (1965), [25] passages which clearly influenced the drafters of *Communio et Progressio*. For example, we are told that partly as a result of 'the spread of knowledge and the speedy diffusion far and wide of habits of thought and feeling' through advances in the media, 'the bonds uniting man to his fellows multiply without ceasing'. (n.6) Again, with advances in the sciences (including the social sciences), in technology and in means of communication, 'heightened media of exchange between nations and different branches of society open up the riches of different cultures to each and every individual, with the result that a more universal form of culture is gradually taking shape, and through it the unity of mankind is being fostered'. (n.54) These statements in *Gaudium et Spes* are, of course, open to the same kind of criticism as is the 'unifying' claim in *Communio et Progressio*, but, when they are read in their total context, it is far more obvious how much their optimistic tone and their stress on the trend towards unity owe to the fundamental theological idea already mentioned. Gregory Baum very rightly points out that the drafters of *Gaudium et Spes* were influenced by the optimistic ethos of the Western bourgeois societies of the sixties,[26] but there has lately been a tendency to overlook just how much these seemingly 'modern' church statements about society owe to ancient ideas in the Church's theological tradition. (*Why* these ideas persist and are used is another question; the only point I am making here is that they *do* persist and *are* used.)

Sociological or theological?

The 'unifying claim' in *Communio et Progressio* – the statement under discussion – is in fact *a theological statement*, not a sociological statement, although that is what at first sight it appears to be. It contains no explicit reference to God or religion and seems merely to be making an observation on the way the media function in society; but it is a 'theological' statement in the sense that it is a statement primarily attempting to project a view of part of the world from a standpoint 'outside' the world, and so is attempting to convey something about life's final meaning. It is a statement attributable to the kind of activity which David Martin has described in Chapter 3,[27] and to the kind of thinking which I have tried to define in the Introduction.[28] That it is a statement of such a kind is not at all apparent until, in the subsequent section of the document, 'The Christian View of the Means of Social Communication: Basic Points of Doctrine', (n.6–18) one reads an account of traditionally-framed salvation-history that is unusual, if not unique, because quasi-scientific concepts drawn from communication theory are being used as the paradigm by which it is expressed. (n.10–11) The problems that crop up in using such a paradigm – there appears, for instance, to be no proper distinction made between the contents and the means of communication – do not concern us here; what is relevant is the juxtaposing of the concepts of 'communication' and 'salvation'. Even so, on a first reading of the document it is only too easy to assume that the Church, having adopted a basically favourable view of the media for quasi-sociological reasons (possibly mistaken quasi-sociological reasons), is here attempting to construct a theological argument to strengthen its claim that the media are 'unifying'. It is only evident that the theological argument in fact comes first when the thinking in *Communio et Progressio* is put in its context – the historical context outlined above. In other words, it is easier to read the document as sociology (clearly bad sociology by sociology's own methodological criteria) decorated with theological trimmings than to read it as what it actually is . . . theology (perhaps quite good theology) with sociological trimmings.

Varieties of unity

But why is this happening? Why are we today more and more often confronting theological utterances of this sort – theological utterances which are to all appearances unfounded sociological utterances? Because *Communio et Progressio* is about the mass media (in other words, about that part of the industrial system which *simultaneously* disseminates the *same* message throughout society), it reveals extra clearly a trend in thinking among theologians which is also present elsewhere but normally only by implication.

At the unreflective level it is not unlikely that we construct our perception of the world through the mediating of the interdependent functions, 'similarity' and 'difference', the boundary distinctions between these two being decided, as in all open systems, by parts of the system itself. But, because we are heirs of the Western metaphysical tradition, the classical antinomy of identity (or *'sameness'*) and of otherness still governs much of our thinking, albeit in a modified form.

Now, as we have already seen, *Communio et Progressio* voices the hope at the core of Christianity, the hope of 'unity'. But since New Testament times there has been a shift in the meaning of 'unity' and in the place of the hope for 'unity' in the Christian proclamation. New Testament 'unity' is two-level. It is *not a state of sameness*, of identity. In the eyes of the New Testament authors 'unity' is seen as a state in which the diverse, hitherto in conflict, has been brought within and is kept within that perfecting orderliness the Israelites called *shalom* ('peace') by the one unique God of Israel, now fully revealed in the person of the crucified-and-risen Jesus Christ (cf. *Ephesians* 4: 1–13; *Colossians* 3: 11–15; 1 *John* 4: 7–12). For these authors the states of being 'in peace' with God (the wholly unique) and of being 'in peace' with redeemed creation (the diverse) are undoubtedly related; in fact, they cannot be separated.

Neither, though, can one replace the other, and this is simply because of the 'total uniqueness' of God, the uniqueness of which this unity is a constant reminder. New Testament 'unity' may even be the sign of contradiction which will bring to judgment a world turned in on itself (cf. *John* 17: 20–26; *Philippians* 1: 27–28). It can be threatening.

The New Testament authors could convey what this unity was in the framework of salvation history, drawing on the language and ideas of covenant theology (cf. *Hebrews* 3: 1–6; 1 *Peter* 1: 22–2: 6). And in the Greek world and later, theology, when speaking of this Christian unity, was able to draw on basic philosophical and cosmological notions of antiquity which did not altogether deprive it of its 'two-level' character. They were notions which in its turn it reinforced. Among the better-known of these was that of a cosmos understood to be a total system of correspondence, of microcosm and macrocosm, and the notions of participation and synthesis. Tradition and liturgy helped to perpetuate these within the Churches (especially in the Roman Catholic and Eastern Orthodox Churches) even when they were losing their hold in a wider society.

However, with theism's decline we perceive a subtle change, at least in Western Christendom. The major transformations that have marked the modern age have been accompanied by a tendency, at least among theologians, to see the Christian proclamation of unity in a fresh context. It would seem to mirror a proclamation of the Enlightenment and the subsequent political and industrial revolutions – their proclamation of the new man's (or the new society's) ability to self-integrate. As heaven on earth promised to appear, did it not seem that the Christian proclamation of harmony and reconciliation was surely one of the most convincing indicators of the persistence of God's relevance and one of the best ways of speaking of God? And when, in the new society, the foundations for optimism were badly shaken, was there not here a golden opportunity for supplying reassurances which would make God's relevance still more evident? Unavoidably, maybe, what has at least been thought to be the Christian idea of unity has, under one disguise or another, occupied an increasingly important place in the theological presentation of reality. But the Christian idea of unity in its ancient 'two-level' version as described above cannot be used as a *means* (as one might use a language laboratory) through which one might 'learn of God'. For in the thinking not only of the New Testament authors but also of the early Church Fathers, God cannot in any way be known apart from that unity; God is absolutely integral to that unity; entering unity of this kind *is* 'entering the life of God'. One cannot *start* from this unity. So the Christian notion of unity has effectively been shorn of its 'two-level' character; it has become increasingly equated with the notion of *'sameness'*. And consequently it is *drives towards sameness* – 'unifying drives' which 'unify' in the modified sense just described – that are, to an unprecedented degree, being read into the world by theologians. This is reflected not so much in the subject-indexes of their books as in the organization of their books and in their vocabulary; and it is evident in its most banal form in some of the official published pronouncements which have come from the churches and which the theologians have done much to draft. It is a phenomenon very different from, for example, the teleological emphasis that characterized the worldview of Aquinas. It belongs to the specifically 'modern' understanding of man that Michel Foucault urges has emerged with the movement of thought 'no longer towards the never-completed formation of Difference but towards the ever-to-be-accomplished unveiling of the Same'.[29]

And now perhaps a cautious answer can be given to the question of why we are today more and more often confronting theological utterances which are to all appearances sociological utterances. For, the more prominent the phenomenon just written about becomes, the more alike the two kinds of utterances are probably going to sound, as the only ready-made categories and thought-forms which lend themselves for theologizing generated by this shift are some of the categories and thought-forms of the human sciences as developed in the late nineteenth and early twentieth centuries. Namely, those of disciplines rooted in an understanding of society in which all the stress is on 'sameness', and of those disciplines based on the presupposition that all things *can* be compared and through comparison basic 'common denominators' can be identified. The 'absolute newness' embedded in the quantum structure of matter was not yet having to be grappled with even by philosophers of science at the time Dilthey was confidently saying:

In the realm of [the] objective mind every individual expression of life represents something common. Each word, each sentence, each gesture or civility, each art work and each historical deed is understandable only because there is something common linking him who expresses himself in them and him who understands. The individual constantly experiences, thinks, and acts in a sphere of what is common, and only in it does he understand.[30]

This answer of ours is not simply a repetition of the familiar observation that 'horizontal Christianity' is in constant danger of turning into 'pop sociology', but is suggesting that, because of a change in ways of theologizing (an outcome of wider changes), it is increasingly difficult not to theologize in what are sociology's categories. It is not implied that a return to the old world-view and its accompanying metaphysical system is either possible or desirable, and neither is it implied that the sociologists are themselves on such firm theoretical ground that they are always going to set the pace. But the present state of affairs would appear to put into question the foundations of what theology claims is specific to it. David Martin, for example, in Chapter 3, defines what is distinctive about the theologian as the asking of his question 'in relation to a particular postulate and a special possibility', namely that 'the con-centrated "image" of meaning and purpose, striving and release, perfection and plenitude' is not merely a social construct or 'an emergent property of the process', but is *'there'*.[31] But, if there is any truth in what I have been saying about trends in theologizing, how much longer will the theologian be able to describe his task in such a way? Is he losing his own tools – his language and his conceptual apparatus? Rather in the same way that most Westerners have already lost adequate systems of significance to which they can attribute the 'experiences of transcendence', which many of them still apparently have?

Ineradicable difference

If we are looking for a solution, the possibilities are limited. Help is not likely to come either from sociologist or theologian. And we cannot foist an alternative way of thinking on our society. The theologian has to work within the parameters imposed by current discourse and at least certain prevailing presuppositions. Yet the way to a firmly-based solution almost certainly starts with a critique by the theologian, for his own benefit only, of some of the ways in which we unreflectingly organize our thinking. For, arguably, all that has gone before in this chapter indicates that in our efforts to understand our world it would be fruitful if we emphasized more than hitherto its 'otherness' and its 'unlikeness', but not merely by trying to 'pull in' rather than 'push back' the boundaries between 'same' and 'contrary' which we project on it.

The examining and working out of such a procedure is, however, first and foremost the philosopher's concern. I cannot do more than point to one example of potentially influential thinking that is already moving in such a direction: some of the thinking of Jacques Derrida, one of the group of avowedly atheist anti-metaphysical modern French thinkers who have been either attacking directly, or else supplying foundations for attacking, basic categories and assumptions that favour the present domination of the 'human sciences'.

Derrida's attempt to give a fresh account of the 'origin of mean-ing'[32] is, I consider, an example of a controversial but potentially stimulating critique of theorists' basic presuppositions which aims to undermine all boundaries of opposition without having as its object the subjection of all things to the 'tyranny of sameness'. It is now almost a commonplace that meaning can only emerge in a context, against a background, but all Derrida's stress is *on the difference, not the alikeness.* As he says, writing of Saussure's semiology, '. . . le système des signes est constitué *par des différences,* non par le plein des termes'.³³ And he argues strongly for the *ineradicability of difference* at the very basis of our world.

Any effort here to summarize Derrida's highly complex thought would be certain to be a distortion. But if it is indeed the mediating of 'difference', of 'otherness', rather than the mediating of 'sameness' (or, for that matter, of 'the contrary'), that is *the* humanizing activity ('humanizing' in so far as it is the activity that brings us into an understanding at depth of 'how things are'), then the emphases must shift in the task of all who are trying to deepen our understanding of what the human condition is . . . and this includes theologians. We can already see this happening in, for example, the writing of Michel de Certeau.³⁴

What, however, is particularly relevant to the problem considered in this chapter is that it would seem likely that stressing the basic ineradicability of difference will lead to a revision of our understanding of what is so close to the heart of our discussion: it will lead to a revision of our understanding of what 'unity' is. It is likely to make clearer that it is not sufficient for human beings (or societies) merely to seek 'conformity' or 'consensus' – which are static phenomena – but that they must also seek unity. And it is likely to lead to an interpretation of what unity is that in fact brings it rather closer to the biblical model (without that model's explicitly theistic associations), and certainly away from the model found in classical sociology, where it tends to be framed in the 'language of sameness', and away from the corresponding theological view of it which I have briefly summed up above. In a few words, it will lead to a way of looking at the world that emphasizes radical distinctiveness as the source of this world's meaning, that will not permit us to search for 'essences', but which is likely to incorporate a model of unity as the state of affairs in which occurs the reconciling and interiorizing of what we continue to experience as diverse meanings. It is the distinct that unites, in an interpretation of reality of this kind.

Now we can move a little closer to the concrete, but still not far enough for this to be a venture into social anthropology (in the British sense) or into political philosophy: we are still only concerned with what this understanding of 'unity' can mean for the sociologist and the theologian. If radical distinctiveness *is* a mark of the state of affairs we denote as 'unity', then, when we speak of 'unity', we are not speaking of a reification of what is common to the

constituents of a given society (cf. the quotation from Dilthey given
above). On the contrary, we are speaking of a state of affairs that
does not lend itself to adequate description in sociological
categories – to being compared, defined and measured in terms of
the society in which it is present. The sociologist can measure
degrees and varieties of consensus, but the tracing of movements
towards or away from unity demands, it seems, the positing of
something not unlike 'the Utopia that evaporated from religion'
which Horkheimer of the Frankfurt School claimed art had preserved,[35] 'that "other" society, beyond the present one,'[36] which
human beings still yearn for, and which this group of Marxists
believed had to be taken into account if major art was to be understood. It would seem that if one ignores that 'Utopia', that 'other
society' which human beings in their specifically human activity try
to be part of, and yet which is always different, always 'ahead' or
'over there', it is similarly likely to be difficult to make good sense of
the surgings and dispersals of what we identify as 'unity'. And here
the boundaries of sociology emerge.

Sometimes these boundaries are clear almost from the start. For
example, the sociologist examining beliefs in objects 'out of this
world' (like gods) is, most of us think, clearly working inside the
boundaries. And many sociologists see aesthetic theory as clearly
outside. But, if what has been said here about 'unity' is true, apparently sometimes sociological interpretation can also be inappropriate or at least very inadequate, even when what is confronting us is
something widely taken to be as much part of the conceptual
apparatus we need, in order to envisage the dynamics of society, as
are 'State', 'commitment' and 'status' – indeed, something so central that every public leader invokes it (although what precisely he is
invoking is often difficult to perceive). As with 'freedom', to
instance a much more obvious example which has not got comparable roots in society's self-understanding, 'unity' can, it seems, be
interpreted more adequately in a 'theological' way, that is, in the
way briefly defined earlier in this chapter – one that posits an
'outside' standpoint. (Ironically, there are sociologists with no love
at all for theology who would warmly agree with this conclusion,
because they would see 'unity' as belonging to a 'pre-scientific
representation of the social world' which has survived as part of the
rhetoric of domination, for, in the words of Mauss, society pays
itself 'in the false coin of its dream'.[37] But I have tried to show that
the notion of 'unity' – or, more exactly, what is probably the most
important version of it for us – is not in fact an archaism of this kind.)

Such a shift in our understanding of 'unity' as has been described
could have many consequences (and it is a shift that is likely to look
increasingly plausible, for the world-view in which it is rooted is

increasingly shared, and 'the recovery of difference' is not a phenomenon known only to a handful of intellectuals living mainly in France). It would, for Christians, have relevance in the conducting of certain types of dialogue of a specifically religious kind and in the growth of Christianity's understanding of its relationship to society. But (and this is of more immediate interest to us) it would also draw fresh attention to the scope of old and new kinds of interpretation. For, without in any way belittling the extent of sociology's contribution to our understanding of our world, it would seem to reveal that the identification and comprehensive description of 'unity' and even 'unifying trends' is still not properly the concern of sociology . . . not even if we discard the ancient theological and metaphysical connotations of the idea of 'unity'. And, more perhaps than any other single factor belonging specifically to the realm of theory, the recognition of this would help to lessen the pressure to reduce theological utterances to the form of 'sociological' utterances.

Whether, in spite of such recognition, the social and cultural pressures are so enormous that this regrettable kind of reduction would nevertheless persist is another question: one that genuinely belongs to the social sciences.

Notes

1 Gill, R. *The Social Context of Theology* (London & Oxford, 1975) Chap. 4.
2 Segundo, J.L. *The Liberation of Theology* (Buenos Aires, 1975); English translation (New York, 1976 & Dublin, 1977) pp. 48–56.
3 Verón, E. 'Ideología y comunicación de masas', in Prieto *et al.*, in *Lenguaje y comunicación social* (Buenos Aires, 1971).
4 Segundo, *op. cit.* p. 48.
5 *Ibid.* p. 66.
6 Chap. 7, p. 132f.
7 Rahner, K. 'The Congregation of the Faith and the Commision of Theologians' (1969); English translation in *Theological Investigations* (London & New York, 1976) Vol. 14, pp. 105f.
8 *Acta Apostolicae Sedis* 63 (1971) pp. 593–656. English translation by the Pontifical Council for the Instruments of Social Communication in A. Flannery (ed.) *Vatican Council II: The Conciliar and Post Conciliar Documents* (Dublin & New York, 1975) pp. 293–349.
9 Cf. Tunstall, J. *The Media are American: Anglo-American media in the world* (London, 1977) pp. 201–214; Brown, R.L. 'Approaches to the Historical Development of Mass Media Studies' in J. Tunstall (ed.) *Media Sociology* (London, 1970) pp. 41–57.
10 Klapper, J.T. *The Effects of Mass Communication* (New York, 1960).
11 Lasswell, H. 'The Structure and Function of Communication in Society' in B. Lyman (ed.) *The Communication of Ideas* (New York, 1948) p. 37.
12 Cf. Curran, J., Gurevitch, M. Woollacott, J. (ed.) *Mass Communication and Society* (London, 1977) p. 3.
13 Murdock, G. and Golding, P. 'Capitalism, Communication and Class Relations' in Curran *et al.* (ed.) *op. cit.* p. 13.

14   Cf. e.g. Elliott, P. *The making of a television series: a case study in the sociology of culture* (London, 1972) esp. pp. 164–6.

15   Cf. Burns, T. 'The Organization of Public Opinion' in Curran et al. (ed.) *op. cit.* pp. 44–69; Westergaard, J. 'Power, Class and the Media' in *ibid.* pp. 95–115.

16   Cf. Katz, E., Blumler, J.G. and Gurevitch, M. 'Utilization of Mass Communication by the Individual' in Blumler & Katz (ed.) *The Uses of Mass Communications* (New York, 1974).

17   Cf. McQuail, D. 'The Influence and Effects of Mass Media' in Curran et al. (ed.) *op. cit.* pp. 82–5; Adorno, T.W. et al. *The Authoritarian Personality* (New York, 1950); Smythe, D.W. 'Some Observations on Communications Theory' *Audio-Visual Communication Review* Vol. 2, 1954, pp. 24–37, repr. in D. McQuail (ed.) *Sociology of Mass Communications* (Harmondsworth, 1972) pp. 19–34; Hartmann, P. and Husband, C. *Racism and the Mass Media* (London, 1974); Husband, C. (ed.) *White Media and Black Britain: a critical look at the role of the media in race relations today* (London, 1975).

18   Cf. Martin, B. and Pluck, R. *A Kind of Believing* (London, 1977); Berger, P.L., Berger, B. and Kellner, H. *The Homeless Mind* (New York & Harmondsworth, 1973).

19   Cf. *The Gutenburg Galaxy* (London, 1962); *Understanding Media* (London, 1964).

20   Cf. Miller, J. *McLuhan* (London, 1971); Winston, B. *The Image of the Media* (London, 1973) pp. 72–81.

21   *A.A.S.* 28 (1936) pp. 249f. English translation by Catholic Truth Society, London, S. 132.

22   *A.A.S.* 49 (1957) num. 13–14. English translation by C.T.S., London, S. 243.

23   English translation in A. Flannery (ed.) *op. cit.* pp. 283–292.

24   Chap. 7, pp. 125–6.

25   English translation in A. Flannery (ed.) *op. cit.* pp. 903–1014.

26   Chap. 7, pp. 125-7, 132f.

27   Chap. 3, pp. 46f.

28   Introduction, pp. 8–9.

29   Foucault, M. *Les Mots et les choses* (Paris, 1966); English translation *The Order of Things* (London, 1970) p. 349.

30   *Gesammelte Schriften* (Göttingen, 1913–67) Vol. 7, pp. 146f; cf. Habermas, J. *Erkenntnis und Interesse* (Frankfurt, 1968); English translation: *Knowledge and Human Interests* (London, 1972) Chap. 7 (English translation of this quotation p. 156).

31   Chap. 3, p. 47.

32   Derrida, J. *De la Grammatologie* (Paris, 1967); *L'Écriture et la différence* (Paris, 1967); 'La Différence' in Tel Quel, *Théorie d'ensemble* (Paris, 1968); cf. Wilden, A. *System and Structure* (London & New York, 1972) pp. 395–400; Kerr, F. 'Derrida's Wake', *New Blackfriars,* No. 653, (Oct. 1974) pp. 449–460.

33   Derrida, 'La Différence', *op. cit.* p. 49.

34   Cf. Kerr, F. 'The "Essence" of Christianity: Notes after de Certeau', *New Blackfriars,* No. 643, (Dec. 1973) pp. 545–556.

35   Horkheimer, M. 'Art and Mass Culture', *Studies in Philosophy and Social Science* IX, 2 (1941).

36   Jay, M. *The Dialectical Imagination* (New York & London, 1973) p. 179.

37   Bourdieu, P. *Esquisse d'une théorie de la pratique* (Geneva, 1972) English translation *Outline of a Theory of Practice* (London & New York, 1977) pp. 20–22, 192f., 195.

Chapter 9

RELATIVIZING THE RELATIVIZERS: A THEOLOGIAN'S ASSESSMENT OF THE ROLE OF SOCIOLOGICAL EXPLANATION OF RELIGIOUS PHENOMENA AND THEOLOGY TODAY

Timothy Radcliffe

THIS book opened with sociologists writing, from different angles, about the ways in which sociology might be a challenge to theology. It is not my intention here to go back over their ground. Mills, in Chapter 8, has tried to illustrate how confused one can sometimes be nowadays about what is 'sociological' and what is 'theological' thinking. It is my aim here to review from a specifically theological standpoint the major issues which have been the concern of this book. First of all we shall look again briefly at the relationship between the sociological explanation of religious phenomena and theological statements about them. Then I shall suggest the limitations of the sociological explanation of *theology itself.* I shall attempt to show why the sociologist is, in reality, neither the theologian's rival nor his executioner, and why, on the contrary, sociological explanation may have an immensely important function within the practice of theology itself.

It is commonly assumed that sociology and theology provide alternative explanations of religious phenomena. Sociology explains what happens by reference to patterns of social interaction; theology by reference to God's intervention. It would follow, of course, that if the sociological explanation was accepted then the theological explanation would be redundant; there would be no need to bring in God at all. But if one conceives of the relationship between sociological and theological statements in this way, then one is being deceived by the superficial resemblance of their language. Theological references to divine intervention are not, or should not be, understood as explanatory at all. Rather, they are claiming that the events in question are, in some sense, revelatory.

Let us take the example of the Exodus. The sociologist could attempt to produce a coherent explanation of the event of the Exodus in terms of the social conditions of Egypt in the thirteenth century BC. He could examine the conflicts between Haipiru and other classes of that society and seek to establish whether they could be identified with the Hebrews of the Bible or not. In principle it might be shown that the Exodus is perfectly comprehensible as one of a number of attempts by oppressed groups within that society to slip across the border and take refuge in the desert. What room would there be left for the theological claim that it was God who led the Israelites out of Egypt? It looks as if the theologian is presenting an alternative explanation of the event, which he would have to justify by demonstrating that there were certain aspects of the Exodus that the sociologist had failed to explain. But this is not the case. The theological claim that it was God who caused the Exodus does not explain how the event happened; it is the recognition of the event as revelatory of God and his purposes. The theological statement is made within the context of a belief in the ultimate destiny of mankind, a destiny that is revealed and achieved in a history. It is claimed that this event is, in some sense, constitutive of this history and revelatory of that destiny. This is not to say that if you were to observe the Exodus you would see the hand of God at work in it, or that the event would have some numinous quality about it that would puzzle the sociologist. The theologian would see just what the sociologist saw, but he would claim to have discerned its significance and its meaning. The point that I am making is not too dissimilar to Evans-Pritchard's insistence that when the Azande explain events in terms of witchcraft they are not rejecting perfectly natural explanations. 'Witchcraft explains *why* events are harmful to man and not *how* they happen. A Zande perceives how they happen just as we do. He does not see a witch charge a man but an elephant. He does not see a witch push over the granary, but termites gnawing away its supports. He does not see a psychical flame igniting the thatch, but an ordinary lighted bundle of straw. His perception of how events occur is as clear as our own.[1]

This distinction between understanding an event, declaring its significance and explaining it, does not mean that the theologian will be utterly indifferent to all possible explanations of religious phenomena, that they are none of his business. Some 'understandings' will clearly exclude some 'explanations'. For example, if I say that God raised Jesus from the dead I am not explaining the emptiness of the tomb but rather articulating the meaning of its emptiness. But my interpretation of the meaning of its emptiness will clearly exclude certain, possibly all, explanations. If someone were to explain that the tomb was empty because the disciples stole the body then this would contradict my understanding of the meaning of the empty tomb.

Let us take a more trivial example in which the relationship between understanding and explanation is more complex. After the first papal election of 1978, while Cardinal Hume was declaring that Pope John Paul I was 'God's candidate', Vatican watchers were carefully analyzing possible voting combinations and producing a fairly coherent explanation of his election. Of course, Hume would not maintain that he was making a serious theological claim, but it is worth asking whether all possible explanations of the event would be compatible with his interpretation. If it emerged, for example, that Luciani had bribed most of the electorate, then Hume might well wonder whether his interpretation was justified, not because he had been confronted with an alternative and more convincing explanation of the event but because the election would have been shown to be an event of a different sort. He had understood the election to be pregnant with meaning, a revelation of God's purpose for the Church, because he believed it to be the election of a good man. If Luciani turned out to be a wicked briber then his election would have been a different event, the election of a bad man. So if there are conflicts between sociological and theological statements about religious phenomena, then this will not be because they are competing as forms of explanation, but because it might so happen that the sociological explanation implied such a radical redescription of the event that the theologian would have to conclude that it was not in fact open to the sort of significance that he had attributed to it. If a sociologist, for example, explained the career of Jesus in terms of the popular Galilean revolutionary movements of his time, if he saw him as just another Zealot, then he would find himself in conflict with the theologians because the life of such a Jesus could not have been open to the sort of significance that the theologian was claiming to find there. The theologian, therefore, would not be ruling out *all* sociological explanations of the career of Jesus, but merely those implying such a radical redescription of who Jesus was that he could not have been revelatory of God in the way that the theologians claim that he was.

It is worth remembering that even sociological theories are not value-free. The explanations proposed always derive from and express some prior implicit or explicit interpretation of the meaning of man's existence and destiny. If this interpretation is in profound contradiction with the professed beliefs of the theologian, then it is likely that the theologian will find that the sociological explanations of the events offered will be in contradiction with his interpretation of their meaning and significance. A Marxist sociological explanation of Christianity will be threatening or useful to the theologian to the extent that the ideology that it expresses and of which it is symptomatic is held to be compatible or incompatible with Christian belief. A radically incompatible interpretation of man's destiny and meaning is likely to beget explanations of religious phenomena with which the theologian is unhappy. Of course, the theologian cannot simply dismiss these explanations by showing that they derive from an unacceptable interpretation of the world. If he accepts the validity of sociology as a discipline he will have to maintain that these explanations can be refuted sociologically.

So far I have been performing a merely negative task by suggesting how sociology and theology do not relate, that is, as alternative forms of explanation. Many sociologists of religion believe that one could describe the relationship between the disciplines more positively as one of complementarity. For example, Robin Gill, in his book *The Social Context of Theology*, maintains that they offer alternative perspectives on the world, that they work in terms of alternative 'as if' methodologies which do not compete but which complement each other. Unfortunately Gill never spells out at length what constitutes the theological perspective and therefore what sort of complementarity it might have with the sociological perspective; but he does give an example which is illuminating. He refers to Maurice Wiles' suggestion that when the theologian considers the doctrine of creation he is obliged to employ two 'stories', the one scientific-historical and the other mythological. He quotes Wiles:

On the one hand we tell the scientific story of evolution; it is the real world as it has developed with which the doctrine of creation is concerned, not with some ideal world of the theological imagination. But in addition we tell a frankly mythological story about the spirit of God moving on the face of the chaotic waters, about God taking the dust of the earth, making man in his own image, and breathing upon him so that he becomes a living soul. If we know what we are doing we can weave the two stories together in poetically creative ways – as indeed the poet combines logically disparate images into new and illuminating wholes.[2]

Like Gill, I accept this description of the task of the theologian, but we interpret Wiles' position quite differently. Gill sees here an example of the complementarity of two 'as if' methodologies, that of the theologian and that of the scientist, and in this a model for the relationship between sociology and theology. He says, 'Wiles' depiction of the theologian's task in terms of "mythology" may or may not be satisfactory. Yet his main point remains. It is important to maintain that the theologian's methodology is complementary, not in opposition, to scientific methodology.'[3] But I understand Wiles to be suggesting that the theologian's task is to weave together the mythological and scientific 'stories' in a creative and illuminating way. The mythological story is not for us a transparent theological statement, and it is certainly not the task of the theologian to repeat it. He has to make sense of it by establishing a relationship between it and contemporary understandings of creation. So what we have here is not an example of the complementarity of the scientific and theological methodologies, but a description of the theologian's task as the establishment of an illuminating relationship between two disparate accounts of the origins of our world. The theologian is only able to perform this task in so far as he can transcend the mythological perspective himself and so bring it into an illuminating relationship with a quite different perspective. The theological 'perspective' is the product of the encounter of these two 'stories'.

The time has come to propose a definition of theology that will enable us to specify its relationship with sociology. Cornelius Ernst defined theology thus: 'Theology is an encounter of Church and world in which the meaning of the gospel becomes articulate as an illumination of the world.'[4] The theologian has the essentially creative task of making sense of the gospel in the light of contemporary experience, and of making sense of contemporary experience in the light of the gospel. His role is not simply to repeat religious formulae, whether they come from the gospels or from his own tradition, but to illuminate them by bringing them into relationship with the contemporary experience of meaning. The New Testament is a theological work precisely because it represents the initial encounter of Church and world, in which the gospel became articulate as an illumination of that world. It expresses that first encounter of the gospel with Judaism and Hellenism. It remains the permanently normative instance of creative transformation. We will all recognize in our respective traditions other, though less normative, theological 'monuments'. For a Roman Catholic one might be that encounter of the gospel and Aristotelianism in the thirteenth century that culminated in the theology of Thomas Aquinas, the disclosure of a new, deep understanding of the gospel and a transformation of Aristotelianism. It should be clear now why I do not think that it is legitimate to talk of a 'theological perspective'. If the task of the theologian is to provoke and enable a mutually illuminating encounter between the gospel and contemporary understandings of man and his destiny, then he cannot bring to that task a ready-made perspective. Whatever perspective may arise must be engendered by the encounter and not brought to it. One might, for example, wish to talk of a Thomist perspective, a Thomist 'way of looking at things', but would it make more sense to say that Thomas shared this perspective with non-Christian Aristotelians or with non-Aristotelian Christians? The question is obviously inappropriate. One might even wish to say that theology does not have a permanent and coherent language of its own. Of course, there is a whole vocabulary of theological words such as 'grace', 'justification', 'salvation', etc., but they only remain properly 'theological' for us as long as they remain capable of making possible that creative encounter.

So theology is not a 'discipline' in any ordinary sense of the word, and its relationship to sociology cannot, therefore, be that of one discipline to another. They are not complementary perspectives or methodologies, for theology, in itself, has neither a particular perspective or methodology. It is rather that praxis or activity by which the meaning of the gospel becomes articulate as the illumination of the world, and by which the meaning that men succeed in making of themselves and their experience is transformed to become a disclosure of that meaning of meaning that we call God.

One might object at this point that it is nonsense to deny that theology is an academic discipline, given that there are, whether one likes it or not, 'professional' theologians, degrees in theology, theological journals and so on. I would reply that these 'theological disciplines' which we find practised in the universities are properly theological not because they employ rational, coherent and critical modes of discourse, but because such forms of discourse, especially philosophy and history, have been important ways in which man has attempted to interpret his experience, and therefore are potentially theological. It follows that the relationship between theology and sociology within our universities will often be that between a philosophical or historical perspective that has been transformed in the light of the gospel and a sociology which has not been so transformed. But there is no reason why sociology itself should not provide an alternative locus for the encounter of gospel and world. One must remember, however, that there are all sorts of other less academic ways in which men seek to make sense of their experience, through poetry, drama, painting, music, etc., and any of these activities are potentially theological in that the meaning they make is capable of disclosing that most ultimate depth of meaning which we believe was revealed in the life, death and resurrection of Jesus Christ. I would not be happy with any definition of theology that excluded, for example, the poems of St John of the Cross, which are the secular love songs he heard outside his prison walls transformed in the light of the gospel.

One might also protest that if one identifies theology as an essentially creative praxis, then one is excluding from the fold all those theologians who write the boring humdrum books that fill the shelves of our theological libraries. I would reply that they can be accepted as genuine theologians only in the sense that they perpetuate or extend some original and creative theological insight. Thus the theological perspectives of Thomas, Luther, Barth, etc., will continue to be explored by their disciples, but many of these disciples will only be creative by virtue of some sort of participation in the original, founding, creative praxis of their masters.

Having made those provisos, I would still wish to assert that theology is, in itself, neither an explanation of the world, nor a perspective, nor a methodology. But the fact still remains that theologians make theological statements. In what sense may sociology be said to explain these statements? Theological statements are, after all, examples of language, and one of the functions of sociology is to explain the relationship between social structures and language. Could sociology therefore demonstrate that theological statements are merely epiphenomenal, the products of patterns of social interaction? Theology may not fear sociology as a rival, but might not sociology relativize theology out of existence?

If theology is the attempt to make sense of the gospel and the world in the mutually illuminating moment of their encounter, then the limitations of sociological explanation will be determined by the extent to which sociology can be held to explain man's attempts to make sense creatively of himself and the world. Theology is as inexplicable in sociological terms as those other activities that man practises when he attempts to explore and establish the meaning of his existence, whether through philosophy, poetry, drama or even sociology! A sociologist who explores the relationship between social structures and language will misunderstand the limitations of the explanations that he proposes if he misconceives the relationship between language and meaning.

A poem or a piece of theology or a play is meaningful not merely in virtue of being an example of a particular language but because of what it *does* with that language. *Hamlet*, for instance, is certainly significant and meaningful as an example of Elizabethan English. If there had not been such a thing as Elizabethan English then there could never have been that play which we call *Hamlet*. A sociologist could establish a relationship between that language and the structures of Elizabethan society, and in that sense he could be said to 'explain' *Hamlet*. But of course this play is not merely an instance of Elizabethan English but a creative use of it. It stretches the language in all sorts of unaccustomed ways, uses metaphors and analogies and poetically engenders new meaning in a way that a knowledge of Elizabethan English would not enable one to anticipate. Therein lies the limitations of sociological explanation confronted with any creative praxis, including theology.

I shall illustrate my thesis by looking at the work of one social theorist, Peter Berger, who does misconceive the relationship between language and meaning and who therefore, I believe, misrepresents the relationship between sociological explanation and theology. It is true that he is primarily concerned not with theology but with religion, but it is clear that he believes that his sort of explanation would apply to theology itself, particularly when he is considering the question of theodicy.

Throughout his book *The Sacred Canopy* Berger makes an

explicit identification between meaning and order or *nomos*. The meaning that man projects upon the universe, the order that he establishes, is always threatened by collapse and potential chaos because of the inability of any order to organize the whole of human experience. Man therefore requires religion to legitimize this projected order, this *nomos*, by claiming that it is inevitable and sacred.

Religion legitimates so effectively because it relates the precarious reality constructions of empirical societies with ultimate reality. The tenuous realities of the social world are grounded in the sacred *realissimum*, which by definition is beyond the contingencies of human meanings and human activity.[5]

Berger therefore maintains that religion is inherently a conservative force, since its function is to consecrate the *status quo*. If the task of religion, and so of theology, is to bestow or reveal some ultimate meaning, and if meaning is the order that society projects upon the universe, then religion cannot but be seen as the consecration of the structures of society.

Can we really be satisfied with such a definition of meaning? Is meaning simply equatable with order? Berger tells us that animals live in perfectly ordered worlds determined by their instinctual structures. Does this mean that the mouse rejoices in a plenitude of meaning that man can never hope to enjoy? On the contrary, I believe that man is only driven to question the meaning of anything and everything because he finds himself at the intersection of many orders, employing many languages, playing many roles. It is the plurality of *nomoi* that provokes the question of meaning. The mouse could never ask about the meaning of being a mouse because he could never be anything else. Because the structures and order of its life are unalterably given, the question of meaning could not arise. Now sociology can demonstrate the relationship between social structures and the various languages that are employed within a society, but it cannot explain the creative interpretations that man makes of his experience when he finds himself at the point of intersection of different roles and discourses. It is precisely at these moments that men find themselves driven to articulate their self-understanding, whether in terms of philosophy, theology or poetry, not through the affirmation of the given orders of meaning but rather through the evocation of an order that cannot be fully stated. If theology, or indeed any other creative praxis, simply legitimized society with all its contradictions and conflicts then it would not give meaning to man's experience. It would simply rule out the question of meaning and make man's experience of meaninglessness appear to be inevitable.

When Berger is considering the role of theology as theodicy, he appeals to the book of Job. But in Job the sufferings of the innocent man are never legitimized by the articulation of an explicit overarching *nomos* in which they are given meaning. These sufferings only make sense in terms of an order, 'the wisdom of God', which can never be made explicit, merely glimpsed. In the final moment of vision, Job confesses: 'I have heard of thee by the hearing of the ear, but now my eye sees thee: therefore I despise myself and repent in dust and ashes.'[6] Berger cites only the second half of Job's confession and claims it as evidence that Job's sufferings are justified by his sinfulness. This is a misinterpretation of the whole book. Job suffers because he and his companions have absolutized a *nomos*, the wisdom tradition, which is unable to interpret his experience and which therefore drives him to accuse God. He only comes to understanding in that vision of God, which explains nothing. The book of Job is not an example of the legitimization of suffering by the affirmation of a *nomos* which confirms the structures of society. It demonstrates the way in which our *nomoi* break down in their attempts to explain. Job passes from explanation to understanding in a moment of vision – from theory to *theoria*.

Berger himself is unable to sustain this oversimple identification of meaning and order. In the second half of the book he operates with an alternative and implicit definition of meaning which might be described as 'self-awareness'. All true knowledge is knowledge of oneself. The ultimate truth is the truth of man himself. This becomes particularly evident in Berger's interpretation of the relationship between religion and alienation. He defines alienation as 'the process whereby the dialectical relationship between the individual and his world is lost to consciousness. The individual "forgets" that this world was and continues to be co-produced by him.'[7] Religion is an alienating force because, by consecrating the meaningful order that man projects upon the universe, it conceals from man the fact that order derives from himself. Thus it induces a 'false consciousness'. The implication is that true salvation, the return to 'true consciousness', is achieved in that moment in which man becomes aware of himself as the origin of the meaningful order that he has projected. The same *nomos* which in the first part of the book was identified with meaning is here claimed to be 'the alien', that which stands between man and true self-awareness. I believe that the plot or play of Berger's book hinges upon the uneasy and shifting relationship between these two definitions of meaning as order and as self-awareness. Meaning as order must always seek to establish itself as total and all-embracing; meaning as self-awareness must always attempt to undermine the facticity and giveness of the projected order. Of course religion and theology have to be identified with meaning as order, since the alternative definition excludes the knowledge of anything other than man himself.

I have attempted this analysis of Berger's text in order to illustrate my thesis that man's attempts to make sense of his experience always involve a creative praxis, in this case involving the play between two definitions of meaning. Sociology can demonstrate the relationship between social structures and forms of language, but man's search for meaning involves an irreducible creativity which it cannot explain. Berger invites us to relativize the relativizers. It would be amusing to do just that and attempt a sociological analysis of *The Sacred Canopy*. Berger was born in Vienna in 1929 and came to America when he was seventeen. His formative years were spent in a highly structured society threatened by *anomie*. He then experienced the transition to a far more fluid, mobile and individualistic society with a different value system and a different conception of meaning. It would be tempting to explain this text as a product of the experience of these two societies, a conversation between a Viennese past and an American present. My thesis is that even if we did produce a convincing sociological analysis of the text we would still have failed to explain what he had done with these experiences. We could analyze what he said in terms of the different social structures in which he had been formed, but we could not explain his creative attempt to make sense of this complex experience. One may either participate in it as an event of meaning or not. Even one's relativizing of the relativizers is limited.

On 30 June 1860, when Wilberforce, the Bishop of Oxford, attempted to refute Darwinism during his confrontation with Huxley in the University Museum, he defined man as *homo poeticus*. Even though I do not agree with Wilberforce's conclusions, I believe that one should justify theology, and indeed any other creative praxis, in the face of any attempt at sociological reductionism, by an appeal to man as 'poetic' or creative. Man is the one who is capable of new meaning. This novelty is achieved through what Eliot called 'the intolerable wrestle with words', through metaphor and analogy, through the creative interplay of different modes of discourse. Any such discourse can be said to be 'theological' when the meaning that it generates is claimed to be revelatory of the meaning of meaning that we call God, when this new meaning is accepted as a disclosure of 'the transcendent novelty of the God who creates, liberates and renews'.[8]

Having suggested what are, I believe, the limitations of the sociological explanation of religious phenomena and of theology, I shall now attempt to say why, nevertheless, I believe sociology to be potentially a very useful and liberating discipline for the theologian. In *A Rumour of Angels*, Berger tells us that 'while other analytical disciplines free us from the dead weight of the past, sociology frees us from the tyranny of the present'.[9] I think that sociology can free the theologian from the tyranny of the past as well. By showing how the theological statements of his tradition are in fact formulated in languages that reflect the social structures of quite different societies, the sociologist can free the theological from the temptation merely to repeat what has been said before. Once the theologian has been brought to see how the language that is used is a human product, the function of particular patterns of social interaction, then he is liberated from naive biblical or dogmatic literalism. Of course, one hopes that this initial distancing of the text is just the first step towards a more profound re-appropriation. But once he has come to discern the strangeness of the language, as the product of an alien way of life, then he might be able to see how it is more than that: that it is a creative and revelatory use of that language. He must let the text be drawn far from him if he is to come close to it again and participate in it as an event of meaning, just as in one's ordinary experience of human relationships one must sometimes discover how different someone is from oneself before one can rediscover a unity at a more profound depth of one's humanity.

Let us take the example of the Chalcedonian Definition. All too often Roman Catholic theologians have given up bibilical fundamentalism, only to cling all the more firmly to dogmatic literalism. But one can only discover a proper loyalty to the Chalcedonian Definition if one has come to understand it not as an eternal solution to the 'problem' of the person of Christ but as an attempt to evoke the mystery of his person through the creative interplay of two quite different theological languages, Alexandrian and Antiochean. These two theological languages, in turn, must be understood as reflecting the two quite different societies that produced them; Alexandria with its philosophical tradition and history of autocratic government, and Antioch with its tradition of rhetoric and democracy. It is only when one has distanced oneself from the text through some such sociological analysis that one can reappropriate the Definition as a subtle and profound attempt to lead one into the mystery of Christ's person through the mutual qualification of these different discourses. One has to lose the text in order to rediscover it as poetic, creative and deeply theological, and thus come to see what loyalty to its insights might demand. The sociologist can liberate the theologian by helping him to let go.

There appear, then, to be two ways in which theology and sociology might relate. First of all, the sociological exploration of the relationship between language and social structures can liberate the theologian from a false understanding of his own tradition. Second, the theologian should recognize that sociology is not merely explanatory. It is one valid way in which man attempts to make sense of himself and his experience. And so sociology can itself provide a locus for the encounter of gospel and world. This encounter would take place not through the theologian importing a particular 'theological perspective', but rather by the internal transformation of sociology itself.

Notes

1   Evans-Pritchard, E.E. *Witchcraft, Oracles and Magic among the Azande* (Oxford, 1937) p. 72.
2   Wiles, M.F. 'Does Christianity Rest on a Mistake?' in S.W. Sykes and J.P. Clayton (eds.) *Christ, Faith and History* (London, 1972) p. 8.
3   Gill, R. *The Social Context of Theology* (London & Oxford, 1975) p. 134.
4   Ernst, C. 'Theological Methodology' in Karl Rahner *et al.* (ed.) *Sacramentum Mundi*, English translation Vol. 6, (London & New York) p. 218.
5   Berger, P.L. *The Sacred Canopy* (New York, 1967); Eng. edn. *The Social Reality of Religion* (Harmondsworth) p. 41.
6   Job 42: 5f. (RSV tr.)
7   Berger, *op. cit.* p. 92.
8   Ernst, C. *The Theology of Grace* (Cork, 1974) p. 80.
9   Berger, P.L. *A Rumour of Angels* (New York, 1968); Eng. edn. (Harmondsworth) p. 62.

Chapter 10

THEOLOGY AND SOCIOLOGY: WHAT POINT IS THERE IN KEEPING THE DISTINCTION?

Antoine Lion

THE debate between theology and sociology in France over the last twenty years or so has been lively, and its history, characterized by polemics, realignments, reciprocal vetoes and laborious attempts at reconciliation, has yet to be written. Much has been said on the respective scope of these two branches of knowledge, on their particular approaches, their possible areas of agreement and their insurmountable differences of opinion.

The question I have taken as a title is not intended to suggest in any way that the debate has been a vain one. My question would be provocative if it was not immediately placed in its precise context, which is that of marxist Christians in France in the past few years. I shall define below which groups of marxist Christians I include under this designation: they will not, incidentally, be restricted uniquely to the 'Marxist Christian Movement' founded in 1975. It will be seen that although only an extremely limited minority of French Christians are concerned, their influence cannot be disregarded.

My argument is as follows: for such Christians the function traditionally carried out by theology is now exercised by other intellectual disciplines, namely sociology and, in a wider sense, the humanities. This is to say that, *for such Christians*, the 'theology – sociology debate' is defunct, relegated to the status of an historical fact, in just the same way – and this is not unconnected – that the ecumenical debate between Catholics and Protestants is no longer of interest to them, since for these groups this distinction has also ceased to be relevant.

I shall begin with a number of reflections on the social function of theology. Then, *à propos* the transformations which French Christianity has undergone, I shall give a brief outline of the Christian groups to which I am referring. After this, I shall be in a position to proceed with my argument and to examine two examples of its application.

A final world of clarification on my own standpoint. It is my intention to view this topic as a 'sociologist' and not as a 'theologian'. I do not claim to be neutral, for I believe this to be neither possible nor desirable, but I have remained on the outside as regards the position of the believer and the language of religion.

Furthermore, the following reflections inevitably have a provisional quality about them; we are far from the end of the discussion.

The social function of the theologian

Theology, like sociology, is a whole series of writings which generate patterns of thought and, as the case may be, practices. The sociological approach to these writings supposes that they be considered as social products and that one can therefore trace the way back from these texts to their authors and the conditions in which they were written. This is why I intend to discuss the *theologian* rather than *theology*.[1]

In the history of Christianity, from the time of John the Divine, author of the fourth gospel, the term theologian can be said to encompass a great variety of people: 'Church Fathers', who were the authors of various texts (treatises, letters, sermons, biblical commentaries), and who often bore ecclesiastical responsibilities; contemplatives, in the Middle Ages particularly, and 'doctors', who aimed to integrate all religious knowledge. From the time of the Council of Trent, in Roman Catholicism, the figure of the guardian and guarantor of orthodoxy emerged, who provided the teachings destined for use by those responsible for the perpetuation of the forms and traditions of the institution (in the seminaries), or who acted as counsellor to the ecclesiastical authorities (such as expert advisor to the Second Vatican Council for instance).

For our purposes here, I shall define the theologian as the author of a reasoned interpretation of the practices and beliefs of a Christian group, founded on the personal adherence ('faith') of the author to this body of practices and beliefs, an adherence which the group acknowledges to be legitimate. More succinctly, I shall define him as the author of a reasoned and authorized interpretation of the practices and beliefs of the group to which he belongs.

My initial premise is therefore that the theologian is connected to a structured group, in the first place by personal membership of this group, for a discussion of practices and beliefs from the outside is not theology.[2] The recognition the group accords to the discussion, normally through tacit or explicit approval of the ecclesiastical authority, also constitutes this connection. If there is no such recognition, because the theologian is disowned by his church, he ceases to exercise a theological function (Loisy, for example). Lastly, let me make it plain that I am dealing with reasoned discourse, and that the discourse of the mystical authors, which operates within a different social logic, can therefore be excluded.

The function of the theologian is explained by the role played by collective memory in the religious groups. Any social group which intends to survive must develop its own collective memory; this anchors the present in a historical context and ensures that the group has a future. In so far as it is constituted by the group, this memory is also a constituent. It is, in addition, the reservoir of social forces that Durkheim attributed too exclusively to the collective conscience. This memory varies with the situations in which the group finds itself in order that it may respond to its current interests, and, in particular, so that it may provide an ideological justification for these situations to the advantage of the dominant faction. It transforms the materials provided by history, eliminating some, inflating the importance of others and is able, if necessary, to invent new material.[3]

A religious group relies upon its memory more than do other groups. A body of original events associated with a 'founder' is the common reference point of its members. In the case of Christianity, the liturgy, sermons, catecheses etc. form the corpus which maintains its knowledge and its memory, and thereby also its common culture. As in all great religions, once the effervescence of the first believers ('the Pentecost', which lends itself excellently to an interpretation in Durkheimian terms) wore off, the original events generated a profusion of interpretations both theoretical and also based on personal experience, according to the social and cultural diversity of the groups which had been the object of Christian preaching. In order to survive and to become unified, at least partially, the Christians had to ensure that knowledge of the founding experience was passed down to later generations. The development and codification of the memory, which was the task of the first leading churchmen, was ultimately entrusted to specialists, and involved the evaluation of the texts recognized to be canonical, the provision of a commentary on the selection of these texts, and the production of new reference texts ('symbols', the first formulations of dogma). A gradual accumulation of texts which accompany the original work then takes place.

The relationship between Christianity and the Bible is a complex one which has been analyzed in detail by Deconchy.[4] The basic dialectic, 'Christianity creates the Bible; the Bible creates Christianity', implies other dialectical relationships, in particular the one Deconchy terms: 'reverence and prudence': 'the Bible says everything but, on that count, it can also be made to say everything and must therefore be used with caution'. Or again: 'everything that should be believed is in the Bible, but not everything in the Bible should be believed'. In fact, the Bible conceals forces which can be subversive: the movements of religious protest or of those which are at variance with the churches which have based themselves upon the Bible are numerous. '[The Church] makes a cult of the Bible because it is the source and origin of its belief. On the other hand, [it] mistrusts the Bible because the biblical text does not possess that degree of technicality which alone could settle questions of adherence and orthodoxy, and because the text frequently reports facts which challenge orthodox social regulations'. (Deconchy p. 255)

A Christian group which is aiming at orthodoxy (and thereby even at orthopraxis) cannot therefore avoid exerting some control over the Bible. Its leaders may even restrict the access of the majority of believers to it through a linguistic barrier, such as the Catholic ban on translations of the Bible into the vernacular. When this was no longer culturally possible, various barriers were erected round the text to regulate access to it: authorized commentaries 'approved by the Holy See', obligatory notes, liturgical settings, and the filtering of lectionaries. To guarantee this protection a body of trusted experts grew up – the biblical scholars.

Apart from safeguarding the founding text they also carried out the task of authorizing all theological publications. An institution must respond to the various social demands which come from its own particular group. It is the task of the theologians to provide such a response and this requires them to find support in the Scriptures. It is with this end in view that they draw upon the Bible.[5] 'The ancient myths and texts are transformed into signifiers with partially new meanings in so far as they have sprung from new social practice. This has been achieved by elaborate and extensive tinkering', writes Casanova.[6] The term 'tinkering' is used here in the sense Lévi-Strauss employs it in *La Pensée sauvage*,[7] that is to say an infinite rearrangement of a finite stock of material by means of various adjustments and combinations for the purpose of achieving combinations which fulfil new requirements. This indicates the other function of the biblical scholar: he provides the theologians of his church with material from the Scriptures which, as a result of his preparatory work is presented in usable form. It is he who coaxes 'biblical facts' to serve the intellectual – or, for that matter ritual – constructs required by the social situation of his church.

What has just been said of the biblical scholar can be extended to cover the theologian. As his training makes him an expert on religious memory, the group to which he belongs assigns a double 'theological task' to him. First of all, he is to explain and make accessible the corpus of texts received from tradition, controlling authorized interpretations, and placing them at the disposal of the ideological needs of the group; similarly, he is to explain traditional rites and practices. Second, he is to examine, in the light of the ideas thus elucidated, questions raised by the social practice of the institution and its members (for instance, the modifications imposed upon the Church) and show that the solutions arrived at are consistent with the data of tradition.

The functions of the theologian are perhaps even more vital for the churches today than in the past, for they no longer possess any means of exercising coercion over practices and beliefs. Now, the only way they can maintain their appeal is by indicating the objective interest they represent for the public, in other words, by showing that they are in line with its social demands. The theologian is thus called upon to make membership of the Church desirable (or rather to provide those responsible for the members and for increasing their numbers with the means of achieving this). As Legendre remarks when speaking of the medieval religious institution, what matters is to 'maintain the belief of its subjects' (unless it has a missionary aim which is nowadays scarcely to be found outside the sects), and the best way of doing this is to 'train people to love Power'.[8]

The ecclesiastical apparatus provides theologians with the means they require to carry out these functions, such as protracted university training, material upkeep, the tools of intellectual work. In exchange for the services he provides, the theologian expects certain rewards in return: recognition of the monopoly of authorized interpreters, titles, congregations, careers, and the instruments for disseminating ideas.

It is self-evident that in part the theologian's work helps to bring about the (religious) legitimacy of his own writings. The fact that he produces meanings places the theologian in a situation of power; not that he is himself the origin of that power, for it is only delegated to him by the authority which recognizes him as a theologian. For an analysis of the relations between the theologian and his church, we can take up Bourdieu's masterly comment on the relations between the academic and the university: 'the cunning logic of the university system by which the institution induces the teacher to serve the institution by enabling him to make the institution serve him, ultimately serves a function of social conservation which is not a feature of the rationale underlying the university system and which in any case it cannot acknolwedge'.[9] As we know, it is the concept of 'symbolical violence' that Bourdieu uses to indicate the power under discussion, in other words, 'any power which succeeds in imposing meanings and in imposing them as legitimate by concealing the presence of force in its relations which forms the basis of its strength'. The force referred to here is that which permits a fraction of the members of the Church to dominate the group as a whole.

In the Roman Catholic Church the status of the men who play this
role is clearly defined; they are the clerics situated within the
ecclesiastical apparatus and who are dependent upon it. In particular, as they themselves have been trained by the system, they, also,
are qualified to carry out the task of training, the institution necessarily making certain it has a monopoly over the provision of people
entrusted with this task. To quote Bourdieu again on the subject of
the university teachers: 'these agents tend to ensure the reproduction of their own value by ensuring the reproduction of the market
on which they have their value'.[10]

This knowledge, which is produced by clerics and for clerics, and
which reaches the majority of the 'faithful' only through various
'pastoral' mediations, has therefore, to the advantage of the clerics,
been based upon dispossessing the laymen of the opportunity to
comprehend practices and beliefs for themselves. It is not my belief
that the recent development of instances of the spread of 'theological competence' among laymen really alters this state of affairs.
Leconte and Rousseau have adequately demonstrated that, when
they do this, 'theologians, ceasing to find in the clergy a satisfactory
or a sufficiently gratifying social base, develop a strategy of recon-
quest'.[11] The relative distribution of knowledge in which they have
been involved would in fact serve to reinsure their power by creating a new social demand for them.[12] The possession of a certain
amount of theological knowledge by laymen would in fact reinforce
the virtual monopoly of the training, which lies in the hands of
theologians who are clerics, and which is a monopoly almost as
rigidly maintained in Roman Catholicism as that which exists in the
practice of the liturgy.[13]

What has been said so far raises the following problem: if every
Christian group requires a theological function which ensures that
there is a clear link between its tradition and its social practice, and
if the theologian we have described belongs to a Christian group
with a religious structure, brought together by a body of common
beliefs and unified by an ecclesiastical authority, how is the theological function taken care of in Christian groups which exist outside
any such structure? But before this can be answered, these groups
must be described.

The marxist Christians: Christians without a church

The groups we shall examine are part of a general proliferation of
different styles of Christian practice which has taken place in France
recently and which is linked with a decline in the social power of the
ecclesiastical institution.[14] It is not simply its influence over society
as a whole which is on the decline and which is distinguished by the

progressive loss of control on the part of the Church of numerous areas of social life – schools, universities, welfare work, the law – but it is the role of the Church in the control of Christian experience itself which has also declined.

Rather than attempting to present an overall picture of the crisis which the ecclesiastical institution and religious beliefs are facing in France, I shall restrict myself to three aspects of it. The first of these is the loss of the power of the Church to confer meaning on the world. In French culture Catholicism has long had a dominant influence on the formation of the general view of reality. Today it is no more than a fragment of contemporary culture and has been extensively devalued by other aspects of that culture. For believers themselves the Church's pronouncements have ceased to be the primary source for the understanding of the world. The second aspect is the loss of the power of the Church to direct social practices. Now bereft of a large number of its institutional links, the Church is witnessing a decline in its influence on French behaviour. Its rites are losing their appeal. This is discernible in the decline of church attendance and the decrease in the practice of *rites de passage* such as baptism, first communion, church marriages and funerals. Its codes of value are less and less respected even by the faithful. The crisis following the publication of the papal encyclical on birth control, *Humanae Vitae,* in 1968, showed that sexual practices were not subject to the injunctions of the magisterium any more than were the revolutions of the planets at the time of Galileo. The third aspect of the crisis is the loss of the prerogative to be the exclusive spokesman on the subject of God. Over recent centuries the Church has lost its acknowledged right to speak in various fields of knowledge which have become secular; now it is in their own domain that religious institutions are witnessing the disappearance of their monopoly over the word. A type of popularization of religions within the social sciences has helped to make the pronouncements of the churches relative. They have even unintentionally become the providers of meanings for socity as a whole. As Michel de Certeau[15] puts it:

Like those majestic ruins from which stones are plundered for the construction of other buildings, in our modern societies Chrisianity has become the supplier of a vocabulary, a treasure trove of symbols, signs and practices put to use again elsewhere. Each person uses them as he sees fit and without the ecclesiastical authority being able to oversee the manner in which they are distributed or provide its own definition of their meaning.

These factors represent some of the underlying causes for the diversification of Christian practice. Whereas certain schisms are occurring within the Catholic system of references (for instance, the so-called 'Lefebvre affair', which can be seen as the reaction of sections of society, whose importance is currently on the decline owing to the fact that the ecclesiastical apparatus, which it more or less controlled, now serves the interest of other sections of society), and whereas the charismatic movement has by and large succeeded in holding its ground in the framework of orthodoxy, numerous fairly unspectacular breaches are taking place through gradual abandonment of membership of the Church.

On the whole such individuals are progressively losing their explicit Christian reference. But in some sections of society a continued interest in Christianity can be observed even though it does not involve religious intermediaries. A new division, not foreseen by the theological movements based upon the distinction between faith and religion, which were fashionable in the 1960s, is taking place between faith and religious practice. The latter can no longer be regarded as an indicator of belief in Christianity as it was in the halcyon days of 'religious sociology'. The crisis in mediation is a function of a more general movement towards the abolition of intermediaries. Immediacy is one of the characteristics of our culture.

While these breakaway groups often involve only a few people, a large number of groups is emerging which are endowed with more or less loose links with the institutional Church. One of the criteria of this link is whether there is a sacerdotal ministry within the group. When this is no longer the case, the expression 'Christians without a church' can, at least within the context of French culture, justifiably be used. One is also obliged to speak of several forms of Christianity rather than one.

It is one of these forms of Christianity without a church that we shall discuss and which will serve as the testing ground for our hypothesis. It involves groups with the two following characteristics. First, they are united by the common political practice of their members who belong to the leftist tendencies associated with remarkable political, social and cultural eruptions of May 1968. Their theoretical reference is marxism as it is interpreted in such circles. And second, they belong to the Christian frame of reference through a complex relationship of criticism and reinterpretation which I shall describe below.

In the post-1968 period, a certain number of groups increasingly distanced themselves from the ecclesiastical hierarchies. At several national meetings between 1970 and 1974 there was evidence, at one and the same time, of a constant uncertainty as to the meaning of their Christian reference (debates on the specific nature of the Christian), and the growing emergence of a political reference which caused tensions. If in fact all the participants declared themselves to be 'leftists', they were nevertheless affected by the split between the Union of the Left and the extreme Left which characterized the French Left at that time.

During the last of these meetings, attended by Christian 'communes' at Dijon in June 1974, one group decided to establish another kind of grouping on a different basis. In the belief that the debate on Christianity was becoming bogged down, it was agreed that the unifying factor would no longer be the Christian reference but political practice. A deliberate shift of opinion was occurring. A meeting of Christians with common political references was turning into a meeting of political militants with common Christian references. It also appeared that such political commitment would no longer be experienced as a kind of consequence of the Christian reference, but, on the contrary, that the attention given to Christianity would be one of the components of the political commitment – in the wide sense – of the participants.

Two meetings (at Chevilly-Larue on the outskirts of the capital in October 1974 and in Paris in January 1975) led to the creation of a new movement which called itself 'marxist Christians'. In Ocober, discussion centred exclusively upon confirming the agreement on the political commitment and views of the participants, the Christian reference being taken as a foregone conclusion to be discussed in detail only at a later date. The movement provided itself with a journal, originally a Protestant monthly publication which had been in existence for a long time and which held similar views, namely *Cité Nouvelle* (current circulation 2,000, with some 1,000 subscribers). Another journal, *La Lettre*, of Catholic origin (current circulation between 3,000 and 3,500, with 2,500 subscribers), soon took up a similar standpoint. And *Cité Nouvelle-Midi*, a regional periodical with a small circulation, is published in Marseilles. Groups have formed in several large towns. With a few exceptions, they have evinced only restricted activity. Elsewhere there are various groups connected with *La Lettre*, which study the Bible. These are more numerous, and have established themselves since 1975. Some hold extensive discussion groups during the holidays.

What we mean by marxist Christians in this context is all those who are included within these trends, and who often have some local common denominator. One might take as the criterion the regular perusal of one of the periodicals mentioned and concrete evidence that the individual subscribes to the ideology in question. No study has been made of these people. On the whole, it would appear that the majority of those who belong to it are of the lower middle class and are usually involved in professional activity of a social kind, such as teachers or social workers. These are socio-professional jobs which foster a strong sensitivity to cultural change and an aptitude for reflecting upon society as well as political commitment. All members of this group have a Christian past one way or another, and they include within their number some priests and pastors. All the groups are urban. They probably contain few people under the age of twenty-five.

It is clear that even if we are going far outside the framework of the marxist Christian Movement properly speaking, the social area in which we are interested involves only very small numbers. When one considers its restricted base, the image of the marxist Christians in the religious arena at present seems striking. There is scarcely a study on Christianity in France, whether in the press or in book forh, which does not include them, and the frequency with which these references appear would seem to be out of proportion with the size of the movement. The title 'marxist Christians', with its association of two terms frequently considered incompatible, has itself often seemed provocative. Whereas marxists and Christians have met in numerous discussions (most frequently among intellectuals), and whereas many works have discussed the dialogue between these two groups, what is proposed here is the possibility that Christians might openly declare themselves to be marxists.

This deliberate interaction was not completely novel, but it bore a novel emphasis. Being marxists, these Christians meant to apply to Christianity the analytical tools and the modes of action associated with their political reference. A text for internal usage accepted at Chevilly-Larue declared: 'We are all determined to fight against the Church as an ideological apparatus against the State; this apparatus constitutes one of the instruments of the ideological hegemony of the ruling class. We are fighting not only the ecclesiastical structure and how it acts, but also *the oppressive and alienating ideological representations* which are conveyed by Christianity.' The words underlined are an amendment of a first draft that read '. . . all ideological representations . . .' The amendment indicated that certain 'representations conveyed by Christianity' may not be alienating and may even be used in a revolutionary type of action. The concrete achievements were more limited than these declarations lead one to expect, including intervention in the problem of legalized abortion, a demonstration of the ambiguities within the government's policy on charities, based on Christian values, and support for the Christians on the left in the Portuguese revolution of 1975. Their national activities have become less frequent, for certain specific problems have occupied their attention in local areas (the question of the free school in Brittany, for example). Political breaks with official Christianity and its influence necessarily led to a criticism of the ecclesiastical institution, yet the marxist Christians, have seldom acted directly against the religious establishment.

Instead, the difficulty of developing an original political line which preserves the specific character of the marxist Christians and their refusal to become directly invovled in ecclesiastical problems have gradually led them to lend increasing importance to another dimension of their activity, to theological work.

Marxist practice and theological function

We have seen that in the groups we have examined it was the political dimension which was stressed originally. In the text from Chevilly-Larue quoted above, the account of the political standpoints occupied a page. The question of the Christian reference was discussed subsequently in a mere three lines: 'Research on faith forms part of our aims: no profession of faith whatever is required *a priori* for joining the struggle by which we are united.'

The movement soon realized that the problem could not be treated in such a perfunctory way. No sooner was their initial political agreement established than the old question which it had presumed settled arose again: in what respect did the fact of being a Christian determine common political affiliations? And what did it mean therefore to be a Christian? In short, the marxist Christians witnessed a renewal of their need for a theological function in the sense we have used it here, namely, an evaluation of the tradition and consistency with the social practices of the group. This requirement is still associated with the movement, as is indicated for example by the following text which occupied a prominent position in the June 1977 edition of *Cité Nouvelle* and which, incidentally, comes from the corresponding movement in Italy:

to fulfil our role, we must subject ourselves to further questioning and cast off all our old clothing in favour of new, not only the old forms of political action but also the old ways of being Christians. We must firmly establish what it means for us to be Christians unless we are to allow this term to become a mere cultural or historical reference (whether personal or collective), or the token of those who are simply interested in Catholic affairs. We must know what to say to comrades who ask us sincerely what we believe in or what it means to have the faith . . .[16]

In terms studded with Christian references, it does indeed indicate a need for theology.

This question cannot be avoided by those who mean to maintain the link between Christianity and marxism. In fact, those who have not been concerned to do so have ultimately become totally involved in practical politics and therefore lie outside the area which interests us. Although, literally, marxist Christians means Christians (subject) who are marxists (predicate), for all those who withdraw from the movement it is the predicate which gets the best of it. In the face of the practical evidence that this represents, the Christian reference fades into the background. The lack of theology is therefore at one and the same time the token and the cause of the loss of credibility which this form of Christianity has suffered.

If theological work is therefore patently essential for the survival of the movement, it remains to be seen what its perspectives are. In the 1976 text already quoted, the movement reached an agreed definition of these aims and I propose to cite it at some length:

On a third level, it is not merely the attitudes or even the structure of the institution which are called into question, but the basic facts of faith transmitted and interpreted by the institution: 'the core of faith'. A link emerges between a certain 'creed' and certain structures of the churches, maintenance of these structures being inseparably linked with the need to reaffirm the intangible nature of this 'creed'. Even the interpretation of the Bible and the tradition seems to be marked by the class character of the social groups and institutions which transmit it: it is a class interpretation, a partisan interpretation. The image of Jesus and of God, the basic concepts of dogma, thereby lose their initial innocence and appear also to be the objects of a necessary and radical criticism. Recent works on the Bible, on liturgical language, and on sin, have by means of a 'materialistic' reading shown up the partisan nature of all statements concerning faith, all ecclesiastical pronouncements and all religious language.

This attitude is characterised at one and the same time by radical criticism of the religious ideology transmitted by the churches or functioning outside them and a rigorous, impassioned investigation of the texts of the Old and New Testaments and the tradition, tending both to show up their contradictions and to bring out what meaning they may have for contemporary revolutionary struggles. This twofold operation of *radical criticism and reappropriation* is generally associated with the sort of radical, revolutionary politics which challenge social relations as a whole.[17]

This text requires some comment. The work of criticism and reappropriation is based upon a theory which stems from practice. The marxist Christians confirm this: 'It is only from a position within this political practice that we can justifiably ask: what do we mean by the word "Christian"?'[18] One of the reference texts used by these movements and which emerged from the assembly of Christians for Socialism at Santiago in Chile in April 1972 had already declared that: 'it should not be thought that the specific character of the Christian contribution precedes revolutionary praxis and that the Christian brings this with him when he engages in the revolutionary struggle. In fact it is during this struggle that his faith reveals that it is able to make contributions that neither he nor anyone else could have predicted from the outside.'[19] It is in fact the political commitment of the marxist Christians which has led them to restore a theological function for which at one time they had thought they had no further use. It was because they were undertaking a radical critique of religious ideology on several fronts that they became involved in a critique of Christianity itself. It was also because the interpretations of the Bible made by theologians and transmitted by the institutional channels (the pastoral and the catechesis) had no connection with their political involvement and even encouraged contrary activity, that they raised the question of new interpretations of the sources. They sought a theory validated by practice.

In his analysis of our culture, Pastor Dumas notes that 'the word truth has been replaced by the word verification'.[20] The criteria for the evaluation of a theory are no longer based on the idealistic distinction between true and false, but on the practice the theory calls forth. The point of reference here is Marx's second thesis on Feuerbach: 'It is in practice that man must prove the truth, that is to say the reality and the power, the practical side of his thought. Consideration of the reality or unreality of thought, independent of practice, is purely academic.'[21]

The tool required for this theoretical formulation is marxism, as the two previous remarks show. Yet one can no more speak of one form of 'marxism' than one can of 'Christianity'. The criticisms these movements have already begun to level at religious dogmatism have made them wary of all dogmatic marxism. In other respects it is appropriate to derive support from theorists who recognize the specific nature of religious phenomena and who do not reduce them to a reflection of the structures. Casanova, for instance, writes that 'social determinants can only become religious determinants if they are reinterpreted according to the demands of the specific logic of the theological areas previously in existence'.[22] This general theoretical reference does not exclude at all the consideration of other, non-marxist approaches. The emergence of a 'continent of desire' in contemporary thought is scarcely even considered by the marxist Christians.

Lastly, the manner in which theoretical reflections are produced, as well as the sympathies of their authors, are always subject to scrutiny both by the authors themselves and by those who receive their texts. Intellectual specialization, which was previously recognized to be necessary, is in process of being excluded, and the debate on the availability of research to all is brought up again and again. The clerical monopoly known to everyone in France with a Christian past, whether they have been clerics or not, places marxist Christians on their guard against any suppression of knowledge by new clerics.

It is clear from this point what criticism can be levelled at theology as we have defined it above, that is, in the context of the contemporary French situation. Its pronouncements are drawn up independently of praxis, without reference to the presuppositions it makes and the conditions in which it is produced, which reveals the apparent innocence of this logocentrism for what is is. The social context of such non-critical pronouncement places it on an ideological level, in keeping with the social interests of the institution which requests and authorizes it. The theologian, whose basis of work is a belief in his mastery of language,[23] can be of no help in ensuring that the theological function required by the groups we are discussing is carried out. And it will frequently have to be carried out in opposition to him. But at all events, this function will not be carried out by 'theology'.

I should like to make this point quite clear by providing two examples of theoretical investigations undertaken by marxist Christians. They involve attempts at 'criticism and reappropriation' of the two great historical phases of the tradition – the periods when the Bible was produced and the history of the Christians since the New Testament.[24]

For some ten years, certain Christian groups, particularly in the JEC,[25] had come up against the contradiction between their marxist political practice and their idealistic religious references. 'Since we did not wish to idealize politics,' writes Clévenot, 'we endeavoured to endow our faith with a materialist theoretical basis. To achieve this, we attempted to go back to the sources, to the Bible.'[26]

Belo, a Portuguese refugee in France and a former Catholic priest, has given the group coherence. He participated in various research groups before publishing his *Lecture matérialiste de l'Evangile de Marc (A Materialist Interpretation of the Gospel of Saint Mark)* in 1974.[27] Although difficult, this large work enjoyed a spectacular success. In 1976 there also appeared a small and much more easily readable work by Clévenot, which on the one hand reiterates Belo's ideas, and also draws upon the work of a Parisian group on David's succession to the throne in Samuel and Kings.[28] This work also had an unexpectedly large sale.

A number of groups sprang up with the idea of either reading these texts or of carrying out direct research on other biblical texts (Genesis, The Song of Songs, Acts, Thessalonians, etc.). Let us quote one item from a group in Nancy as illustration:

Belo's work has arrived at exactly the right moment. It has given us the elements of an interpretation of Mark that we were looking for, that we suspected were present, though we had neither the time nor the means to work them out. There was still a gap between our social practice, often based on marxist analysis, and our reading of the Gospel, which is frequently still blinkered by traditional theological thinking. We had already made some attempts to subject the Gospel to marxist analysis, but these did not get very far. We lacked the file we needed to cut through the bars of our theological prison.[29]

In the preface to his book, Belo announced his intention to 'make it possible for practical politics with revolutionary aims and Christian practice wishing to abandon religion to exist side by side'. (p. 13)

There can be no question here of discussing the ideas of these lines of research. What concerns me is to indicate that, although its conditions of production differ from those of the theologians and although its theoretical and epistemological basis is different, this is indeed an attempt to develop a new understanding of Christianity.

In this research, the term 'materialist' should, it seems to me, be understood in three ways. The text is to be considered first and foremost for its content. Belo provides a very literal translation of the Bible and explains why he does so. It is in order to 'indicate that it is a foreign text, produced in a social context quite different from our own'. His refusal to polish up the translation is therefore a refusal to make the gospel 'modern', to 'make it sound like the word of God speaking to us now'. This refusal should be seen as representing a break with 'theology based on inspiration' which, to recapture the 'word of God' eliminates the text from its setting. (p. 137) Once the text has been freed of the idealistic meanings in which it abounds, and of the presupposition that it contains realities, for which the text is merely what is significant, reading may proceed freely. What one should do, says Belo, is 'to take possession' of the reading, 'as people nowadays speak of students or the working class taking possession of the floor'.[30] Belo draws upon the semiotic analyses of Barthes and Kristeva. Some groups have become involved in the structural analysis of texts (after Greimas), though this appears to be less effective.

The insistence upon interpretation of the text presupposes an explanatory theory of the society in which the text originates; it is *historical materialism* which provides the framework and the theories on the pre-capitalist methods of production which provide the model. This calls in fact for a minute analysis of Palestinian society in the first century. The work of numerous theologians (the Biblical School in Jerusalem for example) could be used here but to a different purpose. In more general terms the aim is to situate the biblical texts in their original social context, thereby indicating the social classes and the ideological presuppositions which were involved in the authorship of these texts.

Lastly, and this is the third meaning of the term 'materialist', there is a concentration upon the *practices* of the agents of the biblical text. A new conception of the relationship between theory and practice thus shows the gospel text to be an account of the practice of Jesus. This practice may be defined as a kind of communism (aiming to abolish the class system) which is non-revolutionary (not intending to seize power) and international in scope (as compared with the peripheral concerns of the Essene or of Zealot nationalism). Such analyses make it possible to attempt to create a 'materialist ecclesiology'. Belo, after evoking the social position of 'the followers of Jesus', which is seen as the meeting ground of 'the poor without the rich, servants without masters, disciples without scribes, young without adults, brothers without fathers, in short the sons of men outside the relations of parenthood and domination' (p. 352), Belo invites us to use the criteria he derives from the practice of Jesus in order to evaluate these forms of Christianity:

the *ecclesia* [Belo uses this term to avoid the associations of the word church] is not only the community in so far as it is an assemblage but designates the *specific practice* of that community which, like faith, hope and charity, is linked on the three planes of politics, ideology and economics. The issue of Christian identity will therefore be stated in terms of ecclesiality and not in the inevitably subjective terms of the question 'do I have faith?' It will then be possible to see whether our own practice, seen in the light of the messianic account, measures up to the structure of *ecclesia*. (p. 359)

This research, which is undertaken without any reference to the dogmatic traditions of a church, employing a theoretical apparatus which also lies outside these traditions, and which is applied to questions raised by the practice of marxist Christians, is therefore central to an interpretation of Christianity.

Furthermore, Belo's study shows that the messianic practice of Jesus cannot be analyzed simply in terms of political categories. It is this practice in fact which underlies the Apostles' faith in the resurrection, after the murder of Jesus (a *murder* 'which is a consequence of the powerful, liberating subversiveness of the practice of severing' (p. 396) and not simply a *death*, as the 'theological' interpretation of the text has it). This is the origin of the hope that the resurrection, seen as the 'raising of the body', can only 'be the result of insurrection'. (ibid.) Has this view a legitimate place within a materialist approach? The numerous questions which have been left open in the work of Belo, as well as the excessively approximative syncretism inherent in the fusion of numerous trends of contemporary culture, mean that this research does not constitute an entirely successful theoretical demonstration. The research is still being carried out, though the practical validation provided by the fact that it has been taken up by groups of militants at grass-roots' level is an indication of its strong points.[31]

Historical research on Christians using the same methodology and based on the same premises is much less advanced. No theoretical work has been produced as yet, and, apart from several documents published by journals associated with the movement, the only sustained work is being carried out by a Parisian group which has been in operation since 1975 and has links with *La Lettre*.[32]

The work stems from the attempt to carry out a materialistic study of the Old Testament and to extend this beyond the New Testament period. The assumption was that, just as 'the Bible' had revealed itself to be an ideological concept which joined together in a specious unity texts of widely differing nature and with sometimes conflicting interests, similarly the notion of the 'Church' served to unify, either retrospectively or in the present, the plurality of forms of Christianity. The research aimed to produce the *histories of the Christians* as opposed to a *history of the Church*. In contrast to the historiography of the ruling sections of society and the ideology they represent, it aims to resurrect traditions of Christian practices in the oppressed sections of society which have been suppressed and so forgotten.

This aim embraced both a fact and a hypothesis. The fact was the absence of a collective memory among marxist Christians, apart from the memory of biblical origins. In the available data on the past twenty centuries they encounter scarcely anything but the traditions (social, institutional, dogmatic, liturgical) of official Christianity to which they are opposed, and so they are unable to find, in the past, any aspirations comparable to their own, and which the biblical corpus preserves in its prophetic traditions. With a very few exceptions, this memory provides them with no support for their present struggles.

The hypothesis formulated in the first part of this chapter is that, for the survival and vitality of a Christian group, a common memory is required. In the political arena in which they operate, the marxist Christians have, moreover, encountered several groups which are dedicated to restoring to the militants a memory of subversive or revolutionary traditions. Examples of these, with varying emphases, are the journals *Cahiers du Forum – Histoire* and *Révoltes logiques*.

The lack of memory is not fortuitous. The Christian past abounds in social movements from which these groups could draw support. But, as I have already stated, Christian memory is preserved by theologians who (at least within a marxist analysis) are seen as maintaining it in the interests of the dominant sectors of society. This memory of order has eliminated the memory of subversion, just as the dominant form of Christianity has eliminated, even to the extent of using physical force, the other forms of Christianity which have challenged it. With their adhernts tried for heresy as criminals, even their memory has been suppressed. The group has begun its task of 're-appropriation' by concentrating on movements with parallels to their own in nineteenth- and earlier twentieth-century France. Research on the confrontation between socialism and Christianity therefore comes up against both the work of suppression carried out by the clergy and the rejection of these movements by the working-class organizations which did not add their support to them. Some of the reasons for this twofold rejection have been sought in the debate between Marx and the Christian communism of Weitling, and Marx's rejection of evangelical dynamism placed at the service of the proletariat which, despite its ambiguities, Weitling's movement was advocating and which might still be recreated nowadays in a different form.

But it seems that here, too, this research which uses historical materialism as the tool of analysis and which endeavours to apply the rigour of the historian, does indeed account for one aspect of what I have termed the theological function, ven if it has no trace of dogmatic presupposition.

If the past did not repeatedly provide evidence of the existence of liberating practices and interpretations in the mobility of Christianity and in conflict with the ecclesiastical powers, marxist Christianity would be unable to find a historical context and its credibility would be compromised.

This history was made up of the repeated collapse of these trends (either because they were suppressed or because they were rendered totally peripheral). The fact that the churches have lost the physical and ideological possibility of eliminating these forms of Christianity today, together with the reflexive tools which have become available, makes it possible to analyze the failures and rethink their causes.

The plurality of different forms of Christianity – the marxist Christians would go so far as to say the plurality of faiths – is demonstrated and explained by these analyses and it compels us to become aware of the choices which have to be made. This historical research which has begun aims to inject dynamism into Christian practice and to endow it with a deeper awareness of those factors which condition it.

Here, too, the theological function which is so vital for the groups of Christians we are studying is carried out neither by theology nor by theologians but by an intellectual approach based on the social sciences.

What is one to conclude? In his speech at the Synod of Bishops in October 1977 Monsignor Nguyen Van Binh, Archbishop of Ho-Chi-Minh-Ville, considered it necessary in his country to 'present the Catholic faith through the medium of marxist language', though without 'making Christianity marxist'. He explained that 'when Aristotelian or existentialist language was used to present the Catholic faith, the faith was not "aristotelianized" or "existentialized".'

Whatever the situation may be in Vietnam, the trends we have examined in France do not make it possible to state the problem in such terms. It is not simply a question of pastors and theologians using a new language, or of trying to do with Marx – and it sometimes seems to be a temptation – what Saint Thomas did with Aristotle. Marxism, as the marxist Christians understand it, is not first and foremost a theory, but practical politics, and it is here that the approach is new in comparison with the intellectual confrontations the Church has experienced throughout its history. Though it does not in any way dispense with the urgency for ensuring that the theological function is carried out, this form of Christianity makes 'theology' and the 'theologian' redundant, at least in the form known to us within the dominant type of Christianity. In that case it is to other disciplines – sociology among them – and to other kinds of praxis that we must look for a replacement.

This does not necessarily mean that the use of other languages and practices – poetic, mystical or symbolical – which is not outmoded among the marxist Christians is discredited. But this was not our subject.

Translated from the French by H.L. Sutcliffe

Notes

1 The same approach, though with different motives, is found in Jossua, J. P. 'De la Théologie au théologien', *Concilium*, supplement to No 60, 1970, pp. 55–60; and in Le Gal, Y. *Question(s) à la théologie chrétienne* (Paris, 1975), particularly the first part, 'La théologie comme problème'.

2 The denominations of the Christian churches only become susceptible to the influence of the theological approaches of other denominations (for example the Catholics' acknowledgement that Luther and Barth are theologians) when awareness that all are Christians supersedes differences between the various institutions.

3 See for example the research on imaginary saints carried out by Delooz, P. *Sociologie et canonisations* (Liège, 1969).

4 Deconchy J. P. *L'Orthodoxie religieuse. Essai de logique psychosociale* (Paris, 1971). Part Three, 'Le Relent messianique et la lecture orthodoxe de la Bible'.

5 A caricature of this relationship between the theologian and the Bible is the remark attributed to a Dominican master of theology, who died some years ago: 'My book is almost finished; I have only to add the biblical quotations.'

6 Casanova, A. *Vatican II et l'évolution de l'Eglise* (Paris, 1969) p. 102.

7 Lévi-Strauss, C. *La Pensée sauvage* (Paris, 1962) pp. 26–33.

8 Legendre, P. *L'Amour du censeur. Essai sur l'ordre dogmatique* (Paris, 1974) cf. pp. 19 and 38.

9 Bourdieu, P. and Passeron, J. C. *La Reproduction. Eléments pour une théorie du système d'enseignement* (Paris, 1970) p. 159.

10 *Ibid.* p. 76

11 Rousseau, A. and Leconte, J. P. 'Les Conditions sociales du travail théologique' *Concilium*, May, 1978.

12 Corroboration of this might be found in the analyses carried out in another field by Roqueplo, P. *Le Partage du savoir. Science, culture, vulgarisation* (Paris, 1974).

13 The very few Catholic laymen who can be found actively engaged in theological writing are almost always university academics and, as such, 'clerics' in a different way. It should be borne in mind that we are discussing the French situation only and Catholicism in particular. Quite different situations are to be found elsewhere, for example in Greece, where the theological function is largely in the hands of lay intellectuals and where it is the inferior cultural level of the clergy which is a problem.

14   From this point onwards, it is mainly to Catholicism that we are referring and, in keeping with general usage in France, 'the Church' will denote the Catholic Church.

15   de Certeau, M. 'La Faiblesse de croire' *Esprit,* April-May 1977, p. 231 (special issue devoted to 'Les Militants d'origine chrétienne').

16   *Cité Nouvelle,* 589, July-August, 1977, p. 10.

17   *Lettre,* 218, October 1976, p. 7.

18   *Cité Nouvelle,* 576, January 1976, p. 1.

19   The final document of the meeting, §3.2. *Information Catholiques Internaponales,* 409, June, 1972, p. 21.

20   *Le Déplacement de la théologie* (Paris, 1977) p. 73.

21   Marx, K. and Engels, F. *Sur la Religion* (Paris, 1968) p. 70.

22   Casanova, *op. cit.* p. 109.

23   See on this topic Y. Le Gal's comments on 'le lien qui unit le parler non-logocentrique à la pratique politique opposée à l'ordre établi'. *Op. cit.* p. 164.

24   It would also have been possible to discuss the research and experiments which have been undertaken in the field of symbolism. On this topic see Cercle Jean XXIII de Nantes, Guichard, J. and C. *Liturgie et lutte des classes. Symbolique et politique* (Paris, 1976).

25   Jeunesse Etudiante Chrétienne.

26   Interview in *Cité Nouvelle,* 577, February 1976.

27   Belo, F. *Lecture matérialiste de l'Evangile de Marc* (Paris, 1974).

28   Clévenot, M. *Approches matérialistes de la Bible* (Paris, 1976).

29   *Lettre,* 224, April 1977, p. 1.

30   Belo, *op. cit.* p. 339.

31   Among the reactions provoked by Belo's work, see document 'C/X ou de Marc à Marx. L'Evangile mis à nu par la subversion de l'exégèse', *Archives de sciences sociales des religions,* 40, July-December, 1975, pp. 119–137.

32   Cf. the documents puiblished in *Cité Nouvelle* in 1975 (Nos 571, 572 and 573) or 'Nous, chrétiens de gauche (1934–1978)', special issue of *La Lettre,* 231, November 1977.

Epilogue

MANY VOICES

Robert Towler

IN the last chapter Antoine Lion wrote about some groups of people
in France who see themselves as both Marxists and Christians, who
are arguing that the distinction between theology and sociology
must be abandoned altogether because, according to Marxism with
its stress upon *praxis*, 'theologizing' as traditionally conceived now
appears to be so very questionable. They are attempting to reappropriate scripture and Christian history using the social sciences as
their tools.

When the first version of the chapter was discussed at the 1978
meeting of the Symposium of sociologists, theologians and
philosophers from which this book has evolved, most of the participants were either critical or sceptical about what these groups
described by Lion were doing. One question especially was asked:
Can what would seem to be an eclectic Marxism and an eclectic
Christianity possibly survive side by side like this except on the
edges of a pluralistic society and of a pluralistic Christian community? There was widespread feeling that simply abolishing theology
would not serve to resolve the tensions which exist at the very centre
of society and at the centre of the Christian community.

Yet the thesis in this last chapter does in fact bring into focus
questions which lie half-hidden behind the whole debate, and these
questions need to be stated explicitly. Can sociology at this time be
used simply as a tool? This is the basic question forced upon us by
both the essentially practical *sociologie religieuse* of Le Bras and
Boulard in France, and also by the high theorizing of Berger in the
USA and Luckmann in West Germany. *Sociologie religieuse* set out
to answer straightforward questions about the state of religion, but
it rapidly became clear that, simply by posing those questions
sociologically, sociology had the potential to be more than a mere
tool, and thus it has exerted much more than a technical influence.
The theoretical essays of Berger and Luckmann, on the other hand,
which regard theology from the exalted heights of a sociological
perspective, make the limitations and deficiencies of sociology all
too clear. Neither theology nor sociology must be allowed to assume
control of the other. The distrust of these small French groups for
the traditional ways of theologizing has foundation, even if one
disagrees with their explanation and with their remedy, for in part it
is a distrust of the customary ways of talking about the relationship
between theology and sociology, as though the theoretical precepts

of one must determine the practice of the other, regardless of which way round the determinism operates.

What, though, is that 'foundation'? One part of it in particular is relevant to the interests of sociologist as well as theologian. It does not seem to be either comic or shocking to many people that large numbers of modern professional theologians have gone through their working lives with only very vague ideas of how the mass of human beings who identify themselves as Christians are 'religious', that is, what in fact they believe and in what way. It is clear that many highly intelligent writers of theology have often not even been aware of the chasm between the orthodoxy they articulate and the patterns of belief of much of the humanity they are indirectly addressing. Is it mistaken to try, in contrast, to articulate 'faith' starting from 'exactly where people are'? Or mistaken to try to build a community's theology 'from the ground upwards', rooting it in *praxis*, after the fashion of the group Lion has written about? Whether mistaken or not, simply by putting these questions to oneself one is likely to become aware of certain assumptions about religious belief which remarkably few church-going people or even students of religion are prompted to question, and yet which my own research indicates badly need to be questioned. What we learn from posing these questions may help to shape the future of the subject of this book.

As a result of my interest in 'common religion' I recently had the opportunity to analyze the four thousand or so letters written to Bishop John Robinson during the storm of controversy which followed the publication in 1963 of his best-selling book *Honest to God*. It enabled me to survey the wrestlings of a wide range of people of all kinds with deeply disturbing theological ideas, and one of the main conclusions of the study was that contemporary religiousness must be understood as something composed of elements drawn from a number of types or syndromes of religious belief: it is probable that there is not just one extant form of religiousness, but at least five.

If this is indeed the case it has serious implications for the conduct of social research into religion. Most empirical studies assume that, very broadly speaking, there is but one form of religion, whose shape they know, and they set out to measure its prevalence; they assume, that is, that they know what beliefs people might hold. The revealing of a variety of forms would have consequences for theology too, however, for the assumption that we know the beliefs people might hold, and that what we need is to find out how many people hold them and how strongly, is an assumption made by others besides social scientists. Social scientists took the assumption in the first place from priests and theologians, but now the priests and theologians appeal to the evidence of social scientific research when they continue to promulgate the myth of a single religious orthodoxy which originated with them and is embraced by more or less all people in the present generation. Thus, for example, the Rev. Don Cupitt was able to write in *The Listener* (18 March 1976):

Christian beliefs are widely held. About 80 per cent believe in God, 64 per cent in Christ as the Son of God, and 40 per cent in an afterlife. Forty-four per cent say they pray regularly, and 58 per cent teach their children to pray. Of those who believe in God, about half take an anthropomorphic view of him, and the others do not.

Mr Cupitt is no more gullible than most clergymen and students of theology in accepting the validity of such statistics; indeed, he is no more gullible than the sociologists who compute and publish them, for I am certainly not accusing the survey researchers of deceit and fraud, but only of naïvety.

A study of contemporary forms of religiousness is therefore as important for the valid pursuit of theology as for sociology. The exact nature of theology is itself distinctly problematical at the present time, of course, and this is only confirmed by the fact that nearly every contributor to this book, sociologist and philosopher as well as theologian, has felt obliged to supply a working definition of theology. I believe that a case can be made for saying that the sociology of religion has something to contribute to an understanding of what theology might be. If by theology we mean the disciplined discussion of knowledge about God, we must recognize that it is composed of a number of separate strands. It has grown into what it is today through many and varied historical processes, and each new turn of events has added something to what was there before, rather than displacing it.

It began as an undifferentiated part of the folklore of every culture. Then, in the Western world, came the theology of prophetic, revealed religion. The prophet brought a message of knowledge not already assumed by people: it was news. A new factor comes into play when religion is a separate and autonomous institution, organized in its own right, as it is not in simple, undifferentiated cultures. We find that the power it possesses by virtue of its autonomy is exploited by the society from which the religious institution has struggled free, and it is a commonplace observation that when Constantine made Christianity the official religion of the Roman Empire, Christianity was more radically affected than was the Empire. Added to the tension within theology between the priest and the prophet, therefore, is the external tension between pope and emperor, between church and state. It is within this context that the orthodox theology, approved and enforced by external, secular authority, comes into existence. At the present time, however, doubt has assumed a new and positive significance for theology. An editorial in *Theology* could say recently (January 1976):

We assume (I believe rightly) that all questions that can be asked should be asked; and that we live in bad faith, as Sartre would say, if we do not ask the questions that we think we must ask.

Theology today asks what people can believe. When theology was part-and-parcel of the folklore of society the man who doubted was regarded as insane; when theology was a revealed message, he was treated as blind and left in his blindness; when theology was orthodox teaching he was exhorted and if necessary threatened; but today the doubter is cajoled and wooed. The result for theology is that, at worst, it seeks its own success as little more than a saleable commodity; at best, it tries to find a mode of expression which is comprehensible to contemporary men and women. A seriously apologetical component enters it. This is not quite the whole story, however, for the past hundred years or so have seen the emergence of theology as an independent academic specialism, with degrees in theology, where previously divinity was assumed to be part of the knowledge possessed by every man of culture. As a result, the debates about what theology should be are in danger of being foreclosed by the easy assumption that theology is what is done by theologians. (A horrifying example of this occurs at the beginning of *The Crucified God* by Jurgen Moltmann, when, with sheer impertinence, he writes: 'It then dawned upon many, and especially upon those on whom the Church depended for its continuance, the students of theology . . .')

There are, then, at least these five strands in theology: folklore; a prophetic message which claims to be self-evidently true; orthodoxy upheld authoritatively; doctrines established on scientific principles; and teaching based on an understanding of what is comprehensible and credible to modern men and women. But concern with what is credible has, in fact, constantly been borne in mind by theology throughout nearly its whole history, if in very different ways, and it is this to which the editorial in *Theology* from which I have already quoted draws attention when it says that one of the present dangers is:

. . . not to recognize the situation in which we live, and therefore to fall out of touch with the life with which theology must be concerned if it is to justify itself. The kind of writing which this produces fails the test of experience. It addresses itself to questions, neds and concerns which men are assumed to have, rather than those which they do have.

Theology, according to this point of view, must be concerned with the fate which has met the traditional religious symbols; the meaning of traditional theological propositions for ordinary people must be known and noted. If theology is to be vital it must be aware of the theological significance of overtly secular images, but it must be aware, also, of the significance of overtly religious images. The religion of ordinary people, the common forms of religiousness, are ignored by theology at the risk of using words and images in a way peculiar to itself. The best work in Church history has always been sensitive to the varieties of religious belief; it is fully recognized that widely disparate versions of Christianity existed in various early churches, and Church history has placed these differences within their proper social context. It has undertaken a similar task of interpretation for every historical period. Theology has not been allowed to simplify the facts of history in the interests of a neat and systematic account of theology's development. But historians do not study the present day, and so contemporary theology can tend to go unchecked.

Together with the undermining of the assumption that there is a single form of religiousness, study of the *Honest to God* correspondence has produced evidence that suggests we are far from clear what kind of affirmation is being made when someone says 'I believe'. There is a case for saying that the nature of belief is a variable. In his book *Belief, Language and Experience* (Oxford, 1972), the anthropologist Rodney Needham has shown, amongst other things, that westerners who study alien cultures make certain assumptions. He points to the general conviction among anthropologists that the 'common intellectual nature of man' is 'intuitively understood' and has 'already been pragmatically established'. And he begins with the following comment:

It has seemed to me that these presumptions are not well founded, and that the essential capacities of man have yet to be empirically determined by comparative investigation. One presumed capacity, which by the frequency with which it is cited claims a special attention, is that of belief. That men can be said to believe, without qualification and irrespective of their cultural formation, is an implicit premise in anthropological writings of the most varied kinds, from abstract and generalizing disquisitions to the most particular of ethnographical reports. (p. 3)

He elaborates his argument by considering in some detail the case of the Nuer, showing that while on the one hand their rich vocabulary has allowed Roman Catholic missionaries to translate the scriptures and the liturgy, and to do so to their complete satisfaction, on the other hand Evans-Pritchard is on record as having reached a contradictory view, namely that:

. . . when we say, as we can do, that all Nuer have faith in God, the word 'faith' must be understood in the Old Testament sense of 'trust' and not in the modern sense of 'belief' which the concept came to have under Greek and Latin influences. There is, in any case, no word in the Nuer language which could stand for 'I believe'. (p. 23)

From here Needham goes on to compare the problem of translating the concept of belief in a number of languages; to explore the various theories of belief; to consider whether it is possible to specify criteria with which to identify belief; to ask whether there is, in any sense, a class of phenomena called beliefs; and to investigate the possibility that believing might be a natural resemblance among human beings. Despite promising leads from certain scholars, in particular from Lévy-Bruhl and from Wittgenstein, his conclusion is that the problem of belief has yet to be addressed successfully. He concludes:

Whereas ethnographers, in particular, have become alert to the dangers of denotative terms such as 'soul', 'gift', 'family', and so on, they have continued in the main to adhere uncritically to a received philosophy of mind, namely that provided by the categories of European languages and the prevailing 'tone of thought' that these express. They recognize that *culture* is differentiated, but they conduct their investigations as though the operations of the mind were undifferentiated. That is, they take it for granted (or at least write as though they took it for granted) that human nature is already adequately charted and determined, so that an ethnographer approaching a foreign culture or an analyst interpreting published reports can assume that the human beings under consideration will have certain well-known logical and psychic capacities that they share with the observer. . . . This tacit presumption is not well founded. . . . The notion of belief is not appropriate to an empirical philosophy of mind or to an exact account of human motives and conduct. Belief is not a discriminable experience, it does not constitute a natural resemblance among men, and it does not belong to 'the common behaviour of mankind'. It follows from this that when other peoples are said, without qualification, to 'believe' anything, it must be entirely unclear what kind of idea or state of mind is being ascribed to them. (p. 188)

It seems to me that if Needham has erred he has erred in not being radical enough in his questioning. I would wish to contend that the problem arises not just with other peoples but within our own culture as well. On the basis of empirical study it is evident that we know pathetically little even about the religiousness which surrounds us.

I think that making good this deficiency promises to be an exciting project for the social scientist and one which may be of no little importance to the theologian. The discussion between a sociologist, a philosopher of religion, and two theologians which constitutes the second half of Chapter 2 of this present book concludes, ironically enough, with the theologians emphasizing the need for theologians to be nearer to, more aware of, and better informed about the actual 'praying, worshipping church'. The study of religious images as they are understood and employed is an authentic part of the study of theology, but it is the study of theology at the practical, grass-roots level. It is what could be called non-normative theology. If the task of prescriptive theology is to teach and proclaim a theology which is true, it is the task of non-normative theology to provide information about practical theologies. And such non-normative theology, I believe, is best undertaken by social scientists working with theologians; for it is social scientists who have tools and skills appropriate to the description of practical religion, and to the analysis of it in relation to its psychological, cultural and social contexts, and also appropriate to the investigation of the variety of connotations of 'believing'.

Of course this is more easily said than done, and contributors to the present volume, besides discussing the role of sociological criteria in theologizing, show the possible confusions which may arise when sociologist and theologian encounter one another, even amicably, and which have their origins in differences in conceptual language and categories.

I anticipate, however, that meeting together to increase understanding of concrete problems, like variations in forms of religiousness, at the very least will benefit individual theologians and sociologists by making them both more wary of their assumptions, and, more substantially, will advance the debates with which this book has been concerned. There is every hope that the debates found here may stimulate us to reflect more deeply on the nature of theology and on the nature of sociology. Nevertheless we should be aware that there are limits to the distance which generalizing can take us, for the issues which have been opened up in these pages will remain open as long as there continue to be distinctly definable disciplines of sociology and theology. There will always be time for other voices.

Which voices will be the next to be heard? An epilogue is the right place for that question to be raised, so I ask whether the next voices may not be more hostile ones? In interdisciplinary discussion perspectives can sometimes, if not always, be best sharpened in abrasive dialogue between scholars looking for conflict rather than for grounds for alliance. I suspect, though, that in the coming years a rather different new voice will be much more urgently needed. The authors of *Sociology and Theology: Alliance and Conflict* have said many things well worth saying, but I think the debate is not likely to advance significantly towards a more creative relationship between the two disciplines until the circle is widened so that sociologist and theologian listen with proper attention not only to each other, but also to ordinary *homo religiosus*.

Select Bibliography

Any bibliography that deals with the relations between two disciplines raises problems of selection over and above those encountered in making a bibliography for one well-established discipline. The task is even more difficult when the interdisciplinary field has scarcely been explored, as is the case between sociology and theology. The number of items available is relatively few; and the choice of books and articles inevitably becomes more subjective when the boundaries are extended. Nevertheless it is necessary to have boundaries and to declare them.

From the very outset the Symposium rejected the idea that the subject of its concern was the sociology of religion 2per se. Clearly the sociology of religion can have, and probably does have at the moment, a considerable influence on theology. In one sense, all the works within the sociology of religion might be said to be influential, and if a very extensive bibliography on sociology and theology is the aim, a large section should be devoted to the sociology of religion. However, such an exercise would detract from the purpose of the Symposium and in any case the reader can refer to a standard bibliography on the sociology of religion, such as that in S. Budd, *Sociologists and Religion*, (Collier-Macmillan, London, 1973). And not only have all references to works on the sociology of religion been generally excluded, but so also have all references to perhaps the two most influential classical writers of the subject, Emile Durkheim and Max Weber. Once again attention is drawn to the bibliography of Durkheim's works on religion in W.S.F. Pickering (ed.), *Durkheim on Religion* (Routledge, London and Boston, 1975); and in the case of Max Weber's thesis on the Protestant ethic and the spirit of Capitalism, B. Nelson's bibliography in *Beyond the Classics?* ed. by C.Y. Glock and P.E. Hammond (Harper and Row, New York, 1973) pp. 113–30, should be consulted. And to those wanting references to Marx's thought and that of his immediate followers attention is drawn to D.B. McKown, *The Classical Marxist Critiques of Religion: Marx, Engels, Lenin, Kautsky* (Martinus Nijhoff, The Hague, 1975). In another direction, all references to pastoral sociology or religious sociology (sociology carried out for the ultimate good of the churches), to the sociology of knowledge, and to liberation theology have also been excluded, unless they deal explicitly with the relations between sociology and theology. (For an extensive bibliography of the subjects just mentioned, see *Sociología de la Religión y Teología: Estudio Bibliográfico. Sociology of Religion and Theology: A bibliography,* Editorial Cuadernos para el diálogo, S.A., Madrid, 1975; and Volume B, 1978.)

In order to differentiate what in our view directly concerns both the relations between sociology and theology, and the influences of the one subject on the other, excluding areas mentioned in the last paragraph, the bibliography is divided into two sections:

1) Sociology and Theology
2) Method and Understanding in Sociology and Theology.

In the first section books and articles have been included which deal explicitly with the relations between the two disciplines. In the second, which is influenced more than the first by subjective criteria, reference is made to items, mostly recent, which deal with either sociology or theology and in which there are implicit influences that the one discipline can have on the other. Even with such a division, however, there are cases when it is difficult to decide into which of the two categories certain items should be placed. In no case has one item been given in both categories.

The compilation of this bibliography is very much a 'Symposium effort' and came out of the 1979 meeting. In particular our appreciation is extended to G. Dekker, R. Gill, and A. Lion for laying the foundations of the bibliography.

Sociology and Theology

BANNING, W. *Theologie en Sociologie. Een Terreinverkenning en Inleiding* (van Gorcum, Assen, 1936).

BANNING, W. *Over de Ontmoeting van Theologie en Sociologie* (Amsterdam, 1946).

BARKER, E. 'Sciences and Theology: Diverse Resolutions of an Interdisciplinary Gap by the New Priesthood of Science', *Interdisciplinary Science Reviews*, 4, 1, 1979.

BARKER, E. 'The Limits of Displacement' (Chap. 1 in this book, 1980).

BAUM, G. 'Sociology and Theology', *Concilium*, 1, 10, 1974, pp. 22–31.

BAUM, G. 'The Impact of Sociology on Catholic Theology', *Proceedings of the Convention of the Catholic Theological Society of America*, 30, 1975, pp. 1–29.

BAUM, G. *Religion and Alienation. A Theological Reading of Sociology* (Paulist Press, New York; Paramus, Toronto, 1975).

BAUM, G. 'The Sociology of Roman Catholic Theology' (Chap. 7 in this book, 1980).

BERGER, P.L. *The Sacred Canopy* (Doubleday, New York, 1967). Eng. edn. *The Social Reality of Religion* (Faber and Faber, London, 1969).

BERGER, P.L. 'A Sociological View of the Secularization of Theology', *Journal for the Scientific Study of Religion*, 6, 1967, pp. 3–16.

BERGER, P.L. 'Sociology and Theology', *Theology Today,* 24, 3, 1967, pp. 329–36.

BERGER, P.L. *A Rumor of Angels* (Doubleday, New York and Pelican, London, 1967).

BERGER, P.L. 'Secular Theology and the Rejection of the Supernatural: Reflections on Recent Trends', *Theological Studies*, 38, 1, 1977 pp. 39–56.

BERGER, P.L. *The Heretical Imperative* (Anchor Press/Doubleday, New York, 1979).

BIROU, A. *Sociologie et religion* (Les Editions Ouvrières, Paris, 1959).

CAIRNS, D. 'The Thought of Peter Berger', *Scottish Journal of Theology,* 27, 2, 1974, pp. 181–97.

CHENU, M.D. 'Sociologie de la connaissance et théologie de la foi', *Recherches et débats,* 25, 1958, pp. 71–4.

DEFOIS, G. 'Sociologie de la connaissance et théologie de la croyance', *Le Supplément,* 112, 1975, pp. 101–25.

DEKKER, G. 'The Relation Between Sociology and Theology' (privately circulated, 1978).

DESROCHE, H. 'Sociologie et théologie dans la typologie religieuse de Joachim Wach', *Archives de sociologie des religions,* 1, 1956, pp. 41–63.

DESROCHE, H. *Sociologies religieuses* (Presses Universitaires de France, Paris, 1968) Chap. 8.

DHOOGHE, J. 'Quelques Problèmes posés par le dialogue entre sociologie et théologie pastorale', *Social Compass,* 17, 2, 1970, pp. 215–29.

DUMONT, F. 'La sociología y la renovacíon de la teología', in *Teología de la renovacíon, 2: Renovacíon de las estructuras religiosas,* (Sígueme, Salamanca, 1972).

EDWARDS, A. 'Life as Fashion Parade: The Anthropology of Mary Douglas', *New Blackfriars,* 58, 682, 1977, pp. 131–39.

FIORENZA, F. 'Critical Social Theory and Christology', *Proceedings of the Convention of the Catholic Theological Society of America,* 30, 1975, pp. 63–110.

FORTMANN, H.M.M. *Als Ziende de Onzienlijke,* II (Gooi en Sticht, Hilversum, 1974).

FRANCO, R. 'Teología y sociología, *Proyección,* 61, 1968, pp. 203–9.

FRIEDRICHS, R.W. 'Social Research and Theology: End of the Detente?', *Review of Religious Research*, 15, 1974, pp. 113–27.

GABLENTZ, H.O. 'Soziologie und Theologie', *Zeitschrift für Evangelische Ethik*, 4, 1960, pp. 56–8.

GARRETT, W.R. 'Troublesome Transcendence: The Supernatural in the Scientific Study of Religion', *Sociological Analysis*, 3, 1974, pp. 169–80.

GESTRICH, C. 'Theologie und Soziologie – Zwei Grenzwissenschaften' in J.M. Lohse (ed.), *Menschlich Sein Mit oder Ohne Gott?* (Kohlhammer, Stuttgart, 1969).

GEYER, H.G., JANOWSKI, H.N. and SCHMIDT, A. *Theologie und Soziologie* (Kohlhammer, Stuttgart, 1970).

GILL, R. 'Berger's Plausibility Structures: A Response to Professor Cairns', *Scottish Journal of Theology*, 27, 2, 1974, pp. 198–207.

GILL, R. *The Social Context of Theology* (Mowbrays, Oxford, 1975).

GILL, R. *Theology and Social Structure* (Mowbrays, Oxford, 1977).

GILL, R. 'From Sociology to Theology' (Chap. 6 in this book, 1980).

GODDIJN, H. and GODDIJN, W. *Sociologie van Kerk en Godsdienst* (Het Spectrum, Utrecht en Antwerpen, 1966).

HAAS, P. de *The Church as an Institution: Critical Studies in the Relation Between Theology and Sociology* (Boek- en Offsetdrukkerij, N.V., Apeldoorn, 1972).

HARRIS, C. 'Displacements and Reinstatements' (Chap. 2 in this book, 1980).

HOLL, A. 'Max Scheler's Sociology of Knowledge and his Position in Relation to Theology', *Social Compass*, 17, 2, 1970, pp. 231–41.

HOLLWEG, A. *Theologie und Empirie. Ein Beitrag zum Gespräch zwischen Theologie und Sozialwissenschaften in den USA und Deutschland* (Evangelisches Verlagswerk, Stuttgart, 1971).

HOUTART, F. *et al. Recherches interdisciplinaires et théologie* (Editions du Cerf, Paris, 1970).

HUDSON, W.D. 'The Rational System of Beliefs' (Chap. 5 in this book, 1980).

HUMMEL, G. 'Religionssoziologie und Theologie: Traditionelle Ansätze und zukünfrige Perspektiven', in U. Mann (ed.), *Theologie und Religionswissenschaft. Der Gegenwärtige Stand ihrer Forschungsergebnisse und Aufgaben im Hinblick auf ihr Gegenseitiges Verhältnis* (Wissenschaftliche Buchgesellschaft, Darmstadt, 1973) pp. 207–21.

HUNTER, D. 'Theology and the Behavioural Sciences', *Religious Education*, 55, 1960, pp. 248–64.

JACKSON, M.J. *The Sociology of Religion. Theory and Practice* (Batsford, London, 1974) Chap. 4.

KAUFMANN, F.-X. Theologie in Soziologischer Sicht (Herder, Freiburg, Basel und Wien, 1973).

LAEYENDECKER, L. 'Sociologie en Theologie', in K. Dobbelaere and L. Laeyendecker, Godsdienst, Kerk en Samenleving (Universitaire Pers, Rotterdam, 1974) pp. 341–61.

de LAVALETTE, H. 'Repères conflictuels. Du champ de la théologie à celui de la sociologie', Recherches de sciences religieuses, 4, 1977, pp. 589–612.

LINDNER, R. 'Uber die Zusammenarbeit von Soziologie und Theologie – eine Auseinandersetzung mit Helmut Schelsky', Zeitschrift für Evangelische Ethik, 10, 1966, pp. 65–80.

LION, A. 'Theology and Sociology: What point is there in keeping the distinction?' (Chap. 10 in this book, 1980).

de LOOR, H.D. 'Soziologie und Theologie', Zeitschrift für Evangelische Ethik, 11, 1967, pp. 159–68.

MANNHEIM, K. Diagnosis of Our Time (Routledge, London and Boston, 1943) Chap. 7.

MARTIN, D. 'The Sociological Mode and the Theological Vocabulary' (Chap. 3 in this book, 1980).

MATHEWS, S. 'The Social Origin of Theology', American Journal of Sociology, 18, 1912, pp. 289–317.

MAYER, H.-C. 'Plädoyer fur die Freiheit der Theologie von der Soziologie', Scheidewege, 4, 2, pp. 179–200.

MEHL, R. 'Bedeutung, Möglichkeiten und Grenzen der Soziologie des Protestantismus in Theologischer Sicht', in 'Probleme der Religionssoziologie', Sonderheft 6 von Kölner Zeitschrift für Soziologie und Sozialpsychologie, 1962, pp. 112–22.

MEHL, R. 'Sociologie du christianisme et théologie', Social Compass, 10, 3, 1963, pp. 285–92.

MILLS, J.O. 'Of Two Minds' (Introduction in this book, 1980).

MILLS, J.O. 'God, Man and Media' (Chap. 8 in this book, 1980).

MONZEL, N. 'Die Soziologie und die Theologen', Hochland, 41, 1948–9, pp. 259–72.

NINEHAM, D. 'A Partner to Cinderella?' in M. Hooker and C. Hickling (eds.), What About the New Testament? (S.C.M. Press, London, 1975).

PANNENBERG, W. 'Signale der Transzendenz – Religionssoziologie zwischen Atheismus und Religioser Wirklichkeit', Evangelische Kommentare, 7, 1974, pp. 151–4.

PANNENBERG, W. Theology and the Philosophy of Science, trans. from German by F. McDonagh (Darton, Longman and Todd, London, 1976).

PELLEGRINO, U. 'Teologia e Sociologia', Atti del XIX Convegno del Centro Studi Filosofici (Morcelliana, Brescia, 1965) pp. 301–7.

PICKERING, W.S.F. 'Theodicy and Social Theory' (Chap. 4 in this book, 1980).

RADCLIFFE, T. 'Relativizing the Relativizers' (Chap. 9 in this book, 1980).

RICHARD, G. *Sociologie et théodicée; leur conflit et leur accord* (Les Presses Continentales, Paris, 1943).

ROUSSEAU, A. 'Emploi du terme "sociologie" dans les textes du magistère central de l'Eglise', *Social Compass*, 17, 2, 1970, pp. 309–20.

ROUSSEAU, A. and LECONTE, J-P. 'Les Conditions sociales du travail théologique', *Concilium*, 135, 1978, pp. 19–27.

SAVRAMIS, D. *Theologie und Gesellschaft* (List Verlag, München, 1971).

SCHELSKY, H. 'Religionssoziologie und Theologie', *Zeitschrift für Evangelische Ethik*, 3, 1959, pp. 129–45.

SCHILLEBEECKX, E. Theological Reflections on Religio-Sociological Interpretations of Modern "Irreligion"', *Social Compass*, 10, 3, 1963, pp. 257–84.

SCHREUDER, O. 'Works on Sociology and Theology', *Social Compass*, 17, 2, 1970, pp. 329–34.

SCHREY, H.H. 'Neuere Tendenzen der Religionssoziologie', *Theologische Rundschau*, 38, 1, 1973, pp. 54–63; and 38, 2, 1973, pp. 99–118.

SEGUNDO, J.L. *Liberatión de la teología* (Ediciones Carlos Lohlé, Buenos Aires, 1975). Trans. J. Drury, *Liberation of Theology* (Orbis Books, Maryknoll, New York, 1976).

SEGUY, J. 'Histoire, sociologie théologie', *Archives de sociologie des religions*, 34, 1972, pp. 132–51.

SHIPPEY, F.A. 'The Relations of Theology and Social Sciences according to Gabriel Le Bras', *Archives de sociologie des religions*, 20, 1965, pp. 79–93.

SIEBERT, R. 'Religion in the Perspective of Critical Sociology', *Concilium*, 10, 1, 1974, pp. 56–69.

SPIEGEL-SCHMIDT, F. 'Theologie und Soziologie' in K.G. Specht *et al.*, *Studium Soziale. Ergebnisse Sozialwissenschaftlicher Forschung der Gegenwart* (Westdeutscher Verlag, Köln, 1963) pp. 385–96.

STROUP, H. 'Theological Implications in Anthropology', *Encounter*, 21, 1960, pp. 464–8.

TOWLER, R. 'Many Voices' (Epilogue in this book, 1980).

TRACY, D., GILKEY, L. and OGDEN, S.M. 'Responses to Peter Berger', *Theological Studies*, 39, 3, 1978, pp. 486–507.

UTZ, A-F. 'Theologie und Sozialwissenschaften' in J. Feiner, J. Trütsch and F. Bückle (eds.), *Fragen der Theologie Heute* (Benziger Verlag Einsiedeln, Zürich und Köln, 1958) pp. 447–62.

VARIOUS 'Research and Debate. Theology and Social Sciences', *Social Compass*, 17, 2, 1970, pp. 261–308.

WHITLEY, O.R. 'Sociological Models and Theological Reflection', *Journal of the American Academy of Religion*, 45, 1977, Supplement J, pp. 333–65.

Method and Understanding in Sociology and Theology

AUDINET, J. 'Action, confession, raison', *Recherches de sciences religieuses*, 4, 1977, pp. 567–78.

BARKER, E. 'Living the Divine Principle: Inside the Rev. Sun Myung Moon's Unification Church in Britain', *Archives de sciences sociales des religions*, 45, 1, 1978, pp. 75–93.

BARKER, E. 'Whose Service is Perfect Freedom: The Concept of Spiritual Well-Being in Relation to the Reverend Moon's Unification Church', in D.O. Moberg (ed.), *Spiritual Well-Being* (University Press of America, Washington D.C., 1979).

BERGER, P.L. 'Sociology in the Theological Curriculum', *Hartford Quarterly*, 1, 1, 1960, pp. 41–5.

BERGER, P.L. 'Note on Sociology and Homiletics', *Hartford Quarterly*, 1, 3, 1961, pp. 113–5.

BERGER, P.L. and LUCKMANN, T. 'Sociology of Religion and Sociology of Knowledge', *Sociology and Social Research*, 47, 1963, pp. 417–27; reproduced in R. Robertson (ed.), *Sociology of Religion: Readings* (Penguin, London, 1969).

BERGER, P.L. and LUCKMANN, T. *The Social Construction of Reality* (Allen Lane, Penguin Press, London, and Doubleday, New York, 1966).

BOURDIEU, P. 'Genèse et structure du champ religieux', *Revue française de sociologie*, 3, 1971, pp. 295–334.

BOURDIEU, P. 'Une Interprétation de la théorie de la religion selon Max Weber', *Archives européennes de sociologie*, 1, 1971, pp. 3–21.

DECONCHY, J.-P. *L'Orthodoxie religieuse, Essai de logique psychosociale* (Les Editions Ouvrières, Paris, 1971).

DEFOIS, G. 'Critique et parole', *Recherches de sciences religieuses*, 3, 1977, pp. 361–86.

DEKKER, G. *Sociologie en Kerk* (Kok, Kampen, 1969).

DESROCHE, H. and SEGUY, J. *Introduction aux sciences humaines des religions*, Symposium recueilli par H. Desroche et J. Séguy (Cujas, Paris, 1970).

ERNST, C. 'Theological Methodology' in K. Rahner and others

(eds.), *Sacramentum Mundi. An Encyclopedia of Theology*, 6 (Burns and Oates, London and Herder, New York, 1970).

FIERRO, A. *The Militant Gospel* (S.C.M. Press, London, 1977).

GILKEY, L. 'Social and Intellectual Sources of Contemporary Protestant Theology in America', *Daedalus*, 96, 1, 1967, pp. 69–98.

GILKEY, L. *Religion and the Scientific Future. Reflections on Myth, Science and Theology* (S.C.M. Press, London, 1970).

GILL, R. 'The Critique of Religious Sociology', *Social Studies*, 3, 2, 1974.

GILL, R. 'British Theology as a Sociological Variable' in M. Hill (ed.), *A Sociological Yearbook of Religion in Britain*, 7 (S.C.M. Press, London, 1974) pp. 1–12.

GILL, R. 'A New Approach to Religions?', *Philosophical Studies,* 23, 1975, pp. 117–28.

GILL, R. *Faith in Christ: Christian Claims in a Changing World* (Mowbrays, Oxford, 1978).

GILL, R. 'Prophecy in a Socially Determined Church', *Theology*, 82, 685, 1979, pp. 24–30.

HINDESS, B. *Philosophy and Methodology in the Social Sciences* (Harvester, Hassocks, 1977).

HOLMER, P.L. *Theology and the Scientific Study of Religion* (T.S. Danison, Minneapolis, 1961).

JAY, M. *The Dialectical Imagination* (Heinemann, London, 1973).

JENSON, R.W. *The Knowledge of Things Hoped For. The Sense of Theological Discourse* (O.U.P., New York, 1969).

KAUFMANN, F.-X. 'The Church as a Religious Organisation', *Concilium*, 10, 1, 1974, pp. 70–82.

LASH, N. *Theology on Dover Beach* (Darton, Longman and Todd, London, 1979).

LEWY, G. *Religion and Revolution* (Oxford University Press, New York, 1974).

MACKAY, D.M. *Human Science and Human Dignity. A Christian Assessment* (Hodder and Stoughton, London, 1978).

MARTIN, D.A. 'The Status of the Human Person in the Behavioural Sciences' in R.H. Preston (ed.), *Technology and Social Justice* (S.C.M. Press, London, 1971).

MARTIN, R. 'Sociology and Theology: Alienation and Original Sin' in D.E.H. Whiteley and R. Martin (eds.), *Sociology, Theology and Conflict* (Blackwell, Oxford, and Barnes and Noble, New York, 1969) pp. 4–37.

MEHL, R. *Traité de sociologie du protestantisme* (Delachaux et Nestlé, Neuchâtel, 1965). Trans. J.H. Farley, *The Sociology of Protestantism* (S.C.M. Press, London, 1970).

NEEDHAM, R. *Belief, Language and Experience* (Blackwell, Oxford, 1972).

OELMÜLLER, W. 'The Limitations of Social Theories' in J. Moltmann and others, *Religion and Political Society*, ed. and trans. in The Institute of Christian Thought (Harper and Row, New York, 1974) pp. 121–69.

RAHNER, K. 'Theology' in K. Rahner and others (eds.), *Sacramentum Mundi. An Encyclopaedia of Theology*, 6 (Burns and Oates, London and Herder, New York, 1970).

ROCHE, D. (ed.) *Ordres et casses. Colloque d'Histoire Sociale. Saint Cloud, 24–25 mai 1967*. Communications réunies par D. Roche et présentées par C.E. Labrousse (Mouton, Paris, La Haye, 1967).

ROUSSEAU, A. and LIENHARD, G. 'Rapports sociaux et systèmes symboliques' in M. Xhaufflaire (ed.), *La Pratique de la théologie politique* (Casterman, Paris, Tournai, 1974).

SCHILLEBEECKX, E. *The Understanding of Faith. Interpretation and Criticism*, Trans. N.D. Smith (Sheed and Ward, London, 1974).

SHINER, L. 'Towards a Theology of Secularization', *Journal of Religion*, 1965, pp. 219–95.

THIBAULT, P. *Savoir et pouvoir. Philisophie thomiste et politique cléricale au XIX° siècle* (Les Presses de l'Université Laval, Quebec, 1972).

TRACY, D. *Blessed Rage for Order* (Seabury Press, New York, 1975).

WACKENHEIM, G. 'Ecclesiology and Sociology', *Concilium*, 10, 1, 1974, pp. 32–41.

WHITELEY, D.E.H. and MARTIN, R. (eds.) *Sociology, Theology and Conflict* (Blackwell, Oxford, and Barnes and Noble, New York, 1969).

WICKER, B. 'Marxist Science and Christian Theology', *New Blackfriars*, 58, 681, 1977, pp. 85–100.

WILES, M. *What is Theology?* (O.U.P., London and New York, 1976).

Index of Authors, Biblical Names and Sources
(Names in the Bibliography have been excluded)

Index of Subjects